pwc

普华永道

普华永道国际财务报告准则实务指引系列（第八册）
PwC IFRS MOA Series (Volume Eight)

Manual of Accounting — IFRS 2012

Chapter 18 - Impairment of assets

国际财务报告准则实务指引

第十八章——资产减值

中英文对照

翻译组主要成员：李宜桦　梁少宝　陈　捷　孙宇辉　唐　昆

中国财政经济出版社

Preface

Businesses around the world are becoming more global and much of the accounting standard-setters' focus today is concerned with global harmonization of accounting requirements. Against this backdrop, International Financial Reporting Standards (IFRS) have become increasingly important as the global business language. IFRS aims to be a comprehensive set of neutral principles that produce consistent, comparable, relevant and reliable financial information useful for investors, lenders, creditors, and those who make decisions in the capital markets. PwC is strongly committed to a common goal of promoting these financial reporting standards to preparers and users.

The IFRS Manual of Accounting is a comprehensive practical guide to IFRS and provides straightforward explanations of how to prepare financial statements in accordance with IFRS, with hundreds of practical examples. The Manual was developed based on the extensive experience of the PwC's global network of firms.

Due to the importance of IFRS for many companies in China and the continued convergence of China Accounting Standards and IFRS, PwC China has undertaken a significant project to translate our IFRS Manual of Accounting into Chinese. We sincerely hope that our IFRS Manual of Accounting with Chinese Translation provides practical insights and can help finance directors, accountants, auditors, analysts and other users of financial statements to bridge the gap between accounting principles and their applications.

Ernest Ip
Senior Partner
PwC China and Hong Kong

前　言

在营商环境日趋国际化的今天，会计规定的全球一致化已经成为会计准则制定者们关注的一个重点。在此背景下，国际财务报告准则（IFRS）作为全球商业语言变得愈发重要。IFRS 旨在成为一套全面的、中性的原则，向投资者、借款方、债权人及其他需在资本市场中作出决策的人士提供一致的、可比较的、相关的及可靠的财务信息。普华永道致力于将这些财务准则介绍给广泛的财务报表编制者及使用者。

英文版的《国际财务报告准则实务指引》（IFRS Manual of Accounting）是对 IFRS 的一份全面性实务指引，对如何按照 IFRS 编制财务报表提供了简明的阐述，并附有诸多实务示例。该指引是基于普华永道全球成员机构网络丰富的经验归纳而成。

鉴于 IFRS 对中国的许多公司的重要性，以及中国会计准则与 IFRS 的持续趋同，普华永道中国启动了这项具有重大意义的项目，即将《国际财务报告准则实务指引》译成中文，并分享给大家。我们诚挚地希望这套中英文对照的《国际财务报告准则实务指引》能够提供实用的见解，为财务总监、会计人员、审计人员、分析人员及其他财务报表使用者们在会计原则与其具体应用之间架起一座桥梁。

叶冠荣
首席合伙人
普华永道中国及香港

Overview/Introduction

Recent years have seen major changes in financial reporting worldwide with the single most important change being convergence around IFRS. There has also been a keen focus to improve the long term development of the CPA profession within China. As the Ministry of Finance and other regulatory bodies continue to promulgate legislation to promote the development of the Chinese CPA profession, we hope the release of our IFRS Manual of Accounting with Chinese Translation will also contribute to this effort.

The Ministry of Finance issued the Accounting Standards for Business Enterprises (hereafter referred to as "China Accounting Standards" or "CAS") in 2006. CAS incorporates all of the principles of IFRS and there has been a continued focus on convergence over the last few years. Additionally, IFRS is becoming increasingly important for many companies in China, including domestic companies seeking to raise capital overseas, as well as for foreign companies that have operations in China. With the continued convergence of CAS and IFRS, the release of our IFRS Manual of Accounting with Chinese Translation brings to China the extensive collective experience of the PwC's global network of firms in applying IFRS.

We hope this Manual will play a part in promoting consistent, comparable, relevant and reliable IFRS financial information and will serve as a reference tool for accounting students, academics, practitioners and users of financial statements in better understanding and implementing IFRS. More importantly, we hope the advice given in this text will assist those dealing with the many issues faced in preparing IFRS financial statements and provide helpful insight to users of such statements.

Raymund Chao
Asia Pacific Assurance Leader
PwC

概述/引言

近年来，全球财务报告领域发生了重大变化，其中最为重要的一项变化是与国际财务报告准则的趋同。同时人们也热切地关注着中国境内注册会计师行业的长期发展。财政部及其他监管机构不断完善法规，推动中国注册会计师行业的发展，我们希望这本中英文对照的国际财务报告准则实务指引能够对此作出贡献。

财政部于2006 年颁布了《企业会计准则》（以下称为中国会计准则，或CAS）。CAS 包含了 IFRS 中的所有原则，且在过去的几年里持续趋同。此外，IFRS 对于中国的许多公司来说越来越重要，包括寻求筹集海外资本的国内公司，以及在中国境内运营的外国公司。随着 CAS 与 IFRS 的持续趋同，本书的发行将给中国读者带来普华永道全球成员机构网络在应用 IFRS 方面积累的丰富的经验。

我们希望本书能够在推广一致的、可比的、相关的以及可靠的 IFRS 财务信息方面起到作用，并且可以作为会计领域的学生、学者、从业人员及财务报表使用者更好地理解及运用 IFRS 的参考工具。更为重要的是，我们希望本指引中提出的建议能够帮助其处理在编制 IFRS 财务报表时遇到的问题，并向此类财务报表使用者提供有用的观点。

赵柏基
普华永道亚太区审计部主管合伙人

How to use this publication

Given the increasing importance of IFRS in China and the continued convergence of CAS and IFRS, the accounting technical team of PwC China and Hong Kong have undertaken a significant project to translate the IFRS Manual of Accounting into Chinese.

The Manual is a practical guide in applying IFRS and the views are based on the extensive experience of the PwC's global network of firms. However, IFRS is not static and is continuously developing. The views on its interpretation and application will adapt and evolve. The views expressed in this Manual are a guide to applying IFRS rather than a set of definitive interpretations. The application of IFRS requires significant judgement and specific facts and circumstances should be carefully considered.

IFRS Manual of Accounting with Chinese Translation will be released in different volumes. Depending on the topic, each release may be a chapter or a combination of a number of chapters from the Manual.

Because of the interdependencies between individual IFRS, there are many cross references between different chapters of the Manual. Although the IFRS Manual of Accounting with Chinese Translation will be released in different volumes, the cross references have been maintained. Users are encouraged to refer to those cross references in other translated chapters or to the English version of the Manual if it helps in their understanding.

This book is the eighth volume of IFRS Manual of Accounting Series with Chinese Translation. The content covers Chapter 18 – Impairment of assets of the English version and its translation. While every effort has been made to ensure an accurate translation, reference should be made to the English version in the event there are any differences between the Chinese and English versions.

使用说明

鉴于 IFRS 在中国愈发重要以及 CAS 和 IFRS 的持续趋同，普华永道中国及香港的会计专业技术支持部门已着手开始了一项具有重大意义的项目，即将国际财务报告准则实务指引译成中文。

国际财务报告准则实务指引是对应用 IFRS 的实务指引，其中的观点是基于普华永道全球成员机构网络丰富的经验。然而，IFRS 不是静止的，而是持续发展的；因此，对 IFRS 的解释和适用会有所改变和发展。本指引表达的观点是对应用 IFRS 的一种指引，而非一套具有决定性的解释。IFRS 的应用需要大量的判断，还应当谨慎考虑特定的事实及所处的环境。

IFRS 实务指引及其中文翻译版将分成多册发行。根据主题，每一册可能是本指引的某一章节或是包含某几个章节。

由于各个 IFRS 准则之间的相互依存，因此本指引中不同的章节会相互参照索引。尽管 IFRS 实务指引及其中文翻译版将分成多册发行，但仍保留此类相互参照索引。如果有助于理解，我们鼓励读者阅读此类相互参照索引时参考其他已翻译的章节或指引的英文版。

本书为普华永道国际财务报告准则实务指引系列（中英文对照）的第八册。内容为英文原版的《国际财务报告准则实务指引》中的《第十八章——资产减值》。我们已尽最大的努力来确保翻译的准确，但中文翻译版与英文版出现不一致时，应参考英文版。

The English version of our IFRS Manual of Accounting Series includes 2 books: IFRS Manual of Accounting and IFRS Manual of Accounting – Financial Instruments with the following chapters.

IFRS Manual of Accounting

Accounting rules and principles

Income statement and related notes

Balance sheet and related notes

英文原版的普华永道国际财务报告准则实务指引系列包括《国际财务报告准则实务指引》和《国际财务报告准则实务指引——金融工具》两本书，其所有章节列示如下：

国际财务报告准则实务指引

会计规则和原则

01 – 引言
02 – 会计原则和国际财务报告准则的适用性
03 – 首次采用国际财务报告准则
04 – 财务报表的列报
05 – 会计政策、会计估计和差错
06 – 恶性通货膨胀
07 – 外币
08 – 保险合同

利润表及相关附注

09 – 收入与建造合同
10 – 分部报告
11 – 职工福利
11A – 职工福利
12 – 以股份为基础的支付（“股份支付”）
13 – 所得税会计
14 – 每股收益

资产负债表及相关附注

15 – 无形资产
16 – 不动产、工厂和设备
17 – 投资性房地产
18 – 资产减值
19 – 租赁会计
20 – 存货
21 – 准备和或有事项
22 – 报告期后事项和财务承诺

IFRS Manual of Accounting—Financial Instruments

合并财务报表

其他主题

国际财务报告准则实务指引——金融工具

Abbreviations and terms used

Accounts	financial statements
AG	Application Guidance
App	Appendix
ARC	Accounting Regulatory Committee
BC	Basis for Conclusions (to an accounting standard)
C	currency unit
Chp	Chapter
chapter (1)	'PricewaterhouseCoopers' Manual of accounting' – chapter (1)
CESR	Committee of European Securities Regulators
CPP	current purchasing power
DP	discussion paper
EBIT	earnings before interest and tax
EBITDA	earnings before interest, tax, depreciation and amortisation
ED	exposure draft
EFRAG	European Financial Reporting Advisory Group
EPS	earnings per share
EU	European Union
FASB	Financial Accounting Standards Board (US)
Framework	Framework for the preparation and presentation of financial statements
GAAP	generally accepted accounting principles (and practices)
IAS	International Accounting Standard (see also IFRS)
IASB	International Accounting Standards Board
IFRIC	International Financial Reporting Interpretations Committee
IFRS	International Financial Reporting Standard (see also IAS)
IG	Implementation Guidance (to an accounting standard)

缩写及词汇对照

财务报表
实施指南
附录
会计监管委员会
（某一准则的）结论基础
货币单位
章
第一章（普华永道《国际财务报告准则实务指引》——第一章）

欧洲证券监管委员会
现行购买力
讨论稿
息税前收益
扣除利息、所得税、折旧和摊销之前的收益
征求意见稿
欧洲财务报告咨询组
每股收益
欧盟
（美国）财务会计准则委员会
编报财务报表的框架

公认会计原则
国际会计准则（亦请参见 IFRS）
国际会计准则理事会
国际财务报告解释委员会
国际财务报告准则（亦请参见 IAS）
（某一准则的）应用指南

para(s)	paragraph(s) of Schedules to the Companies Acts, or IFRSs or IASs or FRSs, or SSAPs, or FREDs, or EDs, or DPs, or text
PPE	property, plant and equipment
US SEC	US Securities and Exchange Commission
SIC	Standing Interpretation Committee of the IASC (see IFRIC)
SPE	special purpose entity
UK	United Kingdom
US	United States of America

段落（公司法、国际财务报告准则、国际会计准则、财务报告准则、会计实务准则、财务报告征求意见稿、征求意见稿、讨论稿或文章中的段落）

不动产、工厂和设备

美国证券交易委员会

国际会计准则委员会的常设解释委员会（参见 IFRIC）

特殊目的主体

英国

美国

Chapter 18 Impairment of assets

Content

第十八章　资产减值

目　录

Objectives and scope of IAS 36

18. 1 IAS 36 ' Impairment of assets ' requires annual impairment tests for certain assets and for any non-financial asset where there is an indicator of impairment.

18. 2 The principle of IAS 36 is that an entity's assets are carried at no more than their recoverable amount. Recoverable amount is the higher of the amount to be realised through the asset's use or sale. Where the carrying value exceeds the recoverable amount the asset is impaired and an impairment loss is required to be recognised. The standard also details the circumstances when an impairment loss should be reversed and lists the disclosures required for impaired assets, impairment losses, reversals of impairment losses and key estimates and assumptions used in measuring recoverable amounts of cash generating units (CGUs) that contain goodwill or intangible assets with indefinite lives. [IAS 36 para 1].

[The next paragraph is 18. 40].

18. 40 IAS 36 contains extensive disclosure requirements. In addition, IAS 1, ' Presentation of financial statements ', requires disclosure of the judgements that management has used in applying the entity's significant accounting policies. IAS 1 also requires disclosure of the key assumptions concerning the future and other key sources of estimation uncertainty at the balance sheet date that have a significant risk of causing a material adjustment to the carrying amount of assets and liabilities within the next financial year. [IAS 1 paras 125]. The judgements and estimates involved in making impairment calculations commonly fall within these IAS 1 requirements in addition to being explicitly required by IAS 36.

18. 41 IAS 36 applies in accounting for the impairment of all assets (including current assets), unless specifically excluded from the standard's scope. Assets that are excluded are:

■ Inventories (dealt with in IAS 2, ' Inventories ').

国际会计准则第36号的目标与范围

18.1　《国际会计准则第36号——资产减值》（“IAS 36”）要求对某些资产以及任何存在减值迹象的非金融资产每年进行减值测试。

18.2　IAS 36的原则是主体的资产以不超过其可收回金额的金额进行计量。可收回金额是通过资产的使用或出售所实现的金额两者之间的较高者。在账面价值高于可收回金额的情况下，资产即发生减值，并应当确认一项减值损失。该准则还详细论述了减值损失应当被转回的情形，并且列出了对于减值的资产、减值损失、减值损失的转回以及在计量包含了商誉或使用寿命不确定的无形资产的现金产出单元（“CGUs”）的可收回金额时所使用的关键估计与假设所要求披露的事项。[IAS 36第1段]。

[下一段是第18.40段]。

18.40　IAS 36包含了大量的披露要求。此外，《国际会计准则第1号——财务报表的列报》（“IAS 1”）要求披露管理层在应用主体的重大会计政策时所运用的判断。IAS 1还要求披露有关未来的关键假设和在资产负债表日存在的估计不确定性的其他关键来源，这些估计不确定性具有会引起资产和负债的账面价值在下一财务年度内作出重要调整的重大风险。[IAS 1第125段]。除了IAS 36有明确要求之外，进行减值计算所涉及的判断和估计通常也属于上述IAS 1的要求。

18.41　除非明确说明被排除在IAS 36的适用范围之外，否则该准则适用于所有资产（包括流动资产）的减值的会计处理。被排除在适用范围之外的资产包括：

■ 存货（适用《国际会计准则第2号——存货》（“IAS 2”））。

- Assets arising from construction contracts (dealt with in IAS 11, 'Construction contracts').
- Deferred tax assets (dealt with in IAS 12, 'Income taxes').
- Assets arising from employee benefits (dealt with in IAS 19, 'Employee benefits').
- Financial assets that are included in the scope of IAS 39, 'Financial instruments: recognition and measurement'. (Examples include cash, debtors and equity investments other than investments in subsidiaries, associates or joint ventures not accounted for under IAS 39).
- Investment property that is measured at fair value (dealt with in IAS 40, 'Investment property').
- Biological assets related to agricultural activity measured at fair value less costs to sell (dealt with in IAS 41, 'Agriculture').
- Deferred acquisition costs and intangible assets arising from an insurer's contractual rights under insurance contracts that are within the scope of IFRS 4, 'Insurance contracts'.
- Non-current assets (or disposal groups) classified as held for sale under IFRS 5, 'Non-current assets held-for-sale and discontinued operations'.

[IAS 36 paras 2, 3 and BCZ8].

18.42 IAS 36 applies to subsidiaries, associates and joint ventures that are accounted for at cost under IAS 27, 'Consolidated and separate financial statements', IAS 28, 'Investments in associates', and IAS 31, 'Interests in joint ventures'. However, this is relevant only to the parent or investing entity's separate financial statements, not to the consolidated financial statements. Impairment of such investments that are accounted for in accordance with IAS 39 is not within IAS 36's scope and is dealt with in IAS 39. [IAS 36 para 4; IAS 39 para 2]. Further guidance is provided in paragraph 18.285.1 onwards.

■ 建造合同形成的资产（适用《国际会计准则第 11 号——建造合同》（“IAS 11”））。

■ 递延所得税资产（适用《国际会计准则第 12 号——所得税》　（“IAS 12”））。

■ 职工福利形成的资产（适用《国际会计准则第 19 号——职工福利》（“IAS 19”））。

■ 包括在《国际会计准则第 39 号——金融工具：确认和计量》（“IAS 39”）适用范围内的金融资产。（例如现金、应收款项以及除了不按照 IAS 39 核算的对子公司、联营或合营的投资之外的权益投资）。

■ 以公允价值计量的投资性房地产（适用《国际会计准则第 40 号——投资性房地产》（“IAS 40”））。

■ 以公允价值减去处置费用后的净额计量的与农业活动有关的生物资产（适用《国际会计准则第 41 号——农业》（“IAS 41”））。

■ 递延获取成本以及在《国际财务报告准则第 4 号——保险合同》（“IFRS 4”）适用范围内的保险合同下由保险人的合同权利所形成的无形资产。

■ 根据《国际财务报告准则第 5 号——持有待售的非流动资产和终止经营》（“IFRS 5”）被分类为持有待售的非流动资产（或处置组）。

[IAS 36 第 2 段、第 3 段，结论基础第 Z8 段]。

18.42　IAS 36 适用于分别按照《国际会计准则第 27 号——合并财务报表及单独财务报表》（“IAS 27”）、《国际会计准则第 28 号——对联营的投资》（“IAS 28”）以及《国际会计准则第 31 号——合营中的权益》（“IAS 31”）以成本核算的子公司、联营和合营。然而，这仅仅与母公司主体或投资主体的单独财务报表有关，并不是针对合并财务报表而言的。那些按照 IAS 39 进行会计处理的投资的减值不包括在 IAS 36 的适用范围之内，而是由 IAS 39 进行规范。[IAS 36 第 4 段、IAS 39 第 2 段]。下文的第 18.285.1 段提供了更多的指引。

18. 43 The standard applies to assets carried at a revalued amount under other IFRSs, such as the revaluation model in IAS 16, 'Property, plant and equipment'. Where the revalued asset's fair value is based on market value the only difference between that value and the fair value less costs to sell will be the direct incremental costs of disposing of the asset. Where these are negligible the recoverable amount (higher of fair value less costs to sell and value in use) will be close to, or greater than, the carrying amount and no impairment test is required. Where, however, the incremental disposal costs are material or where the fair value (carrying value) of a revalued asset is determined on a basis other than its market value the carrying amount may be greater or less than its recoverable amount and the standard should be applied as normal to determine whether or not there is an impairment loss. [IAS 36 para 5].

18. 44 Non-current assets (or disposal groups) held for sale under IFRS 5 are also excluded from IAS 36's scope. A non-current asset (or disposal group) classified as held for sale should be measured at the lower of its carrying amount upon classification as held for sale and fair value less costs to sell. [IFRS 5 para 15]. Immediately before the initial classification of an asset (or disposal group) as held for sale, the carrying amount of the asset (or all the assets in the group) should be measured in accordance with applicable IFRSs. [IFRS 5 para 18]. A plan to dispose of an asset or cash generating unit is an internal indicator of impairment, specifically identified by IAS 36 and so prior to classification as held for sale the asset must be reviewed for impairment under IAS 36. See further paragraphs 18. 248 onwards. [IAS 36 para 12(f)].

Basic principles of impairment

18. 45 An asset may not be carried in the balance sheet at more than its recoverable amount. IAS 36 states that "*If, and only if, the recoverable amount of an asset is less than its carrying amount, the carrying amount of the asset shall be reduced to its recoverable amount. That reduction is an impairment loss*". [IAS 36 para 59]. An asset's carrying amount is the amount at which the asset is recognised after deducting any accumulated depreciation or amortisation and

18.43　该准则适用于按照其他国际财务报告准则（例如，《国际会计准则第16号——不动产、工厂和设备》（“IAS 16”）中的重估价模型）以重估价金额计量的资产。在重估价资产的公允价值是基于市场价值确定的情况下，该价值与公允价值减去处置费用的净额两者之间唯一的差异就是处置该资产的直接增量成本。如果这些成本是可以忽略不计的，则可收回金额（公允价值减去处置费用的净额与使用价值两者中的较高者）将会接近或大于账面价值，因此不需要进行减值测试。然而，如果增量处置费用是相当重要的，或者重估价的资产的公允价值（账面价值）是以其市场价值以外的其他因素为基础确定的，则其账面价值可能会大于或小于其可收回金额，因此，应当像正常情况一样应用该准则确定是否存在减值损失。[IAS 36 第 5 段]。

18.44　IFRS 5 下的持有待售的非流动资产（或处置组）也被排除在 IAS 36 的适用范围之外。被分类为持有待售的非流动资产（或处置组）应当以其在被分类为持有待售时的账面价值和公允价值减去处置费用的净额两者孰低进行计量。[IFRS 5 第 15 段]。某项资产（或处置组）在被初始分类为持有待售之前，应当按照所适用的国际财务报告准则计量该资产（或该处置组中的所有资产）的账面价值。[IFRS 5 第 18 段]。处置某一资产或现金产出单元的计划是 IAS 36 明确识别出的一个减值的内部迹象；因此，在把资产分类为持有待售之前，必须按照 IAS 36 的要求进行减值复核。进一步的讨论参见下文的第 18.248 段。[IAS 36 第 12（f）段]。

减值的基本原则

18.45　资产在资产负债表中不可能以高于其可收回金额的金额计量。IAS 36 指出：“*当且仅当资产的可收回金额小于其账面价值时，应当把该资产的账面价值减记至其可收回金额。该减记金额即为减值损失。*”[IAS 36 第 59 段]。资产的账面价值是该资产扣除任何累计折旧或摊销以及累计的减值损失后所确认的金额。[IAS 36 第 6 段]。

accumulated impairment losses thereon. [IAS 36 para 6].

18.46 An asset's recoverable amount represents its greatest value to the business in terms of the cash flows that it can generate. That is the higher of:

- fair value less costs to sell (the amount for which the asset could be sold in an arm's length transaction between knowledgeable and willing parties, net of estimated costs of disposal); and
- value in use (the present value of the future cash flows that are expected to be derived from the asset. The expected future cash flows include those from the asset's continued use in the business and those from its ultimate disposal. Value in use is explicitly based on present value calculations).

[IAS 36 paras 6, 31].

18.47 An impairment review involves estimating an asset's recoverable amount and comparing it with its carrying value. If the recoverable amount is lower than the carrying value, the asset is impaired and must be written down to the recoverable amount. Impairment cannot be avoided by arguing that the diminution in value is not permanent.

[The next paragraph is 18.53.]

Identifying assets that may be impaired

18.53 IAS 36 requires all assets in its scope to be tested for impairment where there is an impairment indicator. Goodwill, indefinite life intangible assets and intangible assets that are not yet ready for use must also be tested for impairment annually (see para 18.68 below).

18.54 An entity should assess at each reporting date whether there is any indication that an asset may be impaired. If any indication exists the entity should estimate the asset's recoverable amount. The recoverable amount should be compared with the asset's carrying value and if an impairment loss has arisen it should be recognised immediately. [IAS 36 paras 9, 59, 60]. The term 'reporting date' includes not only the year end date, but also interim (half-year or

18.46　资产的可收回金额是指该资产对其所属业务能够产生的现金流量作出的最大的价值。可收回金额为以下两者中的较高者：

- 公允价值减去处置费用的净额（在熟悉情况的交易各方之间自愿进行的公平交易中出售资产并扣除预计的处置费用后的净额）；

- 使用价值（预计资产产生的未来现金流量的现值。预计的未来现金流量包括在业务中持续使用资产所产生的现金流量以及最终处置该资产时所产生的现金流量。使用价值明确以现值的计算为基础）。

[IAS36 第 6 段、第 31 段]。

18.47　减值复核包括估计资产的可收回金额，并将其与该资产的账面价值进行比较。如果资产的可收回金额低于其账面价值，则其发生了减值，且必须被减记至其可收回金额。不能以资产价值的下降并非是永久性的理由来避免减值。

[下一段是第 18.53 段。]

识别可能减值的资产

18.53　IAS 36 要求，其规范范围内的所有资产在存在减值迹象时都要进行减值测试。商誉、使用寿命不确定的无形资产以及尚未达到可使用状态的无形资产还必须每年进行减值测试。（参见下文的第 18.68 段）。

18.54　主体在每个报告日都应当评估，是否有任何迹象表明某项资产可能发生了减值。如果存在任何迹象，主体应当估计资产的可收回金额。应当把资产的可收回金额与其账面价值进行比较，如果出现减值损失，应当立即确认。[IAS 36 第 9 段、第 59 段、第 60 段]。“报告日”不仅包括年终日，也包括中期（半年或季度）报告日。因此，主体每年可能需要进行一次以上的减值测试。

quarterly) reporting dates. Accordingly, an entity may be required to complete an impairment test more than once per annum.

18.55 In assessing whether there is any indication that an asset may be impaired an entity should consider at least the following:

External sources of information, including:

- A decline in the asset's market value that is significantly greater than would be expected as a result of the passage of time or normal use. Changes in market values reflect economic conditions, hence a significant fall in value is worthy of further investigation (at least to consider whether it is relevant) as it could be a symptom of another more pervasive change, for example technological change or a change in demand for the asset's output.

- Significant adverse changes that have taken place or are expected in the near future in the technological, market, economic or legal environment in which the entity operates or in its markets.

- Increases in interest rates or other market rates of return that may materially affect the discount rate used in calculating the asset's recoverable amount.

- The carrying amount of the entity's net assets exceeds the entity's market capitalisation.

Internal sources of information, including:

- Obsolescence or physical damage affecting the asset.

- Significant adverse changes that have taken place or are expected in the near future in the extent to which, or in the way that, an asset is used or expected to be used. This includes the asset becoming idle, plans to discontinue or restructure the operation to which the asset belongs or the asset's disposal. It also includes reassessing the asset's useful life from indefinite to finite.

- Deterioration in the expected level of the asset's performance.

- Management's own forecasts of future net cash inflows or operating profits may show a significant decline from previous budgets and forecasts.

18.55　在评估是否有任何迹象表明某项资产可能发生了减值时，主体至少应当考虑下列因素：

外部信息来源，包括：

■ 资产的市场价值的下跌程度远远高于因时间的推移或者正常使用所预期产生的结果。市场价值的变化反映了经济的情况，因此，对资产价值的大幅下跌值得作进一步的调查（至少要考虑其是否相关），因为这可能是另一影响更加广泛深入的变化（例如科学技术更新或者对资产的产出需求的变化等）的征兆。

■ 主体经营所处的技术、市场、经济或法律环境、或者在其所处的市场上已经发生或者预期在不久的将来即将发生的重大不利变化。

■ 利率或者其他可能对计算资产的可收回金额所使用的折现率产生重要影响的市场回报率上升。

■ 主体的净资产的账面价值超过了其市值。

内部信息来源，包括：

■ 陈旧过时或对资产造成的实体损坏。

■ 资产的使用或者预期使用的方式或者程度已经发生或者预期在不久的将来即将发生的重大不利变化。这些变化包括资产变为闲置、计划终止或者重组资产所属的经营、或者处置资产；还包括对资产的使用寿命从不确定变为确定所作的重新评估。

■ 资产绩效的预期水平出现恶化。

■ 管理层自己对未来的净现金流入或营业利润的预测与之前的预算和预测相比可能呈现出大幅下降的趋势。

[IAS 36 paras 12,14].

18.55.1 Other indicators of impairment that are not specifically mentioned in IAS 36 could be:

- The actual net cash outflows or operating profit or loss may be significantly worse than budgeted.
- Operating losses or net cash outflows are forecast.
- Cash flows for constructing the asset or for maintaining or operating it are significantly higher than those budgeted.

Example 1 – Impairment indicator – reduced selling price of recently acquired asset

Entity A bought (and capitalised) a computer system off the shelf for £2m. Shortly afterwards the manufacturer dropped the selling price to £1.5m.

A change in the market value of an asset is an indicator of impairment.

Example 2 – Impairment indicatior- impairment due to future closure

Entity X is proposing to close a manufacturing unit; this is an indicator of impairment. The closure will take place in two years time during which, for operational purposes, the unit (a separate CGU) will continue to manufacture, buying in raw materials and making sales as normal. Entity X is considering impairment issues. It has fixed assets at the unit whose useful lives are now two years rather than ten years, which they would have been were the unit not being closed. The carrying value of the fixed assets is C100 and the 'normal' depreciation charge is C10 per year. Based on the current year impairment review, there is an impairment attributable to the fixed assets at the present time of C30 and the residual (that is, realisable) value of the fixed assets in two years time is C40.

Under IAS 16, 'Property, plant and equipment', any change in the useful life will be accounted for prospectively. The plant has been reviewed for impairment and an impairment charge of C30 needs to be recorded in the current year. This gives a remaining net book value of C70, in order to

［IAS 36 第 12 段、第 14 段］。

18.55.1　在 IAS 36 中没有特别提及的其他减值迹象可能还有：

- 实际的净现金流出或者营业利润或损失比预算情况糟糕得多。
- 预测到会出现营业损失或净现金流出。
- 为建造资产、维护或者运营资产所发生的现金流量大大超出了预算的支出。

示例 1——减值迹象——最近取得的资产售价下降

主体 A 以 2 百万英镑的价格购买了一个计算机系统的现货（资本化为资产）。不久之后，生产商把该产品的售价降至 1.5 百万英镑。

资产市场价值的变化是一个减值迹象。

示例 2——减值迹象——由于未来停业所导致的减值

主体 X 正在计划关闭一个生产单位，这是一个减值的迹象。这个生产单位将于两年后关闭，在此期间，出于经营的目的，该单位（为一个单独的现金产出单元）将会像在正常情况下一样，继续生产、购买原材料并销售产品。主体 X 正在考虑减值问题。它在这个生产单位所拥有的固定资产的使用寿命现在应该是两年，而不是十年（如果不关闭这个生产单位，它们的使用寿命应该是十年）。这些固定资产的账面价值为 100 元，“正常”的折旧费用为每年 10 元。根据本年度的减值复核，目前归属于这些固定资产的减值为 30 元，而其在两年后的残值（即可实现的价值）为 40 元。

根据《国际会计准则第 16 号——不动产、工厂和设备》，使用寿命的任何变化都按照未来适用法进行会计处理。已经对该工厂进行了减值复核且需要在本年度记录 30 元的减值费用。剩余的账面净值为 70 元，为了确定要记录的折旧费用，必须要减去残值。因此，剩余价值 30 元将会在剩

establish the depreciation charge to be recorded it is necessary to subtract the residual value. This gives a remaining value of C30 to be depreciated over the remaining useful life of 2 years.

18.56 The above list is not exhaustive. Other indicators may be apparent that are relevant to a business' particular circumstances. [IAS 36 para 13]. For example, changes in tax regulations, the impact of publicity over brand names, a change in the proposed use of an asset, an impairment recognised by an associate or the entrance of a new competitor to the market may require the recoverable amount of an entity's assets to be investigated.

Example 1 – Impairment indicator – change in tax legislation

Entity P produces a wide range of drinks and beverages. Its main product is a special filtered beer, whose sales represent 50% of annual revenues. According to the local tax regulation, filtered beers are rated as 'category 4' in the alcoholic beverages tax table. Tax charges are based on four categories 1 (with higher tax charges) to 4 (with lower tax charges). New legislation will shortly come into effect under which all alcoholic beverages will be taxable equally based on the former category 1 tax charge.

In this situation, the change in the country's tax regulations should be considered an impairment indicator. The increase in the tax charge on entity P's products, and specifically over its main product, may have a direct impact on the entity's sales volumes, margins and cash flows.

Management should perform impairment tests, estimating the recoverable amount of its assets, based on the best available information (about fair values, future sales, and the assets' current condition).

Example 2 – Impairment indicator – global competitor starting business in an existing entity's territory

Entity S is the biggest local supermarket chain in country X, a developing country.

Recently, the global chain M, has decided to set up operations in the country. Entity M is well known world-wide, intends to establish its shops close to

余的使用寿命两年内进行折旧。

18.56 上文所列举的并没有穷尽所有的迹象。与某项业务所处的具体环境相关的其他迹象也可能出现。[IAS 36 第 13 段]。例如，税收规定的变化、公众关注度对品牌的影响、资产拟定用途的改变、联营确认了减值、或者新的竞争对手进入市场，都可能需要调查主体资产的可收回金额。

示例 1——减值迹象——税收法规的变化

主体 P 生产各种酒类和饮料，其主要产品是一种特制过滤啤酒，其销售额占年收入的 50%。根据当地的税收规定，过滤啤酒在酒精饮料的税率表上被定级为“第四类”。税负按照从 1（较高税负）到 4（较低税负）为基础分为四类。新的法规不久后即将生效，根据其规定，所有酒精饮料将按照相当于之前的第 1 类所适用的税负征税。

在这种情形下，该国家税收法规的变化应当被认为是一个减值迹象。对主体 P 的产品（具体来说是其主要产品）征税金额的提高，可能对该主体的销量、毛利、现金流量产生直接影响。

管理层应当根据其可获得的最佳信息（有关公允价值、未来销售以及资产目前的状况等）进行减值测试，估计其资产的可收回金额。

示例 2——减值迹象——国际竞争对手开始在主体所在的地区开展业务

主体 S 是在发展中国家 X 中最大的本地连锁超市企业。

最近，一家全球性的连锁企业 M 决定在 X 国开展经营。主体 M 是一家世界知名的企业，其计划在主体 S 的商店附近开设商店，并且为主体 S

entity S's and to offer entity S's customers a wider range of products and international brands. However, management of entity S expects to retain most of its customer base.

In this example, entity M's market entry is an impairment indicator. Management should perform impairment tests, estimating the recoverable amount of its assets, based on the best available information.

Example 3 – Impairment indicator-government price controls

Entity A is a water and sewage entity with a country wide water and sewage network. Although entity A is a listed entity, the government is the controlling shareholder.

Management has asked the government to allow a 3% increase in prices in order to cover recent cost increases. This is a regulated business and any price rise must be authorised by the government. The government has only authorised a 0. 5% price increase.

The fact that the government has not approved the requested price increase is an indication that the entity's assets used in the water and sewage network may be impaired. The assets should be tested for impairment, based on the approved business plans and using the information available regarding prices and the assets' current condition.

Example 4 – Impairment indicator – change of asset's use

Entity X uses asset M to manufacture product A. There has been a significant reduction in demand for product A as a result of a change in consumer taste. Management has not assessed asset M for impairment because it can, subject to minimal reconfiguration, be used in the manufacture of its new product T.

Entity X should review asset M for impairment. The change in use is itself an indicator of impairment. Entity X's management will need to assess the impact of both the change in consumer tastes and the asset's proposed change of use on the asset's recoverable amount.

18. 57 Most of the examples of impairment indicators are self-explanatory. They

的顾客提供更多的产品和国际品牌。然而，主体 S 的管理层预计其能够留住大多数的顾客。

在这个示例中，主体 M 的市场进入是一个减值迹象。管理层应当根据可获得的最佳信息进行减值测试，估计其资产的可收回金额。

示例 3——减值迹象——政府的价格调控

主体 A 是一家从事自来水供应和污水处理的主体，其自来水和污水网络遍布全国。尽管主体 A 是一家上市主体，但是政府是它的控股股东。

管理层请求政府允许其涨价 3%，以弥补近期成本的增加。由于该业务是一项受管制的业务，因此，任何价格的上涨都必须经过政府批准。政府只批准涨价 0.5%。

政府没有批准主体 A 所要求的涨价幅度这一事实，就是主体 A 用于自来水供应和污水处理网络的资产可能发生减值的一个迹象。主体 A 应当根据已批准的经营计划，并使用可获得的有关价格和资产当前状况等信息，对该资产进行减值测试。

示例 4——减值迹象——资产用途的变化

主体 X 用资产 M 生产 A 产品。由于消费者口味的变化，对 A 产品的需求大幅下降。管理层还没有对资产 M 进行减值评估，因为该资产经过最小限度的重新配置之后，可以用于生产其新产品 T。

主体 X 应该对资产 M 进行减值复核。用途发生变化本身就是一个减值迹象。主体 X 的管理层将需要评估消费者口味的变化以及该资产拟定的用途的变化对资产可收回金额的影响。

18.57　大多数减值迹象的示例都是不说自明的。它们反映了直接影响资产或

reflect adverse events or conditions that affect either the assets directly or the business in which they are employed. An impairment test should be performed, if there are any impairment indicators, even when there are conflicting indicators that an asset may, or may not be, impaired.

Example – Impairment indicator – introduction of a superior competitor product

Entity Q produces printers for home computers and has for some time been the market leader. Its chief competitor, entity R, has recently developed a new product that is widely acknowledged as being superior to that of entity Q as it has the ability to also photocopy documents, send and receive facsimile and colour-print photographs.

Entity Q's management has not performed an impairment review on its plant on the grounds that annual production and sales are ahead of budget.

Entity Q should review its plant and equipment for impairment. The change in the market for its product can have a significant impact on the equipment's value based on the economic benefit to be obtained from its continued use.

The existence of a conflicting indicator (sales ahead of budget) is not sufficient to negate the need for an impairment review. Management will be required to assess the impact of this new competing product on demand for its existing product and on expected future cash flows.

18.58 Increases in market rates of interest are identified as an indicator for entities to consider. However, IAS 36 emphasises that increases in short-term interest rates would not necessarily trigger an impairment review. Changes in interest rates need to be considered both in the context of the level of headroom indicated by previous impairment tests and the asset being tested; a long life asset is tested using discount rates that reflect long-term interest rates. A marginal increase in short-term interest rates is unlikely to lead to an impairment charge where there was significant headroom in the last test.

18.59 From 2008 onwards, many entities have been impacted by the global economic crisis. An economic downturn would not always be considered a

所在业务的不利事项或状况。如果存在任何减值迹象，即便是存在冲突的迹象表明资产可能减值、也可能没减值，也应当进行减值测试。

示例——减值迹象——竞争对手推出了更优越的产品

主体 Q 生产为家用电脑配置的打印机，并且长期以来一直在市场上处于领先地位。它的主要竞争对手主体 R 最近开发了一款新的产品，该产品被公认为比主体 Q 的产品更为先进，因为它还能够复印文件、收发传真以及彩打照片。

主体 Q 的管理层还没有对其工厂进行减值复核，理由是其年度的生产和销售都超过了预算。

主体 Q 应当对其工厂和设备进行减值复核。基于设备的经济利益是通过其持续使用而获得的考虑，产品市场的变化能够对该设备的价值产生重大影响。

某一冲突的迹象（销售超过预算）的存在并不足以消除进行减值复核的必要。管理层应当评估这种有竞争力的新产品对其现有产品的需求以及对预期未来现金流量的影响。

18.58　市场利率的提高也被认为是主体需要考虑的一个迹象。然而，IAS 36 强调，短期利率的提高并不会必然导致需要进行减值复核。需要根据过去的减值测试所显示的空间水平和所测试的资产情况而对利率变化的影响作出相关考虑；使用寿命长的资产，要采用反映长期利率的折现率进行测试。在上一次测试存在很大空间的情况下，短期利率的小幅增长不太可能会导致确认减值费用。

18.59　自 2008 年起，许多主体受到了全球经济危机的影响。经济衰退本身并非一定是减值测试的触发事件。但是，构成危机的个别经济现象可能对很

triggering event for impairment testing in its own right. However, the individual economic phenomena that make up the crisis may well be indicators for many entities. The following impairment indicators might be particularly relevant in an economic downturn:

- Actual figures are significantly lower than the original budget.
- Cash flow is significantly lower than earlier forecasts.
- Material decreases in mid-term and/or long-term growth rates as compared to the previous estimates.
- Significant or prolonged decrease in the entity's stock price.
- Market capitalisation less than book value of net assets.
- Announced change in business model, restructuring or discontinued operations.
- Increases in the cost of capital.
- Change of market interest rates or other market rates of return.
- Fluctuations in the foreign exchange rates or commodity prices that impact the entity's cash flows.
- Deferral of investment projects.

This list is not comprehensive. Other indicators may present themselves. The indicators above and in the standard are examples only.

18.63 IAS 36 points out that the materiality concept applies in determining whether an impairment review is required. If previous impairment reviews have shown a significant excess of recoverable amount over carrying amount no review would be necessary in the absence of any event that would eliminate the excess. Similarly, previous reviews may have shown that an asset's recoverable amount is not sensitive to one or more of the impairment indicators listed above. [IAS 36 para 15].

18.64 If there is an indication that an asset may be impaired the standard notes that the useful life, the depreciation method or the residual value for the asset need to be reviewed and adjusted if necessary under the appropriate IFRS (for example,

多主体而言都是减值迹象。下列减值迹象可能与经济衰退特别相关：

- 实际数据较最初的预算出现重大下降。
- 现金流量较早先的预测出现重大下降。
- 中期及/或长期的增长率与原先的估计相比出现重大下降。

- 主体的股票价格出现重大或者持续的下降。
- 净资产的市场价值小于其账面价值。
- 已经公布的业务模式的变化、重组或者终止经营。
- 资本成本增加。
- 市场利率或其他市场回报率的变化。
- 外币汇率或者影响主体现金流量的商品价格的波动。

- 投资项目推迟。

这里并没有列举所有的情况。其他减值迹象也有可能出现。上述迹象以及在该准则中所列举的减值迹象仅为一些示例。

18.63　IAS 36 指出，在确定是否必需进行减值复核时，需要应用重要性概念。如果以前的减值复核已经显示出可收回金额远远高于账面价值，那么在可能会抵销该超出金额的事项没有发生的情况下，减值复核不是必需的。类似地，以前的减值复核可能已经显示出资产的可收回金额对于上文列出的一个或多个减值迹象并不敏感。[IAS 36 第 15 段]。

18.64　如果有迹象表明资产可能发生了减值，该准则要求需要根据适当的国际财务报告准则（例如《国际会计准则第 16 号——不动产、工厂和设备》）对资产的使用寿命、折旧方法或残值进行复核，如有必要，作出调整。即使

IAS 16, 'Property, plant and equipment'). This applies even if no impairment loss is recognised for the asset. [IAS 36 para 17].

18.65 The following table illustrates indicators that have triggered impairment losses being recognised.

Table 18.1 – Impairment losses

Vodafone Group Plc – Annual report and accounts – 31 March 2011

10. Impairment (extract)

Impairment losses

The net impairment losses recognised in the consolidated income statement, as a separate line item within operating profit, in respect of goodwill and licences and spectrum fees are as follows:

		2011(1)	**2010**	**2009**
Cash generating unit	Reportable segment	**£m**	**£m**	**£m**
Italy	Italy	1,050	–	–
Spain	Spain	2,950	–	3,400
Greece	Other Europe (2)	800	–	–
Ireland	Other Europe (2)	1,000	–	–
Portugal	Other Europe (2)	350	–	–
Turkey	Other Europe	–	(200)	2,250
India	India	–	2,300	–
Ghana	Other Africa, Middle East and Asia Pacific	–	–	250
		6,150	2,100	5,900

Notes:

(1) Impairment charges for the year ended 31 March 2011 relate solely to goodwill.

(2) Total impairment losses in the Other Europe segment were £ 2,150 million in the year ended 31 March 2011.

Year ended 31 March 2011

The impairment losses were based on value in use calculations. The pre-tax adjusted discount rates used in the most recent value in use calculation in the year ended 31 March 2011n are as follows:

没有确认资产的减值损失，上述要求也同样适用。[IAS 36 第 17 段]。

18.65　下表举例说明了一些引发确认减值损失的迹象。

表 18.1——减值损失

沃达丰集团公司——年度报告和报表——2011 年 3 月 31 日

10. 减值(摘录)

减值损失

在合并利润表中确认的与商誉、许可证和频占费有关的减值损失净额(作为营业利润中的一个单独的报表项目列示)具体如下：

现金产出单元	报告分部	**2011(1)** **百万英磅**	**2010** **百万英磅**	**2009** **百万英磅**
意大利	意大利	1,050	–	–
西班牙	西班牙	2,950	–	3,400
希腊	其他欧洲国家(2)	800	–	–
爱尔兰	其他欧洲国家(2)	1,000	–	–
葡萄牙	其他欧洲国家(2)	350	–	–
土耳其	其他欧洲国家	–	(200)	2,250
印度	印度	–	2,300	–
加纳	其他非洲、中东和亚太国家	–	–	250
		6,150	2,100	5,900

注释：
(1)截至 2011 年 3 月 31 日止年度的减值费用仅与商誉有关。
(2)截至 2011 年 3 月 31 日止年度其他欧洲国家分部的减值损失总额为 2,150 百万英镑。

截至 2011 年 3 月 31 日止年度

减值损失是基于使用价值的计算而确认的。在截至 2011 年 3 月 31 日止年度最新的使用价值计算中所采用的经调整的税前折现率列示如下：

Con.

	Pre-tax adjusted discount rate
Italy	11.9%
Spain	11.5%
Greece	14.0%
Ireland	14.5%
Portugal	14.0%

During the year ended 31 March 2011 the goodwill in relation to the Group's investments in Italy, Spain, Greece, Ireland and Portugal was impaired by £1,050 million, £2,950 million, £800 million, £1,000 million and £350 million, respectively. The impairment charges were primarily driven by increased discount rates as a result of increases in government bond rates. In addition, business valuations were negatively impacted by lower cash flows within business plans, reflecting weaker country-level macro economic environments.

The pre-tax risk adjusted discount rates used in the previous value in use calculations at 31 March 2010 are disclosed below.

Year ended 31 March 2010

The net impairment losses were based on value in use calculations. The pre-tax adjusted discount rates used in the value in use calculation in the year ended 31 March 2010 were as follows:

	Pre-tax adjusted discount rate
India	13.8%
Turkey	17.6%

During the year ended 31 March 2010 the goodwill in relation to the Group's operations in India was impaired by £2,300 million primarily due to intense price competition following the entry of a number of new operators into the market. The pre-tax risk adjusted discount rate used in the previous value in use calculation at 31 March 2009 was 12.3%.

In addition, impairment losses of £200 million, previously recognised in respect of intangible assets in relation to the Group's operations in Turkey, were reversed. The reversal was in relation to licences and spectrum and was as a result of favourable changes in the discount rate. The cash flow projections within the business plans used for impairment testing were substantially unchanged from those used at 31 March 2009. The pre-tax risk adjusted discount rate used in the previous value in use calculation at 31 March 2009 was 19.5%.

续表

	经调整的税前折现率
意大利	11.9%
西班牙	11.5%
希腊	14.0%
爱尔兰	14.5%
葡萄牙	14.0%

在截至2011年3月31日止年度中，与本集团对意大利、西班牙、希腊、爱尔兰和葡萄牙的投资有关的商誉的减值金额分别为1,050百万英镑、2,950百万英镑、800百万英镑、1,000百万英镑以及350百万英镑。这些减值主要是由于因政府债券利率提高引起的折现率的提高而导致的。此外，业务计划内较低的现金流量也为业务估值带来了负面影响，这反映了国家层面较弱的宏观经济环境。

上一次于2010年3月31日进行的使用价值的计算中所使用的经过风险调整的税前折现率披露如下。

截至2010年3月31日止年度

减值损失净额是基于使用价值的计算而确认的。在截至2010年3月31日止年度使用价值的计算中所使用的经调整的税前折现率列示如下：

	经调整的税前折现率
印度	13.8%
土耳其	17.6%

在截至2010年3月31日止年度中，与本集团在印度的经营有关的商誉的减值金额为2,300百万英镑，其主要是由于大量新的经营者进入市场而带来的激烈的价格竞争所致。在上一次于2009年3月31日进行的使用价值的计算中所使用的经过风险调整的税前折现率为12.3%。

此外，本集团转回了前期确认的与本集团在土耳其的经营有关的无形资产的减值损失200百万英镑。该减值与许可证和占频有关，其转回是由于折现率降低所导致的。减值测试所使用的在业务计划之内的现金流量预测与2009年3月31日所使用的信息相比，并没有实质性变化。在上一次于2009年3月31日进行的使用价值的计算中所使用的经过风险调整的税前折现率为19.5%。

Con

Year ended 31 March 2009

The impairment losses were based on value in use calculations. The pre-tax adjusted discount rates used in the value in use calculation in the year ended 31 March 2009 were as follows:

	Pre-tax adjusted discount rate
Spain	10.3%
Turkey	19.5%
Ghana	26.9%

During the year ended 31 March 2009, the goodwill in relation to the Group's operations in Spain was impaired by £3,400 million following a fall in long term cash flow forecasts resulting from the economic downturn.

In addition, the goodwill and other intangible assets in relation to the Group's operations in Turkey was impaired by £2,250 million. At 30 September 2008, the goodwill was impaired by £1,700 million following adverse movements in the discount rate and adverse performance against previous plans. During the second half of the 2009 financial year, impairment losses of £300 million in relation to goodwill and £250 million in relation to licences and spectrum resulted from adverse changes in both the discount rate and a fall in the long term GDP growth rate. The cash flow projections within the business plans used for impairment testing were substantially unchanged from those used at 30 September 2008.

The goodwill in relation to the Group's operations in Ghana was impaired by £250 million following an increase in the discount rate.

Post balance-sheet events

18.66 Post balance-sheet events may provide indications that an asset was impaired at the year end. However, if the event indicates that the impairment occurred after the year end the indicator is not taken into account, although disclosure in accordance with IAS 10, 'Events after the balance sheet date', may be required.

18.66.1 The impairment test should be updated after the year end only if

续表

截至 2009 年 3 月 31 日止年度

减值损失是基于使用价值的计算而确认的。在截至 2009 年 3 月 31 日止年度的使用价值计算中所采用的经调整的税前折现率列示如下：

	经调整的税前折现率
西班牙	10.3%
土耳其	19.5%
加纳	26.9%

在截至 2009 年 3 月 31 日止年度中，与本集团在西班牙的经营有关的商誉的减值金额为 3,400 百万英镑，其原因为经济衰退所导致的对长期现金流量预测的下降。

此外，与本集团在土耳其的经营有关的商誉和其他无形资产的减值金额为 2,250 百万英镑。于 2008 年 9 月 30 日，由于折现率的不利走向以及低于前期计划的不良业绩，该商誉的减值金额为 1,700 百万英镑。在 2009 财务年度的下半年，由于折现率的不利变化以及长期 GDP 增长率的下滑，与商誉有关的减值损失为 300 百万英镑，而与许可证和占频有关的减值损失为 250 百万英镑。减值测试所使用的在业务计划之内的现金流量预测与 2008 年 9 月 30 日所使用的信息相比，并没有实质性变化。

与本集团在加纳的经营有关的商誉的减值金额为 250 百万英镑，其原因为折现率的升高。

资产负债表日后事项

18.66 资产负债表日后事项可能会提供一些迹象，表明某项资产在年底已经发生了减值。然而，如果这种事项表明减值是在年末之后才发生的，尽管根据《国际会计准则第 10 号——资产负债表日后事项》（“IAS 10”）可能要求对其进行披露，但是在评估某项资产在年底是否发生减值时则不会被考虑。

18.66.1 只有在所依据的假设的重要变化为资产负债表日已经存在的情况提

material changes in assumptions provide additional evidence relating to conditions that existed at the balance sheet date. This requires an analysis of facts and circumstances in order to distinguish between adjusting and non-adjusting information. This is a difficult judgement but a continuation of a previously observed trend does not usually warrant further adjustment as the trend should have been incorporated into the most recent impairment calculation. Currency and foreign exchange movements subsequent to the year end would also seldom be a reason to update year end impairment calculations. However, information available subsequent to the year end that indicates that conditions were much worse than thought might indicate that management should update impairment calculations. For example, an entity might make the following assessments:

- Statistical figures released in February 20X9 on consumer spending in the fourth quarter of 20X8 that indicates a 20 per cent contraction in the relevant industry, whereas the expected figure was 10 per cent, may be an adjusting event. Whether there is an adjustment or not would depend on whether the post balance sheet date information on the out-turn for the year casts doubt on the assumptions made in the forecast cash flows for impairment testing purposes.

- Incremental cash flow forecasts arising from a decision made in January 20X9 to launch a new product is a non-adjusting event.

- Further fall in the oil price in January 20X9 due to the cooling in the economy is a non-adjusting event.

Significant information on changes subsequent to year end should be disclosed in the financial statements if the impact is material.

Example – Customer announces plant closure post-year end

Entity A is a major supplier to a car manufacturer, Entity Z, and its year end is 30 June. In August entity Z announces the closure of its manufacturing plant in the UK in two years' time. As a result of this, entity A's plant and machinery, which is dedicated to supplying entity Z, will have a remaining useful life of only two years. In addition, the company's factory premises will be impaired as they have no alternative use.

供了额外证据的情况下，才应当在年末之后对减值测试进行更新。这要求对事实和所处环境进行分析，以区分调整信息和非调整信息。这是一个很难的判断，但是，以前所观察到的趋势的延续通常不必作出进一步的调整，这是因为该趋势应当已经纳入最新的减值计算中了。年末之后发生的货币和外汇的波动也很少会成为更新年末进行的减值计算的理由。然而，年末之后可获得的信息显示情况远比想象中更为糟糕时，则该信息表明管理层应当对减值计算进行更新。例如，主体可能会作出下列评估：

■ 20X9 年 2 月公布的 2008 年第四季度消费者支出的统计数据表明有关行业下降了 20%，而预期的数字为 10%，这可能是一个调整事项。是否需要调整取决于资产负债表日后取得的有关当年产量的信息是否会对为减值测试所做的现金流量预测中使用的假设产生怀疑。

■ 由在 20X9 年 1 月作出的推出一款新产品的决定所导致的现金流量预测的增加，是一个非调整事项。

■ 由于经济冷却导致的油价在 2009 年 1 月进一步下跌，是一个非调整事项。

有关年末之后发生的各种变化的重大信息，如果其影响是重要的，应当在财务报表中予以披露。

示例——客户宣布在年末之后关闭工厂

主体 A 是汽车制造厂主体 Z 的主要供应商，其财务年度截止日期为 6 月 30 日。八月，主体 Z 宣布将在两年后关闭其在英国的制造工厂。因此，主体 A 的那些专门用于为主体 Z 供货的工厂和机器的剩余使用寿命就只有两年了。此外，由于该公司的工厂用房并没有其他用途，因此也将减值。

Entity Z's decision is an indicator of impairment. If the entity was not aware of the decision until the August announcement, the impairment is a non-adjusting event and should be recognised in the year that entity Z announce its decision.

However, if entity A were aware that entity Z was intending to close its plant (but the announcement had been delayed only for administrative reasons), then it would be appropriate to book an impairment at the year end.

Indicators that develop over time

18.67 Sometimes indicators assume more significance over time, perhaps as general market conditions worsen or as an entity's performance gradually deteriorates. Entities should be alert to such trends and to their potential for becoming indicators of impairment.

18.67.1 Situations exist where impairments are the result of changes in economic conditions or other factors that develop over time. For example, industry trends that indicate a potential decrease in demand for an entity's product do not always develop to the point where an impairment indicator might be identified within one reporting cycle. A situation might exist where the trend in sales has reflected a 5 per cent annual decrease for a few years, or where the market share of the entity's principal products has declined steadily. Any plans for reversing negative trends should be critically evaluated.

Example – Impairment indicator-market trends

An entity is in the business of manufacturing CD players. Industry forecasts indicate a decrease in demand for the entity's product over the next five years due to growth in demand for competing products such as mp3 players, and resurgence in demand for turntables.

Management should consider this trend in assessing impairment. External trends as well as discrete events may indicate that an asset is impaired.

Trends such as overcapacity in a particular industry, or a change in the demand for a product due to technological, market or other conditions, should be considered in assessing impairment. Management's ability and plans to reverse negative trends should be considered in assessing impairment.

主体 Z 的决定是一个减值迹象。如果主体 A 在八月份宣布此事之前一直不知道这个决定，则减值是一个非调整事项，应当在主体 Z 宣布这一决定的年度进行确认。

但是，如果主体 A 知道主体 Z 计划关闭其工厂（但只是由于管理的原因而推迟公布），那么在当年年末确认一项减值是适当的做法。

随着时间的推移所发展的迹象

18.67　有时，或许是随着市场总体情况的恶化，或许是随着主体业绩的逐渐恶化，某些迹象会随着时间的推移而变得更加明显。主体应当对这种趋势以及对其成为减值迹象的潜在可能性保持警惕。

18.67.1　由于经济状况的变化或者随着时间推移而发展的其他因素的变化而导致减值的情形是存在的。例如，行业趋势表明对某个主体的产品的需求会出现潜在的下降，但这未必会发展到在一个报告周期内可能识别出减值迹象的程度。而在销售反映出在最近几年每年下降 5% 的趋势，或者主体的主要产品的市场份额持续稳步下降的情况下，则可能会存在上述情形。任何为扭转不利趋势所作的计划都应当被仔细评估。

示例——减值迹象——市场趋势

某一主体主要从事 CD 机的制造。行业预测显示，由于对 MP3 等竞争产品的需求上升以及对转盘唱机的需求复苏，对该主体的产品的需求在未来 5 年间将会下降。

管理层在对减值进行评估时应当考虑这一趋势。外部趋势以及各种不相关联的事项都可能表明某项资产发生了减值。

在评估减值时应当考虑某些趋势，如在某个特定行业生产能力过剩，或者由于技术、市场或其他情况所导致的对产品需求的变化等。管理层扭转不利趋势的能力和计划在评估减值时也应当考虑在内。

18. 67. 2 A negative trend may reflect overcapacity in a particular industry. There would be little that the management of an individual entity could do to affect pricing in such circumstances, thus increasing the likelihood of impairment. The application of the impairment indicators to a given circumstance should then be considered over a continuum rather than as a single event. Management should have such trend information readily available. It is a matter of judgement as to when a particular trend becomes significant enough to be deemed an impairment indicator.

Annual impairment review for goodwill and certain intangibles

18. 68 Goodwill and intangible assets that are deemed to have an indefinite useful life are tested annually for impairment (irrespective of indicators). [IAS 36 para 10].

18. 69 Intangibles that are not yet ready for use must also be tested annually because they are not being amortised. The ability of an intangible asset to generate sufficient future economic benefits to recover its carrying amount is usually more uncertain before it is brought into use. [IAS 36 para 11].

18. 70 The impairment tests on goodwill and intangibles may be performed at any time in the financial year, provided that the tests are performed at the same time each year. An entity can choose to perform their impairment test at less busy times of the year. Different intangibles and, for goodwill tests, different CGUs may be tested at different times. However, where an intangible or goodwill was recognised during the current financial period it must be tested for impairment before the end of the current period. [IAS 36 paras 10 (a), 96]. If any assumptions change or there is a further impairment trigger prior to the year end, the calculation should be updated accordingly.

Example – Timing of impairment test

Entity A, a telecoms company, has goodwill and intangibles with indefinite useful lives and a 31 December year end. Under IAS 36, these assets are required to be tested annually for impairment irrespective of indictors of impairment. [IAS 36 para 10].

18.67.2　某一不利趋势可能反映了在某个特定行业生产能力过剩。在这种情况下，一个单独的主体的管理层对影响定价无能为力，因此发生减值的可能性增加了。减值迹象在某一特定环境下的应用，应该作为一个连续体而非一个单独事项进行考虑。管理层应当掌握此类容易获得的趋势信息。某一特定趋势何时会变得重要到足以被视为一个减值迹象，是需要运用判断的。

对商誉和某些无形资产的年度减值复核

18.68　对于商誉和那些被认为是使用寿命不确定的无形资产，应当每年进行减值测试（而无论是否存在减值迹象）。[IAS 36 第 10 段]。

18.69　由于尚未达到使用状态的无形资产没有被摊销，因此也必须每年对其进行测试。在某项无形资产投入使用之前，其能够产生足够的未来经济利益以收回其账面价值的能力通常是更加不确定的。[IAS 36 第 11 段]。

18.70　商誉和无形资产的减值测试可以在财务年度中的任何时间进行，但前提是该测试要在每年相同的时间进行。主体可以选择在一年当中的淡季进行减值测试。可以在不同的时间对不同的无形资产和（对商誉的测试而言）不同的现金产出单元进行测试。然而，对于在本财务期间确认的某项无形资产或者商誉，在本期期末之前必须对其进行减值测试[IAS 36 第10（a）段、第96 段]。如果年底之前任何假设发生了变化或者发生了导致进一步减值的触发事件，则应当对计算进行相应的更新。

示例——减值测试的时点

主体 A 是一家电信公司，有商誉和使用寿命不确定的无形资产，财务年度结束日为 12 月 31 日。根据 IAS 36 的要求，无论是否存在减值迹象，这些资产都应当每年进行减值测试。[IAS 36 第 10 段]。

The standard states that it is acceptable to perform impairment tests at any time in the financial year, provided they are prepared at the same time each year. Entity A could perform an impairment review using 30 September balances, which would be the same time as it completes its budgeting process for the subsequent year.

Performing the review based on September balances gives the entity sufficient time before the year end to assess the appropriateness of cash flows, the discount rate and assumptions behind the calculation.

In addition, this provides the opportunity for management to ensure that the key areas of judgement involved in the review are appropriately considered and approved. The standard requires the cash flow projections used to be those most recently approved by management.

Management can additionally start to consider the disclosure requirements, which can be extensive, and have skeleton disclosures prepared before the year end ready to import into the annual report.

If any assumptions change or there is a further impairment trigger at the year end, the calculation is required to be updated.

18. 71 In some circumstances, entities may wish to change the timing of their impairment test. This may be, for example, to align impairment testing with the budget cycle. Paragraph 96 of IAS 36 specifies that the annual impairment test of goodwill is carried out at the same time each year. However, we believe that this is an anti-abuse measure to ensure that the period between impairment tests does not exceed 12 months. To the extent that the period between tests is under one year and the change in not made to achieve a specific result (that is, to avoid an impairment charge) we would consider it acceptable to change the date of the annual impairment test. It would generally not be appropriate to change testing dates in consecutive years. As noted in paragraph 18. 70 above, it would be necessary to perform the impairment test again before the year end if a triggering event occurs after the date of the revised impairment test.

18. 71. 1 If an entity reorganises its structure, this can result in the reallocation of goodwill between CGUs. The annual impairment test may have taken place before

该准则指出，在财务年度中的任何时间进行减值测试都是可以接受的做法，但前提是该测试要在每年相同的时间进行。主体 A 可以使用 9 月 30 日的余额进行减值复核，这个时间与其完成下一年度预算编制过程的时间是相同的。

以九月份的余额为基础作减值测试，使得该主体在年底之前有足够的时间评估减值计算所使用的现金流量、折现率以及所依据的假设的适当性。

此外，在这个时点进行减值测试也为管理层提供了机会，以确保在复核中涉及判断的关键领域经过了适当的考虑和批准。该准则要求所使用的现金流量预测是由管理层最新批准的数据。

另外，管理层还可以开始考虑披露要求（披露的信息可以是非常广泛的），并且在年末之前编制披露框架，使其可以纳入到年度报告中。

如果所依据的假设发生改变或者在年末发生了触发进一步减值的事项，则更新计算结果是必需的。

18.71　在某些情况下，一些主体可能希望改变其减值测试的时点。例如，为了使减值测试和预算周期一致时可能就会出现这种情况。IAS 36 的第 96 段明确指出，商誉的年度减值测试应当在每年相同的时间进行。但是，我们认为这是一个反滥用（即防止随意改变测试时点）的措施，以确保减值测试间隔的期间不超过 12 个月。如果两次减值测试间隔的期间没有超过一年，且该改变并不会导致某一特定的结果（即避免确认减值费用），我们认为改变年度减值测试的日期是可以接受的。然而，连续几年变更测试日期的做法通常是不适当的。正如上文第 18.70 段所述，如果在修订的减值测试的日期之后又发生了某一触发事件，则在年底之前再进行一次减值测试是有必要的。

18.71.1　如果一个主体对其组织结构进行重组，则可能导致商誉在现金产出单元之间的重新分配。年度减值测试可能在重组之前已经进行，这便会引发

the reorganisation. This then raises the question as to whether an additional impairment test will be necessary, under the new CGU structure, prior to the year end. We would not usually consider the reorganisation itself to be an impairment trigger. However, if there were any impairment indicators prior to the year end, it would be necessary to perform an impairment test under the new CGU structure. Furthermore, the entity may wish to perform an impairment review under the new structure. In such a situation, the entity might consider changing the date of the annual impairment test if the circumstances are in line with those discussed in paragraph 18.71 above.

18.72 The requirement for an annual impairment test of goodwill and intangibles with indefinite useful lives or that have yet to be brought into use is in addition to the overriding requirement to test those assets whenever there are indications of impairment. Where an indicator of impairment exists, goodwill and intangible assets requiring annual impairment reviews may need to be tested for impairment more than once a year.

Example – Timing of impairment review

An entity in the automotive component supply business has a 31 December year end. The annual impairment review was carried out in September 20X8 in line with budgeted information. However, in October 20X8, two major customers announced a shut down of their sites for a prolonged period. This is an indicator of impairment and, therefore, the entity re-performed the impairment test in October 20X8 based on updated forecasts.

Interim reporting

18.72.1 IAS 34, 'Interim financial reporting', requires that the same impairment testing, recognition and reversal criteria are applied at interim reporting dates as are required at the end of the financial year. An entity will not necessarily have to make a detailed impairment calculation at the end of each interim period. An entity should review for indications of impairment at each interim reporting date to determine whether such a calculation is needed.

一个问题，即是否有必要在年底之前根据新的现金产出单元结构再做一次额外的减值测试。通常情况下，我们不认为重组本身是一个减值的触发事件。然而，如果在年底之前存在任何减值迹象，则根据新的现金产出单元结构进行减值测试就是有必要的了。此外，主体可能希望根据新的结构执行减值复核。在这种情形下，如果符合第 18.71 段中所讨论的情况，主体可能可以考虑改变年度减值测试的日期。

18.72 除了存在减值迹象时要进行减值测试这一最重要的要求之外，对于商誉以及使用寿命不确定的无形资产或者尚未达到可使用状态的无形资产而言，年度的减值测试是一项额外的要求。在存在减值迹象的情况下，对于要求每年进行减值复核的商誉和无形资产而言，可能需要在一年内进行一次以上的减值测试。

示例——减值复核的时点

某主体从事汽车零件供应业务，财务年度结束日为 12 月 31 日。该主体在 20X8 年 9 月进行年度减值复核，与预算信息保持一致。然而，在 20X8 年 10 月，两个主要客户宣布长期关闭其经营场所。这是一个减值迹象，因此，该主体在 20X8 年 10 月根据更新后的预测重新执行了减值测试。.

中期报告

18.72.1 《国际会计准则第 34 号——中期财务报告》（“IAS 34”）要求，在各个中期报告日适用的减值测试的要求以及确认和转回的条件与财务年度末所适用的是相同的。主体不必在每个中期的期末都做一个详细的减值计算。主体应当在每个中期报告日复核是否存在减值迹象，以确定是否需要做这样的计算。

Measuring recoverable amount

General matters

18.73 Recoverable amount is defined as the higher of an asset's fair value less costs to sell and its value in use. [IAS 36 para 6]. This reflects the greatest value of an asset in terms of the cash flows that can be derived from it, either by selling it or by continuing to use it in the business.

18.74 Both fair value less costs to sell and value in use can be difficult to determine in practice. It may be possible to determine fair value less costs to sell even if an asset is not traded in an active market (see para 18.124 for further detail). Sometimes it will not be possible to make an estimate of fair value less costs to sell as there is no basis for making a reliable estimate. In these circumstances recoverable amount should be determined by estimating the asset's value in use. [IAS 36 para 20]. Estimating value in use is a matter of judgement, not fact, requiring estimates of cash flows many years into the future and determining appropriate discount rates to bring them back to their present values. The objective is to make estimates as realistic as possible.

18.75 It is not always necessary to calculate both measures when performing an impairment review. If an asset's fair value less costs to sell or it's value in use exceeds the asset's carrying amount the asset is not impaired and there is no need to estimate the other amount. [IAS 36 para 19].

Example – Value in use less than fair value less costs to sell

Entity A is involved in the generation and distribution of electricity. Management is reviewing all of its assets for impairment as a result of a fall in the market price of electricity. One of the entity's power stations is two years old, has a carrying value of C2.5m and a value in use of C2.2m taking into account the revised electricity price. The market for these assets is an active one, as investors are keen to enter the market to pursue the opportunities arising from market deregulation. A similar asset was recently sold to a US-

可收回金额的计量

一般事项

18.73　可收回金额的定义为资产的公允价值减去处置费用后的净额与其使用价值两者之间的较高者。[IAS 36 第 6 段]。这反映了某项资产在从将其出售或者在业务中对其持续使用所能获得的现金流量方面的最大价值。

18.74　在实务中，公允价值减去处置费用后的净额和使用价值可能都很难确定。即使某项资产没有在活跃市场中进行交易，确定其公允价值减去处置费用后的净额也是有可能的（更多详情参见第 18.124 段）。有时候，估计公允价值减去处置费用后的净额是不可能的，这是因为缺乏作出可靠估计的基础。在这种情况下，应当通过估计资产的使用价值来确定其可收回金额。[IAS 36 第 20 段]。对使用价值的估计是判断的问题，而并非事实，这要求估计未来许多年的现金流量，并且确定适当的折现率以把它们折算为现值。其目标是使估计尽可能地切合实际。

18.75　当执行减值复核时，并不总是必需计算这两种计量结果。如果某项资产的公允价值减去处置费用后的净额或者其使用价值超过了该资产的账面价值，则该资产没有发生减值，也无需再估计其他金额。[IAS 36 第 19 段]。

示例——使用价值低于公允价值减去处置费用后的净额

主体 A 从事发电和供电业务。由于市场电价下跌，管理层正在复核其所有资产的减值情况。主体 A 的一个发电站刚刚使用了两年，账面价值为 2.5 百万元，考虑了调整之后的电价计算的使用价值为 2.2 百万元。因为有其他的投资者希望能够进入这个市场以寻求放松监管所带来的机会，因此这些资产存在一个活跃的市场。最近，有一个类似的资产以 2.6 百万元的价格销售给了一家美国的跨国电力公司。可直接归属于处置的增量成本估计为 50,000 元。

based global power utility for C2.6m. The estimated incremental costs that would be directly attributable to the disposal are C50,000.

Management has no intention of selling the power station and is proposing to recognise an impairment charge based on its value in use.

This is not correct: management should not recognise an impairment charge as the recoverable amount (the higher of value in use and fair value less costs to sell) exceeds the carrying amount. Management could recover the asset's carrying amount if it chose to sell it rather than use it in its operations, therefore, no impairment would be recorded in this situation.

18.75.1 If value in use is found to be lower than the asset's carrying amount, the asset should not automatically be written down to value in use. Before a write-down is booked, the asset's fair value less costs to sell also needs to be estimated in order to determine recoverable amount (being the higher of fair value less costs to sell and value in use).

18.76 Estimates, averages or computational short-cuts may provide a reasonable approximation of the detailed computations otherwise required by the standard to determine fair value less costs to sell or value in use. [IAS 36 para 23]. For example, it may be apparent from a review of financial data that an asset's value in use will clearly either exceed its carrying value or be exceeded by its fair value less costs to sell. In that case, a detailed calculation of value in use is not required.

18.77 Where there is no reason to believe that an asset's value in use materially exceeds its fair value less costs to sell, the asset's recoverable amount may be taken to be its fair value less costs to sell. This will often be so where an asset is to be disposed of. Its fair value less costs to sell and value in use will generally be approximately the same, because value in use then reflects mainly the net cash proceeds expected from the asset's disposal. [IAS 36 para 21]. In such a situation, the asset is not included in the assets of a CGU, even though it might otherwise have been included had it not been held for disposal. Instead the asset is considered separately, its recoverable amount is taken as its fair value less costs to sell and this is compared to its carrying value with any resulting impairment loss being recognised immediately.

管理层并无意图出售这个发电站，因此拟根据其使用价值确认一项减值费用。

这一做法是不正确的：管理层不应当确认减值费用，这是因为其可收回金额（使用价值与公允价值减去处置费用后的净额两者之间的较高者）超过了其账面价值。如果管理层选择出售该资产，而不是在经营中继续使用，则可以收回其账面价值。因此，在这种情况下，无需记录减值。

18.75.1　如果发现资产的使用价值低于其账面价值，不应当自动地把资产减记至其使用价值。减记资产的账面价值之前，还需要对资产的公允价值减去处置费用后的净额进行估计，以确定可收回金额（为公允价值减去处置费用后的净额与使用价值两者之间的较高者）。

18.76　估计、平均或者简便的计算方法可能能够为本准则所要求的确定公允价值减去处置费用后的净额或者使用价值的详细计算提供合理的近似值。[IAS 36 第 23 段]。例如，通过复核财务数据可以很明显地看出，资产的使用价值将会明显超过其账面价值，或者资产的公允价值减去处置费用后的净额明显超过使用价值。在这种情况下，使用价值的详细计算就不是必需的了。

18.77　如果没有理由认为资产的使用价值显著超过其公允价值减去处置费用后的净额，则可能会把公允价值减去处置费用后的净额作为资产的可收回金额。将要被处置的资产往往就属于这种情况。在这种情况下，一般而言，资产的公允价值减去处置费用后的净额和使用价值是近似相同的，这是因为此时的使用价值反映的主要是从资产处置中预期收到的现金净额。[IAS 36 第 21 段]。即使该资产在还没有处于持有待处置状态时是包括在某一现金产出单元中的，但是在这种情况下，它也不应当再被包括在该现金产出单元的资产中了。相反，该资产应当单独进行考虑，其可收回金额为其公允价值减去处置费用后的净额，该金额与资产的账面价值进行比较，出现任何减值损失需要立即确认。

18.78 The starting point for determining the recoverable amount in impairment testing is at the level of individual assets, unless the asset does not generate cash inflows that are largely independent of other assets or groups of assets. Where it does not generate such independent cash flows recoverable amount is determined for the cash generating unit (CGU) to which the asset belongs. A CGU is the smallest identifiable group of assets that generates cash inflows that are largely independent of the cash inflows from other assets or groups of assets [IAS 36 para 6]. A CGU can be a single asset.

Example – Test impairment at the individual asset level where possible

An item of PPE (machine B) is one of the assets used within a CGU. Machine B has become redundant and is being abandoned by management. The recoverable amount of machine B's CGU (which is profitable) exceeds its carrying amount.

Impairment should be identified at the individual asset level, where possible. Management should recognise an impairment loss for machine B, as its carrying amount is above recoverable amount.

The recoverable amount should be calculated for the CGU to which the asset belongs only where the recoverable amount for the individual asset cannot be identified. Machine B is being abandoned and, therefore, will no longer be one of the assets used within the CGU. Therefore, machine B is tested for impairment on its own, if its recoverable amount can be estimated.

18.79 IAS 36 excludes from its scope non-current assets (or disposal groups) classified as held for sale in accordance with IFRS 5, 'Non-current assets held for sale and discontinued operations'. A plan by management to dispose of an asset or group of assets is an indicator of impairment. This will usually be well before the held for sale criteria under IFRS 5 are met. Assets or CGUs are tested for impairment when the decision to sell is made. The impairment test is updated immediately before classifying as held for sale under IFRS 5. IFRS 5 requires an asset held for sale to be measured at the lower of its carrying amount and its fair value less costs to sell. The carrying amount that will be used in this measurement will be the adjusted carrying amount after the impairment test has been completed. See further chapter 26.

18.78 在进行减值测试时，确定可收回金额的起点是在单项资产的层面确定，除非该项资产不能产生在很大程度上独立于其他资产或资产组就能产生的现金流入。如果单项资产不能产生此类独立的现金流量，则可收回金额按照该项资产所属的现金产出单元（“CGU”）进行确定。CGU为最小的可识别的资产组，该资产组产生的现金流入在很大程度上独立于其他资产或资产组所产生的现金流入［IAS 36 第6段］。CGU可以是一项单独的资产。

示例——在可能的情况下，在单项资产层面执行减值测试

某固定资产（机器B）是在某一CGU中的一项资产。机器B已经成为多余的设备且正处于被管理层废弃的过程中。机器B所属的现金产出单元（处于盈利状态）的可收回金额超过其账面价值。

在可能的情况下，应当在单项资产的层面识别减值。由于机器B的账面价值超过了其可收回金额，管理层应该对其确认一项减值损失。

只有在单项资产的可收回金额无法识别时，才应当计算该资产所属的CGU的可收回金额。机器B正处在被废弃的过程中，其不再属于CGU中所使用的资产。因此，如果机器B的可收回金额能够估计，则应当对其本身进行减值测试。

18.79 IAS 36将按照《国际财务报告准则第5号——持有待售的非流动资产和终止经营》（“IFRS 5”）被分类为持有待售的非流动资产（或处置组）排除在了其规范范围之外。管理层处置某项资产或资产组的计划是一个减值迹象。通常情况下，在符合IFRS 5所规定的持有待售的标准之前便已是一个减值迹象。当作出出售的决定时，就应当对资产或者CGU进行减值测试。在按照IFRS 5分类为持有待售之前，应当立即对减值测试进行更新。IFRS 5要求对持有待售的资产应当按照其账面价值和公允价值减去处置费用后的净额两者孰低进行计量。在这一计量中所使用的账面价值将是完成减值测试之后经过调整的账面价值。进一步的讨论请参见第二十六章。

[The next paragraph is 18.81.]

18.81 Where an entity has an asset that is included in a CGU because it does not generate cash flows independently, its recoverable amount would generally be determined at the CGU level to which the asset belongs. However, this does not apply where the asset's fair value less costs to sell is higher than its carrying amount or where the asset's value in use can be estimated as being close to its fair value less costs to sell and the fair value less costs to sell can be determined. [IAS 36 para 22].

Example – Building considered separately for impairment testing

A CGU includes a head office building and that asset has a readily determinable market value. The head office building will be considered separately from the CGU for the purpose of impairment testing if its market value (less costs to sell) is clearly higher than its carrying amount. In this case, it will be possible to compare the recoverable amount with carrying amount for the individual asset, because the fair value less costs to sell is determinable. If the head office building had a market value that was less than the carrying amount then the CGU to which the asset belongs would need to be tested for impairment as the head office does not generate cash flows independently.

18.81.1 Where an asset's recoverable amount has been separately considered from the CGU to which it belongs, if the CGU is tested for impairment then no part of any impairment loss relating to the CGU is allocated to the asset if it would reduce the carrying amount of the asset below its fair value less costs to sell. [IAS 36 para 105]. Furthermore, the carrying amount of each asset within the CGU is reduced to the higher of its fair value less costs to sell and value in use. Any unallocated impairment is reallocated to the CGU's non-monetary assets, subject to the same limits. This could result in an iterative process, continuing until the impairment charge is fully allocated or until each of the CGU's non-monetary assets have been reduced to the higher of each asset's fair value less costs to sell, value in use and zero. The recognition of an impairment does not, however, result in the recognition of a liability, unless it meets the definition of a liability under another IFRS standard, for example an onerous contract under IAS 37, 'Provisions, contingent liabilities and contingent assets'. It is, therefore, possible that some of

［下一段是第 18. 81 段。］

18. 81　在主体拥有一项资产，因为其不能产生独立的现金流量而被包括在某一 CGU 中的情况下，一般而言，该资产的可收回金额应当在其所属的 CGU 的层面确定。然而，在该项资产的公允价值减去处置费用后的净额高于其账面价值，或者能够估计资产的使用价值接近于其公允价值减去处置费用后的净额且该公允价值减去处置费用后的净额可以确定的情况下，这一要求并不适用。［IAS 36 第 22 段］。

示例——考虑单独进行减值测试的建筑物

某个 CGU 中包括总部办公大楼，且该资产的市场价值随时可以确定。如果总部办公大楼的市场价值（减去处置费用）明显高于其账面价值，则在做减值测试时，会把其从 CGU 中分离出来而单独进行考虑。在这种情况下，把单项资产的可收回金额与账面价值进行比较是有可能的，这是因为其公允价值减去处置费用后的净额是可确定的。如果总部办公大楼的市场价值低于其账面价值，则需要对该资产所属的现金产出单元进行减值测试，这是因为总部办公大楼无法单独产生现金流量。

18. 81. 1　在某项资产的可收回金额已经从其所属的 CGU 中分离出来而单独考虑的情况下，对该 CGU 做减值测试时，如果与该 CGU 相关的任何减值损失的部分会导致资产的账面价值低于公允价值减去处置费用后的净额，则该减值损失都不会分配给该项资产。［IAS 36 第 105 段］。此外，该 CGU 内每项资产的账面价值都要被减低至其公允价值减去处置费用后的净额与使用价值两者中较高的金额。任何未分配的减值都会按照同样的限制重新分配至 CGU 中的各项非货币资产。这可能导致出现一个反复的过程，并且会一直持续到减值费用被全部分配完毕或者该 CGU 中的每一项非货币资产都已经被减记至其公允价值减去处置费用后的净额、使用价值和零三者之间的较高金额为止。然而，除非符合另一个国际财务报告准则中对于负债的定义（例如，《国际会计准则第 37 号——准备、或有负债及或有资产》（“IAS 37”）下的亏损合同），否则确认减值费用并不会导致确认一项负债。因此，某些减值损失没有被确认是可能的。

the impairment loss will not be recognised.

Example – Impairment of individual assets in a closure

An entity is closing a division after the year end. No provision has been made for redundancies at the year end, because the announcement of the closure was not made until after the year end. However, the entity is looking at impairment of the division's assets. The plant and equipment is likely to be impaired as the recoverable amount is expected to be lower than the carrying amount, but the property is expected to be sold at a profit (the entity will start to look for a buyer after the year end).

In determining the charge for impairment at the year end does the entity consider the total assets of the division including the property as one CGU or look at individual assets? The profit expected to be made on the property is large enough to offset the impairment on the plant.

Assets should be individually considered for impairment if there is any indication that the asset is impaired. In this case the plant and equipment is impaired and the impairment should be booked in the current year financial statements. No impairment charge would be recognised in respect of the property.

18.82 If a CGU has goodwill allocated or other intangible assets with indefinite lives, the standard permits the most recent detailed calculation of recoverable amount made in a previous period to be used in the current period if the following conditions are met:

- For goodwill allocated to a CGU and those intangibles that do not generate cash flows independently of other assets and are, therefore, tested as part of a CGU
  - The assets and liabilities of the CGU, to which such goodwill or intangibles were allocated, have not changed significantly since the last impairment test.
  - The most recent impairment test resulted in an amount that exceeded the CGU's carrying amount by a substantial margin.
  - Analysis of events that have occurred and changes in circumstances since the last review indicate that the likelihood that the current recoverable amount of the CGU would be less that its carrying amount is remote.

示例——由于关闭而引起单项资产的减值

某个主体将会在年末之后关闭一个部门。由于年末之后才宣布关闭的决定，因此在年末并没有对遣散员工计提任何准备。然而，该主体正在考虑该部门资产的减值情况。由于可收回金额预期会低于账面价值，厂房和设备可能要减值了，但是其房产预期会被出售且有盈利（该主体在年末之后即将开始寻找买家）。

在年末确定减值费用时，该主体应当把这个部门包括房产在内的全部资产作为一个 CGU 考虑，还是应当把各个单项资产分别考虑？出售房产预期产生的利润足以弥补厂房的减值。

如果有任何迹象表明一项资产发生了减值，则应当对各项资产分别考虑减值。在这个案例中，厂房和设备发生了减值，因此应该在当年的财务报表中记录减值。对于房产，则无需确认减值费用。

18.82　如果一个 CGU 有分摊而至的商誉或者其他使用寿命不确定的无形资产，如果符合下列条件，该准则允许在本期间使用前一期间所做的最近一次的可收回金额的详细计算：

- 对于分摊给某一 CGU 的商誉和那些由于独立于其他资产就不能产生现金流量而要作为 CGU 的一部分进行测试的无形资产：
  - 该分摊了商誉或无形资产的 CGU 中的资产和负债自上次减值测试之后没有发生重大变化。
  - 最近一次的减值测试得出的金额远远超过了该 CGU 的账面价值。
  - 对在上一次减值复核之后所发生的事项以及环境变化的分析显示，该 CGU 当前的可收回金额低于其账面价值的可能性是很小的。

- If an intangible asset is assessed for impairment as a single asset (that is it generates cash flows independently of other assets and is not, therefore, reviewed for impairment as part of a CGU):
  - The most recent impairment test resulted in an amount that exceeded the asset's carrying amount by a substantial margin.
  - Analysis of events that have occurred and changes in circumstances since the last review indicate that the likelihood that the asset's current recoverable amount would be less than its carrying amount is remote.

[IAS 36 paras 24, 99].

[The next paragraph is 18.98.]

Cash-generating units

General principles

18.98 The recoverable amount of an individual asset cannot be determined if the asset does not generate cash inflows from continuing use that are largely independent from those from other assets and its value in use cannot be estimated to be close to its fair value less costs to sell. In such cases, value in use and, therefore, recoverable amount can be determined only for the asset's CGU. [IAS 36 para 67]. Note, however, that where the fair value less costs to sell of an individual asset is known and is in excess of the carrying amount the asset is not impaired.

18.99 Where the recoverable amount cannot be estimated for individual assets, it should be estimated for groups of assets that generate cash flows that are largely independent of each other. These are referred to as cash generating units (CGUs). Where an impairment review of a CGU is required, it should cover all its tangible assets, intangible assets and attributable goodwill. The carrying value of each CGU containing the assets and goodwill being reviewed should be compared with the higher of its value in use or fair value less costs to sell (if fair value less costs to sell can be measured reliably). [IAS 36 para 20].

Example – Asset that does not generate separate cash flows

An entity owns and operates a large waste recycling plant and a private

■ 如果某项无形资产作为单项资产进行减值评估（即其独立于其他资产就能产生现金流量，因此不作为 CGU 的一部分进行减值复核）：

■ 最近一次的减值测试得出的金额远远超过了该资产的账面价值。

■ 对在上一次减值复核之后所发生的事项和环境变化的分析显示，该资产当前的可收回金额低于其账面价值的可能性是很小的。

[IAS 36 第 24 段、第 99 段]。

[下一段为第 18.98 段。]

现金产出单元

一般原则

18.98 如果一项资产从其持续使用中不能产生在很大程度上独立于其他资产所产生的现金流入，并且估计该资产的使用价值与其公允价值减去处置费用后的净额并不接近，则该单项资产的可收回金额无法确定。因此，在此类情况下，只能确定该资产所属的 CGU 的使用价值和可收回金额。[IAS 36 第 67 段]。然而，需要注意的是，如果某一单项资产的公允价值减去处置费用后的净额已知并且大于其账面价值，则该资产没有发生减值。

18.99 在单项资产的可收回金额无法估计的情况下，应当估计能够产生在很大程度上彼此独立的现金流量的资产组的可收回金额。这些资产组被称为不同的现金产出单元（CGUs）。在必须对某一 CGU 做减值复核的情况下，该复核应当涵盖其所有的有形资产、无形资产以及可归属于该 CGU 的商誉。（如果公允价值减去处置费用后的净额能够可靠计量），应当把所复核的、含有资产和商誉的每个 CGU 的账面价值与其使用价值和公允价值减去处置费用后的净额两者中的较高者进行比较。[IAS 36 第 20 段]。

示例——不产生单独现金流量的资产

一个主体拥有并经营一个大型废物回收工厂，并且拥有一条私有铁路，

railway that transports the processed waste in containers from the plant to the main public rail network. The private railway could be sold only for scrap value and the railway does not generate cash inflows from continuing use that are largely independent of the cash inflows of the plant as a whole.

It is not possible to estimate the recoverable amount of the private railway, because the value in use of the railway cannot be determined. The scrap value of the railway is below its carrying value. The entity, therefore, estimates the recoverable amount of the CGU (the plant as a whole) to which the railway belongs.

[The next paragraph is 18. 102.]

Identifying CGUs

18. 102 Identifying CGUs is the first key step in carrying out impairment reviews. This establishes the level of aggregation at which impairment reviews would normally be carried out.

18. 103 A cash generating unit (CGU) is defined as "*···the smallest identifiable group of assets that generates cash inflows that are largely independent of the cash inflows from other assets or groups of assets*". [IAS 36 para 6].

18. 104 The higher the level of aggregation the greater is the risk that impairment losses on unprofitable assets might be masked by unrecognised increases in value of profitable ones. Hence, impairment reviews should be carried out at the lowest level that generates largely independent cash flows.

18. 105 Cash inflows are cash flows received from external parties. The independence of cash flows will be indicated by various factors including, for example, by product lines, businesses, individual locations, districts or regional areas or how management makes decisions about continuing or disposing of the entity's assets and operations. [IAS 36 para 69]. Management's day to day operation of the business may not reflect the legal structure through which the operations are conducted.

18. 105. 1 Individual hotels usually generate income that is largely independent of others and their performance is monitored closely by management on an individual

用于把装于集装箱内的经过加工的废物从工厂运送到主要的公共铁路网络。该铁路只能以报废价值出售，并且从其持续使用中不能产生在很大程度上独立于整个工厂所产生的现金流入。

估计这条私有铁路的可收回金额是不可能的，这是因为其使用价值无法确定。这条铁路的报废价值低于其账面价值。因此，该主体应当估计该铁路所属的 CGU（整个工厂）的可收回金额。

[下一段是第 18.102 段。]

识别现金产出单元

18.102　进行减值复核时，识别 CGU 是第一个关键步骤。它确定了在正常情况下应该要在哪一个集合层面上执行减值复核。

18.103　现金产出单元（CGU）的定义是："……*能够产生在很大程度上独立于其他资产或资产组所产生的现金流入的可识别的最小资产组*。"[IAS 36 第 6 段]。

18.104　在集合程度越高的层面进行减值测试，那些并不赢利的资产的减值损失可能被未确认的赢利资产的价值增加所掩盖的风险也就越大。因此，应当在能够产生在很大程度上独立的现金流量的最低层级执行减值复核。

18.105　现金流入是指从外部各方收到的现金流量。包括如生产线、业务、单独的场所、地区或区域、或者管理层如何对继续经营或处置主体的资产和经营作出决策在内的各种因素都可以显示现金流量的独立性。[IAS 36 第 69 段]。管理层对业务的日常经营可能并没有反映出从事经营的法律架构。

18.105.1　通常情况下，每个不同的酒店都能够赚取在很大程度上独立于其他酒店收入的收入，并且管理层会分别对每个酒店各自的业绩进行密切监督。

basis. It is, therefore, probable that they form individual CGUs, even if there are central sales and marketing and finance functions.

18.106 If there is an active market for the output produced by an asset or by a group of assets, that asset or group of assets should be identified as a CGU, even if some or all of its output is used internally. This is because there is an active external market for each stage of production. Each stage should, therefore, be regarded as a CGU, with value in use based on management's best estimate of future cash flows. Where some of the output is used internally, management should use its best estimate of future arm's length prices for that output:

- To estimate the future cash inflows that relate to the sale of the output by the CGU to the entity's other CGUs (when determining the value in use of the CGU that produces the output).
- To estimate the future cash outflows that relate to the purchase of the output by the other CGUs (when determining the value in use of those other CGUs).

[IAS 36 para 70].

18.107 This provision of the standard is particularly relevant for vertically integrated operations, for example in the oil or mining industry, where there is likely to be an active market for the product.

Example – CGUs in a vertically integrated group

Entity P is a vertically integrated electricity utility. It has three distinguishable businesses: generation, distribution and supply. There are active markets for the output of the generation and distribution businesses. The generation business sells power to the distribution business, which distributes electricity to the supply business. Internal transfer pricing approximates market price.

Each business is considered a separate CGU.

Management should use external prices when determining value in use for a CGU in a vertically-integrated operation.

18.108 In such situtations market prices are used because the asset or group of assets could generate cash inflows that are independent of those of the other assets or groups

因此，即使存在集中管理的销售、市场营销以及财务等职能部门，每个酒店很可能会构成一个单独的 CGU。

18.106　如果某一资产或资产组所生产的产品存在活跃市场，即使这些产品中有部分或者全部都是供内部使用的，也应当把该资产或资产组识别为一个 CGU。这是因为对于生产的每一个阶段都有一个活跃的外部市场。因此，每个生产阶段都应当被视为一个 CGU，其使用价值基于管理层对未来现金流量的最佳估计确定。在部分产品供内部使用的情况下，管理层应当运用其对该产品未来的公平价格的最佳估计：

- （当确定生产该产品的 CGU 的使用价值时）估计与该 CGU 向主体的其他 CGU 销售该产品相关的未来现金流入。
- （当确定其他 CGU 的使用价值时）估计与其他 CGU 购买该产品相关的未来现金流出。

［IAS 36 第 70 段］。

18.107　该准则的这一规定与垂直一体化经营特别相关，例如，在石油或者采矿行业，其产品可能就存在活跃市场。

示例——垂直一体化经营的集团中的 CGUs

主体 P 是一个垂直一体化经营的电力公司。它有三个可以区分的业务：发电、配电和供电。发电和配电业务的产品存在活跃的市场。发电业务将电力销售给配电业务，配电业务把电力配送给供电业务。内部转移价格和市场价格近似。

每个业务都被认为是一个单独的 CGU。

管理层在确定垂直一体化经营中的某个 CGU 的使用价值时，应当使用外部价格。

18.108　在此类情形下应当使用市场价格，其原因是该资产或资产组可以产生独立于属于该主体的其他资产或资产组的现金流入的现金流入。可以通过

of assets belonging to the entity. It could do this by selling on the active external market the output it presently sells to other parts of the entity. [IAS 36 para 71].

18.108.1 Paragraph 70 of IAS 36 is written with reference to situations where there is an active market for the output generated by an asset. Active market is defined in paragraph 6 of IAS 36 as a market where the items traded are homogenous, willing buyers and sellers can normally be found at any time and prices are available to the public. In some situations, corporate assets could potentially generate independent cash inflows in an active market but it may not be appropriate to apply paragraph 70 of IAS 36. An example of this is a corporate asset such as an office building. This is illustrated in the example below.

Example – No active market for output produced by a corporate asset

Entity A owns a 20 floor office building that is in good condition. The building is half-rented to third parties and half-rented to a subsidiary within Entity A's group as a corporate asset. The building has no special recognition value. The portion rented to the subsidiary is accounted for under IAS 16, 'Property, plant and equipment', and the other portion is treated as an investment property in accordance with IAS 40, 'Investment properties'. Entity A uses the cost model for the investment property. The recoverable amount of the investment property is lower than its carrying amount, but the CGU to which the own-use portion of the property belongs is profitable.

We would consider that there are two reasonable approaches:

(a) the whole building is an asset that cannot be tested for impairment on a stand-alone basis and the building is, therefore, tested for impairment as part of a larger CGU; or

(b) the rented portion of the building is tested as a separate CGU and the own-use portion of the building is a corporate asset that is allocated to the relevant CGU for impairment testing.

Approach (a) is that outlined in illustrative example E to IAS 36. We would also consider approach (b) to be acceptable to the extent that the cash flows from the different portions of the building are largely independent of one another (as they are in this example).

在活跃的外部市场上出售目前出售给主体内部其他业务的产品而产生现金流入。[IAS 36 第 71 段]。

18.108.1　IAS 36 第 70 段涉及了一项资产生产的产品存在活跃市场的情况。根据 IAS 36 第 6 段的定义，活跃市场为这样一个市场：市场中交易的项目是同质的，通常可在任何时候找到自愿交易的买方和卖方并且价格是公开的。在某些情形下，总部资产也可能在活跃市场中潜在地产生独立的现金流量，但是对它而言，应用 IAS 36 第 70 段的要求可能是不适当的。办公楼就是总部资产的一个例子，请看下文的说明性示例。

示例——总部资产产出的产品不存在活跃市场

主体 A 拥有一栋 20 层的办公楼且其状况良好。该大楼有一半出租给第三方，另一半作为总部资产出租给主体 A 集团内的一家子公司。该大楼无特殊确认价值。出租给子公司的部分按照《国际会计准则第 16 号——不动产、工厂和设备》进行会计处理，而其他部分作为投资性房地产按照《国际会计准则第 40 号——投资性房地产》进行会计处理。主体 A 使用成本模式对投资性房地产进行核算。该投资性房地产的可收回金额低于其账面价值，但是该房地产自用部分所归属的现金产出单元是盈利的。

我们认为存在以下两种合理的处理方式：

(a) 整栋大楼是一项无法对其单独进行减值测试的资产，因此，应当将该大楼作为更大的 CGU 中的一部分而对其进行减值测试；或者

(b) 将该大楼的出租部分作为一个单独的 CGU 进行测试，而自用部分作为总部资产，将其分摊至相关的 CGU 进行减值测试。

方法（a）是在 IAS 36 的说明性示例 E 中所概述的方法。如果该栋大楼的不同部分产生的现金流量在很大程度上是彼此独立的（如本例所示），则我们认为方法（b）也是可以接受的。

18. 109 The flow chart below gives guidance on determining the level at which to perform an impairment test, whether it is at the individual asset or CGU level.

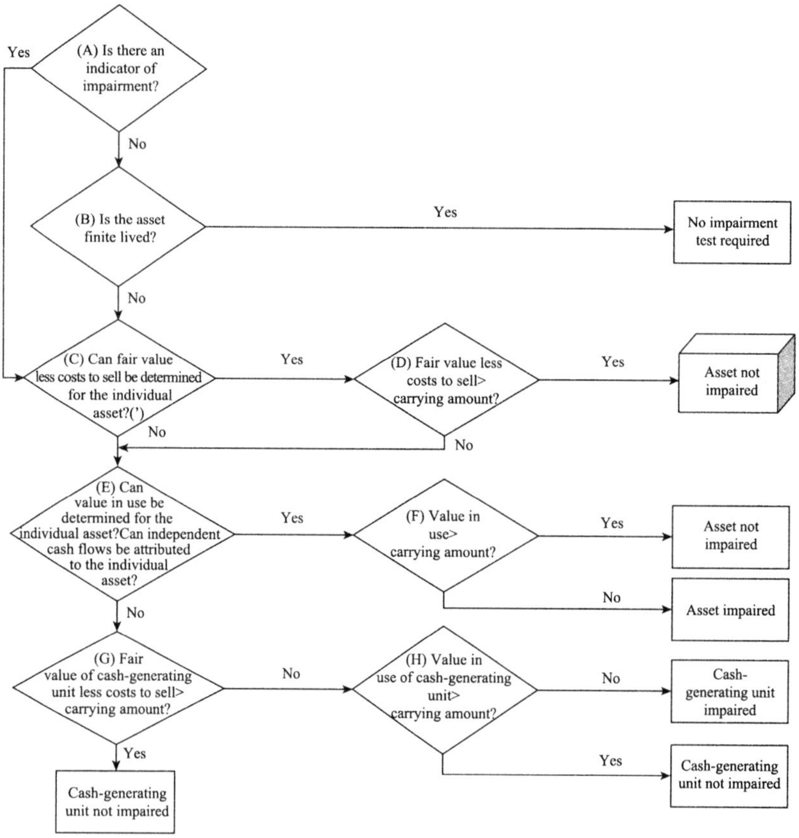

[The next paragraph is 18. 111.]

18. 111 Identifying CGUs requires judgement. [IAS 36 para 68]. The standard includes examples to illustrate how CGUs may be identified in various situations and to highlight factors that an entity may consider in identifying CGUs.

Example 1 – Determination of CGU

Entity H uses asset O to manufacture plastic components that are sold to third parties. Entity H's management has discontinued production of the components as a result of a fall in demand and has reconfigured the asset for use in the manufacture of product T. Revenues from the sale of product T

18.109 以下的流程图为确定在哪一层面（即在单项资产还是 CGU 层面）执行减值测试提供了指引：

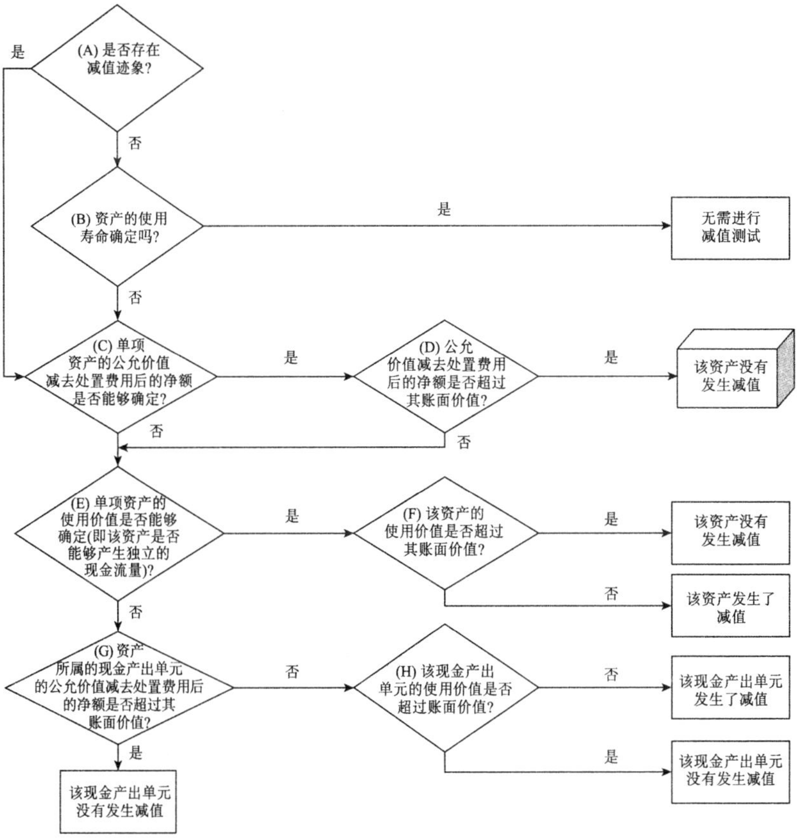

[下一段是第 18.111 段。]

18.111 识别 CGU 需要运用判断［IAS 36 第 68 段］。该准则中包含了很多示例，以说明在各种不同的情形下如何识别 CGU，并且强调主体在识别 CGU 的过程中可能需要考虑的因素。

示例 1——CGU 的确定

主体 H 用资产 O 制造塑料零件，然后出售给第三方。由于需求下降，主体 H 的管理层已经停止了塑料零件的生产，并且对资产进行重新改装以用于制造产品 T。产品 T 的销售收入不能直接归属于其生产过程中所使用的任何一项资产。

cannot be directly attributed to any single asset used in its manufacture.

Asset O will only render economic benefit as part of product T's CGU. As revenues from the sale of product T cannot be directly attributed to any asset, asset O will be tested for impairment as part of T's CGU. It is not possible to determine fair value less cost to sell for asset O.

The value in use of the entire CGU will be compared with the carrying value of the entire CGU including asset O in order to identify any impairment.

Example 2 – Integrated businesses treated as country CGU's

Entity A, a telecommunications entity, owns an integrated voice and data network over several countries. The network is connected end-to-end over entity A's footprint. Each country network comprises city rings, regional rings and a long distance network.

The network assets and associated revenue streams in each country are recorded and monitored independently.

Entity A makes decisions on the deployment of resources on a geographic basis. Entity A can distinguish between voice and data revenues. However, because the voice and data networks are integrated it is not possible to identify specific assets or groupings of assets that generate either voice or data revenues.

In these circumstances, Entity A should classify each country as a separate CGU. Entity A can reliably identify and measure cash flows generated from each country's asset base. This represents the smallest identifiable group of assets that generate independent cash flows that are monitored by management.

Entity A cannot reliably measure and does not monitor separately the cash flows from the city and regional rings or from the long distance network. Furthermore, while entity A can identify revenue from voice and data services separately, it cannot attribute those cash flows to distinct network assets. The appropriate CGUs are therefore on a country-by-country basis.

[The next paragraph is 18.114.]

18.114 A further example in the illustrative examples in the standard considers vertical integration.

资产 O 将只作为产品 T 所属的 CGU 的一部分而产生经济利益。由于产品 T 的销售收入不能直接归属于任何一项资产，因此资产 O 将会作为产品 T 所属的 CGU 的一部分而进行减值测试。确定资产 O 的公允价值减去处置费用后的净额是不可能的。

应当把整个 CGU 的使用价值与包括资产 O 在内的整个 CGU 的账面价值进行比较，以识别是否发生了减值。

示例 2——作为国家 CGU 处理的一体化业务

主体 A 是一家电信主体，其拥有一个覆盖了几个国家的一体化语音和数据网络。这个网络在主体 A 所涉足的范围内以端对端的方式连接在一起。每个国家的网络都由城市环网、地区环网和长途网络组成。

每个国家的网络资产和相关收入都是单独记录和监督的。

主体 A 以地理分布为基础而作出配置其资源的决定。主体 A 能够区分语音收入和数据收入。但是，因为语音网络和数据网络是一体化的，识别出分别产生语音收入或数据收入的专门资产或资产组是不可能的。

在这些情况下，主体 A 应当把每个国家划分为一个单独的 CGU。主体 A 能够可靠地识别并计量每个国家的资产所产生的现金流量。这代表了能够产生受管理层监控的独立现金流量的可识别的最小资产组。

主体 A 不能可靠地计量也没有分别监控城市及地区环网或者长途网络所产生的现金流量。此外，即使主体 A 能够单独识别语音收入和数据收入，其也不能把这些现金流量归属到性质不同的网络资产上。因此，适当的 CGU 是以每个国家为基础确定的。

[下一段是第 18.114 段。]

18.114　在该准则的说明性示例中给出了另外一个有关垂直一体化经营的示例。

Example – Vertically integrated CGU's

The reporting entity has two plants. Plant A produces raw material that is sold to plant B of the same entity. The raw material is sold by plant A to plant B at a price that transfers all the margins to plant A. 60% of plant A's production is sold to plant B and 40% is sold to external customers outside the reporting entity. 80% of plant B's production is sold to external customers of the reporting entity.

The issue is to determine the CGUs for plant A and plant B when:

- Plant A could sell its production in an active market instead of to plant B.
- There is no active market for the production of plant A.

In the first situation there is an active market for plant A's production so it is likely that plant A is a separate CGU. (See para 18.91 above). Plant B would also be a separate CGU, because it sells 80% of its output externally and so generates cash flows that are largely independent of the cash flows from the other assets of the reporting entity. In the financial forecasts and budgets used for determining value in use for both plant A and plant B the internal transfer prices for the production sold by plant A to plant B should be adjusted to arm's length prices.

In the second situation there is no active market for the output of plant A and the cash inflows of plant A depend on the demand for the product sold by plant B. Plant A does not generate cash flows that are largely independent of the cash flows of assets operated by plant B. Also the two plants are managed together, as the use of internal transfer prices demonstrates. Therefore, the two plants should be treated as one CGU.

18.115 The standard contains two further practical examples. The first concerns magazine titles and the second is a building that is half rented to others and half occupied for own use. Each of these further examples illustrates the principles described above.

Example 1 – Magazine titles that are separate CGU's

In this example the entity owns 150 titles, 70 of which were purchased and 80

示例——垂直一体化的 CGU

报告主体有两个工厂。工厂 A 生产原材料，该原材料会销售给同一主体下的工厂 B。工厂 A 向工厂 B 销售原材料的价格会把所有的毛利都转移给工厂 A。工厂 A 60% 的产品销售给工厂 B，其余的 40% 销售给报告主体以外的外部客户。工厂 B 80% 的产品都销售给报告主体以外的外部客户。

问题是在下列情况下，如何确定工厂 A 和工厂 B 的 CGU：

- 工厂 A 可以在一个活跃市场上销售其产品，而不销售给工厂 B。
- 工厂 A 的产品没有活跃市场。

在第一种情况下，工厂 A 的产品存在一个活跃市场，因此工厂 A 有可能是一个单独的 CGU。（参见上文第 18.91 段）。工厂 B 也是一个独立的 CGU，因为其 80% 的产品是对外销售，因而能够产生在很大程度上独立于该报告主体的其他资产的现金流量。在确定工厂 A 和工厂 B 的使用价值所使用的财务预测和预算中，工厂 A 向工厂 B 销售产品的内部转移价格应当调整为公平价格。

在第二种情况下，工厂 A 的产品不存在活跃市场，因此工厂 A 的现金流入取决于工厂 B 所销售的产品的需求。工厂 A 不产生在很大程度上独立于工厂 B 运营的资产所产生的现金流量的现金流量。此外，正如其使用内部转移价格所揭示的，这两个工厂是一起管理的。因此，应当把这两个工厂作为一个 CGU 处理。

18.115　该准则还给出了另外两个实务中的示例。第一个是有关杂志刊名的，第二个是有关一半出租一半自用的建筑物的。这两个示例都对上述原则作了进一步的举例说明。

示例 1——作为单独的 CGU 的杂志刊名

在这个示例中，主体拥有 150 个刊名，其中 70 个是从外部购入的，80 个

were created internally. The costs of purchasing the 70 titles are capitalised as an intangible and the costs of creating titles internally are written off. Cash inflows from sales and advertising are separately identifiable for each title. Titles are managed by customer segments. The level of advertising income for a title depends on the range of titles in the customer segment to which the title relates. The management policy is to abandon titles before the end of their useful economic lives and replace them with new, internally generated titles for the same customer segment.

In this situation the standard concludes that individual titles are CGUs. This is because cash inflows for each individual title can be identified, even though the advertising income for each title may be influenced by the range of titles in the customer segment to which it belongs. In addition, although titles are managed by customer segment, decisions to abandon titles are made on an individual title basis.

Example 2 – Part of property does not generate independent cash flows

The entity owns an administrative building that, following a down sizing of the entity's operations, is half owner occupied and half rented out to a third party on a five year lease. It is not possible to sell an individual portion of the building or to lease it out separately under a finance lease. In this situation, the standard concludes that because the building's primary purpose is for corporate administration, it cannot be considered to generate cash flows independent of the entity's cash flows as a whole. Therefore, it is likely that the CGU for the building is the entity as a whole. The building is not held as an investment and, therefore, it would not be appropriate to determine the building's value in use based on projections of future market related rents. However, the rentals received would be included in the cash flows of the entity as a whole when determining its value in use as a CGU.

Depending on the facts and circumstances, it may also be acceptable to separate the two halves of the building for impairment testing purposes, treating the half rented portion of the building as a separate CGU and the owner occupied half as a corporate asset to be tested for impairment within a larger CGU (see para 18.108.1).

是自创的。购买70个刊名所花费的成本资本化为无形资产，而自创刊名的成本都被核销了。每个刊名由销售和广告产生的现金流入都是可以单独识别的。这些刊名是按照不同的客户分部进行管理的。某个刊名取得的广告收入的水平取决于与该刊名有关的客户分部中的刊名的范围。管理层的政策是在这些刊名的经济使用寿命结束之前将其放弃，并且用一些新的、针对同一客户分部的自创刊名取而代之。

在这种情况下，该准则得出的结论是，每一个刊名都是一个CGU。这是因为，即便每一个刊名的广告收入可能会受到其所属的客户分部内刊名范围的影响，但是每一个刊名所产生的现金流入都是可以识别的。此外，尽管这些刊名是按照客户分部进行管理，但是放弃这些刊名的决定是在每一个标题的基础上作出的。

示例2——建筑物中的一部分不产生独立的现金流量

主体拥有一栋行政办公楼，由于主体经营规模缩减，该栋大楼一半自用，另一半出租给了第三方，且租赁期为五年。将该栋大楼中某一单独部分对外销售或者以融资租赁的方式单独出租都是不可能。在这种情况下，该准则得出的结论是，因为该办公楼的主要目的是为总部管理，不能认为它能够产生独立于主体整体的现金流量的现金流量。因此，该办公楼的CGU很可能就是该主体整体。该办公楼并不是作为一项投资而持有，因此，根据未来市场相关的租金情况来确定该办公楼的使用价值是不适当的。但是，在确定CGU的使用价值时，应该要把所收到的租金包括在主体整体的现金流量中。

取决于事实和所处环境的不同，为减值测试目的而将该大楼分为两部分也是可以接受的做法，即将该大楼出租的部分作为一个单独的CGU，而将自用的部分作为总部资产，在一个更大的CGU中进行减值测试（参见第18.108.1段）。

18. 116 CGUs should be identified on a consistent basis from one period to the next for the same assets or types of assets unless a change is justified. [IAS 36 para 72]. If an asset is moved to a different CGU or the types of assets that are aggregated for the asset's CGU have changed and a material impairment is recognised or reversed, the entity should describe the current and former way of aggregating assets and the reasons for the change. [IAS 36 paras 73, 130].

18. 117 Assessing recoverable amount for an individual CGU is difficult in situations where management has multiple assets and has the ability to choose the assets that are used. An example is a power station where management can choose to switch on/off different nuclear reactors. Each nuclear reactor can be identified as a single CGU, but it would not be appropriate to assess the recoverable amount of each individually. Management should, therefore, treat the individual CGUs as inter-linked and test for impairment together rather than individually. Multiple, inter-changeable assets are often monitored and managed together in other sectors such as shipping and the airline industry.

18. 118 The interaction of vertically integrated operations and IFRS 8, 'Operating segments', is considered from paragraph 18. 225. 11.

[The next paragraph is 18. 123. 1.]

Indefinite-lived intangible assets

18. 123. 1 A cash-generating unit is defined as the smallest group of assets that generate cash inflows that are largely independent of each other. A brand is normally used to support production of a branded product and the revenues from sales of the branded product are not capable of being split between revenue for the brand and revenue for the costs of production. Brands are typically not a CGU under IFRS and should not be tested alone. The brand should be tested with the associated manufacturing CGU or group of CGU's. There may be some circumstances, where there is no indicator of impairment, where it may not be necessary to test the brand at the CGU level.

Example – Indefinite-life intangible asset

An entity has a brand with an indefinite useful life that does not generate

18.116　除非改变是合理的，否则从一个财务期间到下一个财务期间，对于相同的资产或者相同类别的资产应当按照一致的基础识别 CGU。[IAS 36 第 72 段]。如果某项资产被归入了另外一个 CGU，或者为资产阶段 CGU 中的其他资产构成发生了变化，并且导致确认或者转回了重大的减值，主体应当对当前及过去采用的资产汇总方式以及该方式发生改变的原因进行描述。[IAS 36 第 130 段]。

18.117　在管理层有多个资产并且有能力对所使用的资产进行选择的情况下，评估单个 CGU 的可收回金额是很困难的。发电站的管理层可以选择打开或者关闭不同的核反应堆就是这样一个示例。每个核反应堆都可以被识别为一个单独的 CGU，但是，分别评估每个核反应堆的可收回金额是不适当的。因此，管理层应当把每个单个的 CGU 作为一个相互链接的整体一起进行减值测试，而不是分别进行测试。在其他行业（例如海运以及航空公司等），可以互换的多个资产通常也都是被一起监督和管理的。

18.118　垂直一体化经营和《国际财务报告准则第 8 号——经营分部》（"IFRS 8"）的相互影响在第 18.225.11 段及其下文进行讨论。

[下一段是第 18.123.1 段。]

使用寿命不确定的无形资产

18.123.1　现金产出单元被定义为能够产生在很大程度上相互独立的现金流量的最小资产组。一个品牌通常会被用来支持该品牌产品的生产，品牌产品的销售收入并不能在品牌产生的收入以及产品生产成本产生的收入之间进行区分。一般而言，在国际财务报告准则下，品牌不是一个 CGU，因此不应当单独对其进行测试。品牌应当和与其相联系的从事制造的 CGU 或 CGU 组一同进行测试。在某些环境下，可能会有因为没有出现减值迹象，而可能未必需要在 CGU 层面对品牌进行测试的情况。

示例——使用寿命不确定的无形资产

某一主体拥有一个使用寿命不确定的品牌，因为该品牌只能用于对该主

independent cash flows since it is only used for marketing products produced by the entity. There is no indicator for impairment, but because the useful life is indefinite, the brand must be tested annually.

The only circumstances under which the brand can be tested for impairment as an individual asset rather than as part of a CGU are when all of the following conditions are met:

- The asset has an indefinite useful life.
- There is no indicator of impairment (that is, annual test).
- Fair value less costs to sell can be determined for the brand.
- Fair value less costs to sell exceeds the carrying amount, that is, there is no impairment.

All other conditions will lead to testing the brand at the level of the CGU.

[The next paragraph is 18.124.]

Fair value less costs to sell

18.124 The definition of fair value less costs to sell (FVLCTS) is "…*the amount obtainable from the sale of an asset or cash generating unit in an arm's length transaction between knowledgeable, willing parties, less the costs of disposal*". [IAS 36 para 6]. IAS 36 provides a hierarchy of sources for fair value less costs to sell.

18.124.1 The best indicator of fair value less costs to sell is the price in a binding arm's length sale agreement adjusted for the costs of disposal. [IAS 36 para 25]. If there is no binding sale agreement but the asset is traded in an active market, the current market price or the latest transaction price, less costs to sell, should be used. [IAS 36 para 26].

18.124.2 An active market is defined in the standard as a market where the following conditions exist:

体生产的产品进行市场营销，因此不产生独立的现金流量。目前并未出现减值迹象，但是因为该品牌的使用寿命是不确定的，因此必须每年对其进行测试。

唯一可以把该品牌作为一个单项资产而不是 CGU 的一部分进行减值测试的情况，会出现在下列条件被同时满足的时候：

- 该资产的使用寿命不确定。
- 不存在减值迹象（即年度测试）。
- 该品牌的公允价值减去处置费用后的净额可以确定。
- 公允价值减去处置费用后的净额大于账面价值，即没有发生减值。

所有其他条件的出现，都会导致在 CGU 的层面对该品牌进行测试。

[下一段是第 18.124 段。]

公允价值减去处置费用后的净额

18.124　公允价值减去处置费用后的净额（“FVLCS”）被定义为：“*……在熟悉情况的交易各方之间自愿进行的公平交易中通过销售资产或者现金产出单元所能获得的金额，减去处置费用后的净额*”。[IAS 36 第 6 段]。IAS 36 为公允价值减去处置费用后的净额提供了一个数据来源的层级。

18.124.1　公允价值减去处置费用的最佳指标是具有约束力的公平销售协议约定的价格，并根据处置费用进行调整。[IAS 36 第 25 段]。如果没有具有约束力的销售协议，但是该资产是在活跃市场中进行交易的，则应当使用当前的市场价格或最新的交易价格减去处置费用后的净额。[IAS 36 第 26 段]。

18.124.2　在该准则中，活跃市场被定义为存在下列条件的市场：

- The items traded on the market are homogeneous.
- Willing buyers and sellers can normally be found at any time.
- Prices are available to the public.

[IAS 36 para 6].

There are very few assets tested for impairment under IAS 36 that are traded in an active market as defined by the standard.

18.124.3 If there is neither a binding sale agreement nor an active market, then fair value may be estimated as the amount that the entity could obtain from the asset's disposal in an arm's length transaction based on data from recent market transactions. In determining this amount an entity should consider evidence from recent transactions for similar assets in the same industry. Fair value less costs to sell should not reflect a forced sale unless management is obliged to sell immediately. [IAS 36 para 27]. If the asset or CGU has been acquired recently, the purchase price adjusted as appropriate for any costs to sell may be an approximation of fair value less costs to sell absent information to the contrary.

Example – Recent market transactions in different territories

Entity A is doing its annual impairment test of goodwill allocated to a group of cash generating units based on fair value less costs to sell. Management was looking for recent market transactions in its country and did not find any.

Entity A's management should look further than the home market. The standard refers to "*recent transactions for similar assets within the same industry*". That means management should also look in other territories. When evaluating the outcome of a transaction in another country, the specifics due to the other political and economical environments should be taken into account.

18.124.4 Where there is an asset for which there is no active market, such as goodwill attaching to a business, then fair value less costs to sell may still be derived using estimation techniques such as a discounted cash flow analysis. The

■ 在该市场中进行交易的项目是同质的。

■ 在正常情况下，可以随时找到自愿交易的买方和卖方。

■ 价格是公开的。

［IAS 36 第 6 段］。

很少有根据 IAS 36 的要求进行减值测试的资产是在该准则所定义的活跃市场上进行交易的。

18.124.3　如果既没有具有约束力的销售协议、也不存在活跃市场，则公允价值可以估计为以从最近发生的市场交易取得的数据为基础，主体在公平交易中处置该资产可能得到的金额。在确定这一金额时，主体应当考虑同行业类似资产在最近的交易中取得的证据。除非管理层有立即出售的义务，否则公允价值减去处置费用不应当反映强制销售。［IAS 36 第 27 段］。如果资产或 CGU 是最近才购买的，则在没有相反信息的情况下，购买价格根据处置费用作适当调整后可能是与公允价值减去处置费用后的净额近似的金额。

示例——在不同地区发生的最近的市场交易

主体 A 正在根据公允价值减去处置费用后的净额对分配给一组现金产出单元的商誉作年度减值测试。管理层曾经寻找过其所在国家最近的市场交易情况，但是没有任何发现。

主体 A 的管理层应当不仅仅只关注国内市场。该准则所指的是“*同一行业中类似资产最近的交易情况*”，其意味着，管理层也应当在其他国家寻找相关资料。当评估另一个国家发生的交易的结果时，应当考虑其他的政治和经济环境所导致的特殊情况。

18.124.4　在某项资产没有活跃市场的情况下（例如依附于某项业务的商誉），可能仍然要使用如折现现金流量分析等估值技术才能得到公允价值减去处置费用后的净额。所使用的折现现金流量技术应当结合市场参与者在估计

discounted cash flow techniques used should incorporate assumptions that market participants would use in estimating the asset's fair value (such as revenue growth, profit margins, exchange rates and so on).

Some of the restrictions imposed by IAS 36 on assumptions inherent in the value in use calculations do not apply to fair value less costs to sell and, hence, a valuation on a fair value less costs to sell basis might be higher.

18.124.4.1 Management will have to determine the inputs into the discounted cash flow analysis including establishing a discount rate to use for the discounted cash flow.

Example – Establishing the discount rate

Entity A has a capital structure of 25% equity: 75% debt. Its post tax weighted average cost of capital is 8%. Most of entity A's competitors have a capital structure of 40% equity: 60% debt and a weighted average cost of capital of 10%. Entity A's management propose to use their own cost of capital as a starting point for determining an appropriate discount rate to use in their impairment reviews.

Entity A's management should not use entity A's own cost of capital as a starting point for determining an appropriate discount rate. The potential willing purchaser, who must be considered in determining fair value, is likely to have a cost of capital in line with the majority of the industry participants. Entity A's management should use the normal industry capital structure of 40% equity: 60% debt and a WACC of 10% in determiningthe appropriate discount rate to use when calculating fair value.

18.124.6 In assessing fair value less costs to sell, there are a number of valuation methodologies that are used to assess the value of a business. More than one methodology is normally used to ensure that the valuations are cross checked and considered in light of all appropriate market evidence. (Note that, the replacement cost method is not appropriate for the purpose of impairment testing, as it does not reflect the economic benefits recoverable from use or disposal). [IAS 36 para BCZ 29].

该资产的公允价值时将会采用的假设（如收入增长、毛利率以及汇率等）。

IAS 36 对于在使用价值的计算中固有的一些假设所设定的某些限制并不适用于公允价值减去处置费用，因此，以公允价值减去处置费用后的净额为基础估算的价值可能会更高。

18.124.4.1　管理层必须要确定输入到折现现金流量分析中的各项输入值，其中包括确定折现现金流量所使用的折现率。

示例——确定折现率

主体 A 的资本结构为权益和债务的比例为 25%∶75%。其税后加权平均资本成本为 8%。主体 A 的大部分竞争对手的资本结构都是权益和债务的比例为 40%∶60%，且加权平均资本成本为 10%。主体 A 的管理层打算使用其自身的资本成本作为确定其在减值复核中使用的适当的折现率的起点。

主体 A 的管理层不应当使用其自身的资本成本作为确定适当的折现率的起点。在确定公允价值时必须要被考虑的潜在的自愿交易的购买方，很可能会使用与大多数行业参与者一致的资本成本。在确定计算公允价值时所使用的适当的折现率时，主体 A 的管理层应当采用正常的行业资本结构（即权益和债务的比例为 40%∶60%）以及 10% 的加权平均资本成本。

18.124.6　在评估公允价值减去处置费用后的净额时，有很多估值方法会用于评估业务的价值。通常情况下，会使用一种以上的方法，以确保不同方法下的估值结果之间互相检查并且考虑了所有适当的市场证据。（值得注意的是，出于减值测试的目的，重置成本法并不是一个适当的方法，这是因为它不反映从使用或处置资产中所能够收回的经济利益）。［IAS 36 BC 第 Z29 段］。

18.124.7 In practice, a first assessment of the valuation is performed using cash flows from management. There must be, where appropriate, market evidence to support the key assumptions underpinning the cash flow analysis; for example, growth rates may be considered by benchmarking to industry/analyst reports. If certain of the assumptions used are not those that a market participant would use, those cash flows must be adjusted to take into account the assumptions that are supported by market evidence.

18.124.8 The cash flows to be used in a discounted cash flow prepared to determine fair value less costs to sell will be different from those in a value in use calculation. Any differences in the assumptions in the cash flows used for the fair value less costs to sell compared to the cash flow forecasts used in the value in use analysis need to be considered for reasonableness. The assumptions could also include restructurings, reorganisations or future investments (that would be excluded from a value in use calculation). If all rational market participants would be expected to undertake these expenditures and reorganisations in order to extract the best value from the purchase and, hence, they would have been factored into the acquisition price. In addition, as fair value less costs to sell is a post-tax measure, tax cash flows, whilst excluded from a VIU calculation, are included in the FVLCS calculation.

Example – Expenditure that rational market participants would expect

Entity S is running a number of casinos. It is currently operating its head office function from two separate buildings in different locations as a result of historical acquisitions. The cost of exiting the smaller building is not considered to be significant.

The annual goodwill impairment test is based on a fair value less cost to sell basis using a discounted cash flow model.

The lease costs of the second premises should not be included in the cash flows. Operating a head office from two offices is considered unusual, and a buyer of the business would be likely to immediately cancel the second lease especially when the benefit outweighs the cost of exiting.

Restructuring activities that are expected to enhance the value of a business are

18.124.7　在实务中，使用从管理层得到的现金流量对估值作第一次评估。在适当的情况下，一定要有市场证据来支持现金流量分析所依据的那些关键假设；例如，可以把行业或分析报告作为基准来考虑增长率。如果所采用的某些假设并不是市场参与者将会采用的，则必须对这些现金流量进行调整，以使其考虑那些被市场证据所支持的假设。

18.124.8　为确定公允价值减去处置费用后的净额而编制的折现现金流量中所使用的现金流量与使用价值的计算中所使用的现金流量是不同的。确定公允价值减去处置费用后的净额时所使用的现金流量依据的假设与在使用价值分析中所使用的现金流量预测相比有任何差异，都需要考虑其合理性。假设也可以包括重组、重新安排组织机构或者未来投资（这在使用价值的计算中将会被排除在外）。如果预期所有理性的市场参与者们都会承担这些支出并进行改组，以从购买中获取最优价值，那么它们可能已经成为购买价格的考虑因素了。此外，公允价值减去处置费用后的净额是一个税后计量指标，与所得税有关的现金流量会包括在公允价值减去处置费用后的净额的计算中，但是会在使用价值的计算中被排除在外。

示例——理性的市场参与者们预期会发生的支出

主体S经营着几家赌场。由于历史上所作收购的原因，该主体目前分别在位于不同地点的两栋大楼内行使其总部的职能。退出较小的一栋楼需要花费的成本并不重大。

商誉的年度减值测试是以使用折现现金流量模型计算的公允价值减去处置费用后的净额为基础进行的。

不应该把第二栋建筑物的租赁成本包括在现金流量中。在两个办公地点行使总部的职能是不常见的，因此该业务的买方很可能马上取消对第二栋建筑物的租赁，特别是当其利益超过退出费用的时候。

在确定公允价值减去处置费用后的净额时，那些预期会提高某项业务的

taken into account when determining fair value less costs to sell.

18.124.8.1 It is important that, when comparing carrying amount with recoverable amount, entities ensure that the carrying amount of the CGU being tested for impairment is calculated consistently with the cash flows included in the fair value less costs to sell calculation. For example, if the cash flows include working capital and tax then the carrying amount of the CGU should also include the working capital and tax balances.

18.124.9 If comparable transactions in similar assets or businesses are available, they should be used as market evidence. Consideration should be given to the comparability of the acquired asset/business to the asset/CGU being tested, for example, adjustments for factors such as size, growth expectations, profitability and risk will need to be considered. This evidence might arise in the implied multiple of earnings before interest, taxes, depreciation and amortisation (EBITDA) or revenue that was paid in a comparable transaction, which when applied to the current model (and adjusted for points of difference) provides support for the valuation. For example, if there are a number of recent transactions in comparable entities where the price paid is six times EBITDA and management has produced a valuation that is ten times EBITDA, then the external data would appear not to support the assumptions made in the valuation. Care is needed in selecting comparable entities; risk profile and size may well be more important than geography. Care is also needed to avoid selection bias, if one transaction in ten provides some support for the EBITDA multiple, but the same transaction is regarded in the financial press as an over-payment and an isolated example, then it should not be used.

18.124.10 As a cross-check, it will be useful to benchmark the fair value less costs to sell of a CGU to multiples implied by quoted comparable companies, although consideration will need to be given to comparability in terms of size, growth expectations, profitability, risk etc. In the unlikely event that a benchmark or comparable transactions do not exist, any possible external evidence (growth rates, industry trends, etc.) will be used to support the cash flow projections prepared by management.

18.124.11 It is almost always possible to determine fair value less costs to sell.

价值的重组活动会予以考虑。

18.124.8.1　当把账面价值与可收回金额进行比较时，很重要的一点是，主体要确保被减值测试的CGU的账面价值与公允价值减去处置费用后的净额的计算中所包括的现金流量的计算口径一致。例如，如果现金流量包括营运资金和所得税，则CGU的账面价值也应当包括营运资金和所得税余额。

18.124.9　如果能够获得类似资产或者业务的可比交易信息，则应当把这些信息作为市场证据而使用。应当考虑所购买的资产或者业务与被测试的资产或者CGU的可比性；例如，需要考虑对诸如规模、增长预期、营利能力以及风险等因素所作的调整。隐含的扣除利息、所得税、折旧和摊销之前的收益（“EBITDA”）的倍数或者在可比交易中已经支付的收入可能就是这样的证据，在将这些指标应用到现有模型（并对差异进行调整）时，其为估值提供了支持。例如，如果在可比主体最近发生的很多交易中，所支付的价格是EBITDA的六倍，而管理层计算的估值中使用的是EBITDA的十倍，则该外部数据将会显示出其并不支持估值中所做的假设。在选择可比主体时需要小心，风险状况和规模可能比地理分布更加重要。为避免选择上的偏见也需要谨慎，如果十个交易中的其中一个为EBITDA的倍数提供了一定支持，但是财经新闻认为该交易超额偿付并且只是一个个例，则不应当使用该交易的信息。

18.124.10　尽管需要考虑在规模、增长预期、盈利能力和风险等方面的可比性，但是，作为互相检查，以所引用的可比公司的隐含倍数为基准，将某一CGU的公允价值减去处置费用后的净额与其进行比较是很有用的。在不存在基准或者可比交易这一不太可能出现的情况下，任何可能的外部证据（增长率、行业趋势等等）都将被用于支持管理层所做的现金流量预测。

18.124.11　确定公允价值减去处置费用后的净额几乎都是有可能的。如果使

If fair value less costs to sell is used then the carrying value of the asset or CGU being tested for impairment should be determined on a consistent basis.

Example – Comparing like with like

Entity T usually tests its goodwill on a pre-tax value in use basis. Since this year the value in use test would lead to an impairment and the fair value less costs to sell is expected to be different to the value in use, a post-tax fair value less costs to sell value needs to be determined. What are the consequences for the carrying amounts of the assets tested?

It is important to compare like with like. Whereas value in use is a pre-tax model, fair value less costs to sell is a post-tax model. So in a fair value less costs to sell model the carrying amount tested should include current and deferred tax assets / liabilities. A value in use model would exclude such amounts.

Another consequence is that another discount rate must be used. For a fair value less costs to sell test, this would need to be a post-tax rate. A post-tax discount rate is usually readily available at the market and is, therefore, less of a problem to determine than the pre-tax discount rate.

18.124.11.1 When determining the ceiling to be used for the recoverable amount of an asset, it is not appropriate to use depreciated replacement cost as a proxy for fair value less costs to sell. This is because replacement cost measures the costs of an asset and not the future economic benefit recoverable from the asset's use and/or disposal. [IAS 16 para BCZ28f]. However, the use of depreciated replacement cost may be acceptable when allocating impairment losses to assets in a CGU. See from paragraph 18.246.

18.124.12 If fair value less costs to sell is found to be lower than the asset's carrying amount, it should not automatically be written down to that value. Before a write-down is booked, the asset's value in use also needs to be estimated in order to determine whether it is higher than its carrying amount. If it is, then no impairment write-down is required. Management should also explain the difference between value in use and fair value less costs to sell.

用公允价值减去处置费用后的净额，则进行减值测试的资产或者CGU 的账面价值也应当按照一致的基础确定。

示例——同类比较

主体 T 通常按照税前的使用价值为基础对其商誉进行测试。由于今年使用价值的测试可能会导致发生减值，然而公允价值减去处置费用后的净额预期与使用价值不同，因此需要确定税后的公允价值减去处置费用后的净额。这会对所测试的资产的账面价值产生什么样的后果？

同类比较是很重要的。鉴于使用价值是依据税前模型计算，而公允价值减去处置费用后的净额是依据税后模型计算，因此，在公允价值减去处置费用后的净额的模型中，被测试的账面价值应当包括当期所得税资产或当期所得税负债以及递延所得税资产或递延所得税负债。而使用价值模型则会把此类金额排除在外。

另外一个后果就是必须使用另外一个折现率。对于公允价值减去处置费用的测试，需要使用税后折现率。税后折现率通常在市场上是很容易取得的，因此，在确定时所产生的问题会比确定税前折现率时产生的问题要少。

18. 124. 11. 1　当确定用于某项资产的可收回金额的上限时，使用折旧后重置成本作为公允价值减去处置费用后的净额的代用品是不适当的。这是因为重置成本计量的是资产的成本而不是从该资产的使用以及/或者处置中可收回的未来经济利益。[IAS 16 BC 第 Z28f 段]。但是，当将减值损失分配给一个CGU 的各项资产时，使用折旧后重置成本是可以接受的。参见第 18. 246 段及其下文的讨论。

18. 124. 12　如果发现公允价值减去处置费用后的净额低于资产的账面价值，不应当将账面价值自动地减记至该较低的价值。在减记账面价值之前，还需要估计资产的使用价值，以确定该使用价值是否高于其账面价值。如果高于，则无需因减值而减记账面价值。管理层还应当对使用价值与公允价值减去处置费用后的净额的差异作出解释。

Value in use

18. 124. 13 The definition of value in use is "*the present value of the future cash flows expected to be derived from an asset or cash generating unit*". [IAS 36 para 6].

18. 124. 14 Calculating value in use involves the following processes:

- Estimating the future cash flows expected to be derived from the asset.
- Estimating the potential variation in the amount and timing of the future cash flows.
- Taking account of the time value of money (discounting), using current market risk-free interest rates.
- Estimating the price for bearing the uncertainty inherent in the asset, for example whether the asset will perform as intended.
- Taking account of other factors such as illiquidity, which would be reflected by the market in pricing the future cash flows expected to be derived from the asset.

[IAS 36 para 30].

18. 124. 15 The future cash flows to be derived from the asset include the cash flows from the asset's continuing use and those that will arise from the asset's disposal at the end of its useful life. The time value of money is then taken into account by discounting those future cash flows using a current market rate of interest. [IAS 36 para 31].

18. 124. 16 Risks related to expected variations in the amount or timing of cash flows, uncertainty inherent in the asset and other factors such as illiquidity may be reflected in the calculation either by adjusting the cash flows or by adjusting the discount rate. Clearly if cash flows are adjusted the discount rate should not be adjusted and *vice versa* as otherwise there would be double counting of the risk. Whichever approach is adopted the result of the calculation should be a figure that represents the present value of the expected future cash flows, reflecting the

使用价值

18.124.13　使用价值的定义为："*预期从资产或现金产出单元产生的未来现金流量的现值。*"［IAS 36 第 6 段］。

18.124.14　使用价值的计算涉及以下步骤：

- 估计资产预期产生的未来现金流量。
- 估计未来现金流量在金额和时间上可能出现的潜在变化。
- 采用当前市场上的无风险利率考虑货币的时间价值（折现）。
- 估计承担了资产中固有不确定性的价格，例如资产是否按照原定计划使用。
- 考虑其他因素，如流动性不足等，这可能会反映在市场对预期从资产中获取的未来现金流量的定价中。

［IAS 36 第 30 段］。

18.124.15　资产预期产生的未来现金流量包括从该资产持续使用中产生的现金流量，也包括在该资产的使用寿命结束时将其处置所产生的现金流量。然后，通过使用当前的市场利率对这些未来现金流量进行折现，来考虑货币的时间价值。［IAS 36 第 31 段］。

18.124.16　与现金流量在金额或时间上的预期变化、资产固有的不确定性以及其他因素（如流动性不足等）有关的风险，在计算中可以通过调整现金流量或者调整折现率予以反映。有一点是很明确的，即如果对现金流量进行了调整，就不应当调整折现率，反之亦然，这是因为如果同时调整了现金流量和折现率，就可能是对风险作了重复计算。无论采用哪种方法，计算结果都应当是一个体现了预期现金流量现值的数字，它反映了对所有可能结果的加权平均值。［IAS 36 第 32 段］。

weighted average of all possible outcomes. [IAS 36 para 32].

[The next paragraph is 18. 164.]

Calculating value in use

18. 164 Determining value in use involves estimating the future cash flows that are expected to arise from the asset or CGU being tested for impairment. The cash flows consist of those expected to arise from the continued use of the asset or CGU in its current condition and those, if any, expected to result from its ultimate disposal. An appropriate discount rate is then applied to those cash flows to arrive at their present value. [IAS 36 para 31].

18. 164. 1 IAS 36 provides detailed guidance on the principles to be applied when calculating value in use. In some industries, specific valuation models are used for internal purposes. An example of this is the use of the Dividend Discount Model in the financial services sector. There are numerous variations of the Dividend Discount Model, some discounting only future expected dividend receipts and others based on a more detailed analysis of recoverable value. Regardless of the name, it is important to understand the basis for any valuation model used. Internal valuation models may be adopted to calculate the value in use of a CGU for purposes of impairment testing provided they are consistent with the principles and requirements of IAS 36 as outlined in the paragraphs that follow.

Basis for estimates of future cash flows

18. 165 Relevant cash flow forecasts should be made on the basis of *reasonable* and *supportable* assumptions that represent management's best estimate of the economic circumstances that will prevail over the remaining life of the asset or CGU. Where a CGU has goodwill/ intangible assets with indefinite lives, the cash flow forecast should be into perpetuity. This is typically achieved by identifying a 'steady state' set of assumptions for the cash flows in the last year of the forecasts and applying a terminal value multiple to those cash flows. See further discussion in paragraph 18. 168. If the CGU has no goodwill allocated to it, the cash flows

[下一段是第 18.164 段。]

使用价值的计算

18.164　确定使用价值涉及对进行减值测试的资产或者 CGU 预期产生的未来现金流量进行估计。现金流量由对资产或者 CGU 在其目前的状况下持续使用而预期产生的现金流量以及预期从其最终处置所得到的现金流量（如有）两部分组成。之后，再使用某一适当的折现率将这些现金流量折算为现值。[IAS 36 第 31 段]。

18.164.1　IAS 36 对于在计算使用价值时所运用的原则提供了详细的指引。在某些行业，内部会使用一些特殊的估值模型。在金融服务行业使用的股利折现模型就是这样一个示例。股利折现模型有很多变型，其中有些只对未来预期收到的股利进行折现，而另一些则会基于对应收价值所作的更加详细的分析进行计算。无论模型的名称是什么，了解所有估值模型的基础是很重要的。出于减值测试的目的，可以采用内部模型计算某一 CGU 的使用价值，但前提是这些模型要与在其所适用的有关段落中所概述的 IAS 36 的原则和要求相一致。

估计未来现金流量的基础

18.165　相关的现金流量预测应当基于*合理且有依据的*假设作出，这些假设体现了管理层对于在资产或者 CGU 的剩余使用寿命内普遍存在的经济环境所作的最佳估计。在 CGU 有商誉或者使用寿命不确定的无形资产的情况下，现金流量预测应当是永续的。在典型的情况下，这可以通过对所作预测的最后一年的现金流量识别出一组“稳定状态”的假设，并且用一个终值乘以这些现金流量来实现。进一步的讨论参见第 18.168 段。如果 CGU 没有分配给它的商誉，则现金流量应当以该业务（其使用寿命可能不是不确定的）中使用寿命最长的资产的使用寿命为限。现金流量应当以管理层正式批准的最近的预

should be limited to the life of the longest lived asset in the business which may not be indefinite. The cash flows should be based on the most up-to-date budgets and forecasts that have been formally approved by management, but should exclude estimated future cash inflows or outflows expected to arise from future restructurings or from improving or enhancing the asset's performance (see from para 18.223 below). Projections based on these budgets and forecasts should cover a maximum of five years, unless a longer period can be justified. [IAS 36 para 33(b)]. Any budgets that have been revised must be approved by management before they can be used in the value in use calculation. Greater weight should be given to external evidence. [IAS 36 paras 33(a), 38].

Example – Fair value less costs to sell more appropriate than value in use

Entity A has determined that CGU Z's fair value less costs to sell is lower than its carrying amount. However, based on its VIU CGU Z would not be impaired. The VIU was determined using a business plan that had not been finally approved by management.

The VIU has not been determined correctly; a non-approved business plan does not represent a reliable source of information. It may be subject to change, for example because senior management disagree with the figures presented and the assumptions used.

The only reliable information available would be CGU Z's fair value less costs to sell, if the business plan is not yet approved. An impairment loss should, therefore, be recognised.

18.166 In assessing whether the assumptions it uses in its forecasts are reasonable, management should examine the causes of differences between actual cash flows and past projections. The current assumptions should be consistent with past actual outcomes except where circumstances have changed or subsequent events have occurred that make this inappropriate. [IAS 36 para 34]. For example if actual cash flows have consistently been below projected cash flows, management should build in a greater degree of conservatism to the current cash flows unless it can identify specific reasons for the shortfall and satisfy themselves that those reasons no longer apply. Estimated cash flows (and discount rates)

算和预测为基础，但是估计预期从未来重组或者改善或提高资产绩效所产生的未来现金流入或者流出应当被排除在外（参见第 18.223 段及其下文）。除非能够证明更长的期间是合理的，否则基于这些预算和预测所做的现金流量预计应当涵盖的期间最多为五年。[IAS 36 第 33（b）段]。任何已经修改过的预算，在其可以用于使用价值的计算之前，都必须经过管理层的批准。对于外部证据应当给予更多的重视。[IAS 36 第 33（a）段、第 38 段]。

示例——公允价值减去处置费用后的净额比使用价值更加合适

主体 A 已经确定，CGU Z 的公允价值减去处置费用后的净额小于其账面价值。然而，根据其使用价值计算，CGU Z 可能并没有发生减值。使用价值是采用管理层尚未最终批准的业务计划确定的。

该使用价值的确定是不正确的；一个未经批准的业务计划不代表信息的可靠来源。该业务计划可能会面临改变，例如，由于高级管理层不同意所列报的数字或者所使用的假设而需要改变。

如果业务计划尚未获到批准，那么唯一可以获得的可靠信息就是 CGU Z 的公允价值减去处置费用后的净额。因此，应当确认一项减值损失。

18.166 评估在其预测中所使用的假设是否合理时，管理层应该检查实际的现金流量和过去的预计之间的差异原因。除非环境已经发生了改变，或者发生了后续事项使得原来的假设不再合适，否则当前的假设应当与过去的实际结果一致。[IAS 36 第 34 段]。例如，如果实际的现金流量一直低于预计的现金流量，管理层应当对当前的现金流量采取更加保守的态度，除非其能够识别现金流量不足的具体原因并且使其相信那些原因不再适用了。估计的现金流量（以及折现率）应该是不带有偏见的，并且不包括与所测试的资产无关的因素。[IAS 36 附录 A 第 A3 段]。

should be free from bias and factors unrelated to the asset in question. [IAS 36 App A para A3].

Example – Use of reasonable and supportable forecasts

Entity E owns 90% of its subsidiary L. Entity E's management has approved the group's five year business plan, which also includes information regarding entity L.

Entity L's management has prepared its own budgets, which are more aggressive than those approved by its parent entity's management.

In this situation, entity L should use the business plan approved by entity E, to determine its assets' value in use.

Estimated cash flows should be based on budgets approved by management. Where there are two sets of budget information, question is raised as to which should be used for the purposes of impairment testing. In such a situation, it is important to understand the reason behind the differences in the two budgets.

Entity E's management may have included in its assumptions, information not yet disclosed to entity L's management. Alternatively, entity L's management may have prepared the more aggressive budget to try and set a challenging 'stretch' target for their workforce. The cash flows used in the impairment calculation should be those that represent the most reasonable and supportable forecast approved by management. Although entity L's management has prepared its own budgets, the group's official estimates are those included in entity E's approved business plan. In this situation, we would, therefore, expect entity E's budget to be used unless it could be supported that the budget set by entity L's management was more in line with actual expectations of future trading.

18.166.1 Where the economic environment in which an entity operates has become more volatile in the period since the budget/ forecast was approved by management, it may be appropriate to revise the forecasts made. The forecasts that are incorporated into the value in use calculation should be based on the latest

示例——使用合理且有依据的预测

主体 E 拥有其子公司 L 90% 的权益。主体 E 的管理层已经批准了该集团的五年业务计划，其中也包括了有关 L 的信息。

主体 L 的管理层已经编制了其自身的预算，该预算比其母公司主体的管理层所批准的预算更加激进。

在这种情况下，主体 L 应当使用主体 E 所批准的业务计划来确定其资产的使用价值。

估计的现金流量应当以管理层所批准的预算为基础。当存在两套预算信息的情况下，就会产生一个问题，即出于减值测试的目的，应当使用哪一套信息。在此类情况下，了解两套预算存在差异的原因是很重要的。

主体 E 的管理层可能已经在其假设中包括了尚未对主体 L 的管理层披露的信息。或者，主体 L 的管理层可能已经编制了更加激进的预算以为其全体员工尝试并建立一个具有挑战性的延伸目标。在减值计算中所使用的现金流量应当是体现了经过管理层批准的最合理且最有依据的预测的现金流量。尽管主体 L 的管理层已经编制了其自身的预算，但是该集团正式使用的估计是那些包含在主体 E 的经批准的业务计划中的信息。因此，在这种情况下，除非能够证明主体 L 的管理层所制定的预算更加符合未来交易的实际预期，否则我们会预期主体 E 的预算将会被采用。

18.166.1　在主体经营所处的经济环境在预算或者预测被管理层批准之后的一段期间内变得更加不稳定的情况下，对于所作的预测进行修改可能是适当的做法。纳入使用价值计算的预测应当以管理层批准的最新预算为基础而编制。然而，很重要的一点是，基于执行减值测试时的经济情况来看，在那些

management approved budgets. However, it is important that the forecasts in those budgets are considered reasonable and supportable based on the economic conditions at the time the impairment review is performed. The inputs into the forecast should be benchmarked against available market data. Management should reassess the forecast assumptions based on their best estimates, even if the level of uncertainty is likely to be higher in the year of assessment compared to prior years.

18.166.2 The assumptions used in the forecast should be reasonable and supportable. In periods of uncertainty:

- Management assumptions should be consistent with market evidence, such as independent macro-economic forecasts, industry commentators or analysts, brokers' analysis and other third-party experts. Greater weight should be given to any external evidence that is available.

- Any differences between the forecast's underlying assumptions and market evidence should be analysed and understood. Management may find it helpful to explain these differences in disclosures or other material accompanying the financial statements.

- Management should analyse any differences between fair value less costs to sell and value in use and ensure they are supportable.

18.167 The period covered by cash flow forecasts must relate to the useful lives of the assets or CGU being reviewed for impairment. However, periods covered by detailed formal budgets and plans will vary in different companies and industries. In some, cash flows cannot be predicted with much certainty beyond short periods and the standard acknowledges this by imposing a limit of five years. Management may use a longer period where appropriate, but only where management can demonstrate its ability, based on past experience to forecast cash flows accurately over the longer period. [IAS 36 para 35].

18.168 The useful lives of the assets concerned may extend far beyond the period covered by formal budgets and plans. It is then necessary to extrapolate the formal cash flow projections into the future using reasonable broad assumptions about growth and future prospects. The standard places constraints on those assumptions that should be complied with in most circumstances. As noted earlier,

预算中所作的预测应当是合理且有依据的。预测中的输入值应当以可以获得的市场数据为基准。即使评估当年的不确定性程度比前几年更高，管理层也应当以其最佳估计为基础对预测所用的假设进行重新评估。

18.166.2 预测中所使用的假设应当是合理且有依据的。在存在不确定性的期间：

- 管理层的假设应当与市场证据（例如独立的宏观经济预测、行业评论员或分析师、经纪人的分析以及其他第三方专家）一致。对于任何可以获得的外部证据都应当给予更多的重视。

- 应当分析并了解预测所依据的基本假设与市场证据之间存在的任何差异。管理层可能会发现，在财务报表披露的信息或者其附带的其他材料中对这些差异进行解释是很有帮助的。

- 管理层应当对公允价值减去处置费用后的净额与使用价值之间的任何差异进行分析，以确保它们是有据可依的。

18.167 现金流量预测所涵盖的期间必须与被进行减值复核的资产或者 CGU 的使用寿命相关。但是，详细的正式预算和计划所涵盖的期间，因公司和行业的不同而各有差异。在某些公司和行业，无法对超过短期的现金流量作出确定地预测，该准则设定了五年的限制来确认这个问题。在适当的情况下，管理层可以使用更长的期间，但是这仅限于管理层基于过去的经验，能够证明其有能力准确地预测更长期间内的现金流量的情况。[IAS 36 第 35 段]。

18.168 有关资产的使用寿命可能远远长于正式的预算和计划所涵盖的期间。这样就有必要使用有关增长和未来前景的合理的广泛假设，将正式的现金流量预计外推至更远的将来。该准则对于那些假设设定了一些限制，这些限制在大多数情况下都应当被遵守。如上文所述，在 CGU 的账面价值中包括了商誉或者经济使用寿命不确定的其他固定资产的情况下，使用价值的计算将会

where the carrying value of a CGU includes goodwill or other fixed assets with an indefinite useful economic life, the calculation of value in use will include an estimated value of the CGU's cash flows relating to the indefinite period beyond that covered by detailed cash flow projections. This is the terminal value that represents the net present value of cash flows beyond the formal budget period. It may be calculated by applying a terminal value multiple to, say, the cash flows expected in the last year (CF) covered by the entity's explicit forecasts, by using the formula $CF \times (1 + g)/(r-g)$, where r is the discount rate and g is the estimated longer term annual rate of growth in the cash flows (constraints on long-term growth rates are considered below). The terminal value calculated as at the end of the period covered by formal budgets and plans is discounted to its present value.

18.169 There are no restrictions on growth rates in the period that is covered by formal budgets and plans. In that initial period the cash flows will reflect the variability in growth rates that is included in the entity's explicit forecasts. However, the cash flows for periods beyond those covered by formal budgets and plans – whether they cover the full five years or a shorter period-should assume a steady or declining growth rate. This rate will not exceed the long-term average growth rate for the product, industries, country or countries in which the business operates or for the market in which the asset is used. [IAS 36 para 33a].

18.170 Whilst this restriction is aimed at preventing short-term difficulties from being overridden by over-optimistic long-term forecasts, the theory is that in the long run a business has no right to assume it can out-perform the economy as a whole. It is also prudent in the light of an uncertain future. The standard notes that a higher rate may be used only if it is justified, for example by objective information about patterns over a product or industry lifecycle. It also notes that where conditions are very favourable, competitors are likely to be attracted into the market, thus restricting growth of the entity's business. Entities, therefore, will have difficulty in exceeding the average historical growth rate over the long-term (say 20 years). [IAS 36 paras 36, 37].

18.171 There may be situations where it would be unrealistic to cap the growth assumptions (that is, defaulting to a restricted steady or declining growth rate)

包括与详细的现金流量预计所涵盖的期间之外的不确定期间有关的该 CGU 的现金流量的估计价值。这是一个终值，其代表了正式预算期限之外的现金流量的净现值。它可以采用终值乘以比如说主体明确的预测所涵盖的最后一年度预期的现金流量（CF），用公式 $CF \times (1+g)/(r-g)$ 进行计算，其中 r 为折现率，g 为估计的在更长期间的现金流量的年度增长率（对于长期增长率的限制在下文进行讨论）。在正式预算和计划所涵盖的期间的期末计算的终值会被折现为现值。

18.169　对于在正式的预算和计划所涵盖的期间内使用的增长率并没有限制。在该初始期间，现金流量将会反映包含在主体明确的预测中的增长率的可变性。但是，对于超出正式预算和计划所涵盖的期间（无论该预算和计划会涵盖整整 5 年或者是一个较短的期间）的现金流量，则应当假定增长率是稳定的或者是下降的。这一增长率将不会超过其产品、行业、主体业务经营或者资产所处市场所在的一国或多国的长期平均增长率。[IAS 36 第 33a 段]。

18.170　这个限制为的是防止过于乐观的长期预测忽视了短期困难，其理论是，从长远来看，一项业务没有权利假定自己可以超越整体经济环境而进行运营。从未来不确定性的角度看，这也是谨慎的做法。该准则注意到，只有在能够证明更高的比率是合理的情况下（例如，取得了有关某产品或者行业生命周期模式的客观信息），才能使用该比率。该准则还注意到，在条件非常有利的情况下，竞争对手很有可能被吸引进入市场，从而会限制主体业务的增长。因此，主体将难以超过长期（比如说 20 年）的历史平均增长速度。[IAS 36 第 36 段、第 37 段]。

18.171　可能会存在这样的情形，即对五年后的增长假设加一个上限（也就是说，默认一个限制性的稳定或者下降的增长率）是不现实的。例如，这种

after five years. This might be the case, for example, where a CGU with products under development may be expected to incur losses for two or three years and be followed by several years of significant growth as the new products reach the market – thus cash flow forecasts with explicit growth assumptions may exceed five years. However the circumstances for overriding the presumed five year cut-off should be exceptional.

Composition of estimates of future cash flows

18.172 The composition of the cash flows used to estimate value in use need to be considered carefully. It is important, for example, to ensure that they are comparable with the basis on which the carrying amounts of the CGUs have been established, so that omissions or double-counting that would lead to errors in the calculations are avoided.

18.173 The cash flows should include:

- Projections of cash inflows from the continuing use of the asset or the activities of the CGU.
- Projections of cash outflows necessarily incurred to generate the cash inflows from continuing use of the asset or CGU (including cash outflows to prepare the asset for use) and that are directly attributable to the asset or CGU.
- Projections of such cash outflows that are indirectly attributable (such as those relating to central overheads), but that can be allocated on a reasonable and consistent basis to the asset or CGU.
- Net cash flows expected to be received (or paid) for the disposal of assets or CGUs at the end of their useful lives.
- Cash outflows to maintain the operating capacity of existing assets, including, for example, cash flows for day-to-day servicing.

[IAS 36 paras 39, 41, 49].

18.173.1 Cash flow projections used to measure value in use should be based on reasonable and supportable assumptions of the set of economic conditions that will

情况有可能出现在下列情况，某些正在开发中的产品所属的 CGU 可能预期在未来的两至三年内发生亏损，而在接下来的几年中其盈利会因为新产品进入市场而有大幅增长——因此，有明确增长假设的现金流量预测可能会超过五年。但是，超过假定的五年期限的情况应当是例外情况。

估计未来现金流量的构成

18.172　应当认真地考虑估计使用价值所使用的现金流量的构成情况。例如，很重要的一点是，要确保这些现金流量和已经确定的 CGU 的账面价值的基础是可比的，从而避免由于漏记或者重复计算所可能导致的计算错误。

18.173　现金流量应当包括：

- 从资产的持续使用或者 CGU 的活动中产生的预计现金流入。
- 为从资产或者 CGU 的持续使用中产生现金流入而必须发生的预计现金流出（包括为使资产能够使用所作的准备工作而发生的现金流出），并且这些现金流出可以直接归属于该资产或 CGU。
- 不是直接归属于资产或者 CGU、但是能够按照一个合理及一致的基础分配给该资产或者 CGU 的预计现金流出（例如与集中发生的管理费相关的现金流出）。
- 在资产或者 CGU 使用寿命结束时对其进行处置所预期收到（或支付）的净现金流量。
- 维持现有资产的运营能力所产生的现金流出，包括日常维修的现金流量等。

[IAS 36 第 39 段、第 41 段、第 49 段]。

18.173.1　用于计量使用价值的现金流预计应当以体现了在该预计以及资产的剩余使用寿命期间存在的整个经济情况的合理并且有依据的假设为基础。

exist over the period of the projections and the asset's remaining useful in life. [IAS 36 para 33].

[The next paragraph is 18. 173. 3.]

18. 173. 3 The cash flows will be determined and influenced by the following factors:

- Sales volumes: determined by current demand, market share, growth in market size, advertising effects, competition. Growth in sales volumes should be restricted to existing capacity and should not anticipate future capital expenditure that might expand capacity.
- Sales prices: determined by current prices, competition, promotions, inflation.
- Operating costs: determined by prices of goods and service consumed, level of activity, discounts available, competition among suppliers, inflation.
- Other cash flows: decommissioning costs, disposal proceeds, costs necessary to get assets under construction ready for use.

18. 173. 4 The predictions must be prepared for the asset's remaining life, but should not exceed five years unless a longer period can be justified. [IAS 36 para 33(b)]. The cash flows should not reflect restructuring plans to which management is not committed or future expansion plans and any associated increases in revenues or decreases in costs. Predictions of future sales growth and reductions in production costs should reflect existing technology and processes.

18. 174 The cash flows should exclude cash flows relating to financing (which include interest payments), since liabilities are excluded from the carrying amount and because the cost of capital is taken into account by discounting the cash flows. In theory, tax cash flows should also be excluded, because the standard requires value in use to be calculated on the basis of discounting pre-tax cash flows at a pre-tax discount rate (see para 18. 219). (In practice, however, value in use is often likely to be derived from post-tax cash flows discounted at a post-tax discount rate, (see para 18. 219)). [IAS 36 paras 50, 51].

［IAS 36 第33段］。

［下一段是第18.173.3段。］

18.173.3　现金流量将由下列因素确定并受其影响：

- 销量：由目前的需求、市场占有率、市场规模的增长、广告效果以及竞争确定。销量的增长应当被限制在现有的生产能力上，而不应当预期发生可能会扩大生产能力的未来资本支出。
- 销售价格：由目前的价格、竞争、促销以及通货膨胀确定。
- 经营成本：由所耗费的商品价格和服务价格、活动水平、可以获得的折扣、供应商之间的竞争以及通货膨胀确定。
- 其他现金流量：弃置费用、处置收入、为在建资产达到使用状态而发生的必要费用。

18.173.4　必须对资产的剩余使用寿命进行预测，但是该期限不应当超过五年，除非能够证明一个更长的期间是合理的。［IAS 36 第33（b）段］。现金流量不应当反映管理层尚未作出承诺的重组计划或者未来的扩张计划以及与之相关的收入的增加或者成本的降低。对未来销售的增长和生产成本的降低的预测应当反映现有的技术和工艺。

18.174　由于账面价值中并没有包括负债，并且资本成本已经通过对现金流量进行折现予以考虑，因此现金流量不应当包括与融资有关的现金流量（包括支付的利息）。从理论上说，与所得税相关的现金流量也不应当包括在内，这是因为该准则要求按照税前折现率对税前的现金流量进行折现为基础计算使用价值（参见第18.219段）。（然而，在实务中，使用价值经常可能是按照税后折现率对税后的现金流量进行折现而得出的（参见第18.219段））。［IAS 36 第50段、第51段］。

18. 175 Cash flows relating to assets that generate cash flows independently of other assets are excluded from the forecasts (because they are also excluded from the carrying amount of a CGU). Examples would include financial assets such as receivables. Similarly, cash outflows relating to obligations that have already been recognised as liabilities would be excluded, as the related liability is excluded from the CGU. This ensures that like is compared with like. Examples of such liabilities include payables, pensions or provisions. [IAS 36 para 43]. However, in practice, cash inflow and outflow items such as trade receivables and payables (that are expected to generate cash flows equal to their carrying amounts) *can* be included in the calculations if it is easier to allocate them to individual CGUs. The assets and liabilities are then included in the carrying value of the CGU and the respective receipts and payments are also included in the value in use calculation-again to treat like with like. [IAS 36 para 79]. This inclusion of balances simplifies the preparation of the working capital forecasts and should not make any difference to the impairment calculation. This is explored further from paragraph 18. 180. 1.

18. 176 Cash flows that are to be incurred before an asset or CGU is ready for use or sale should be estimated and included in the forecast provided that the project is already in progress. Examples might be future cash flows relating to a building under construction or a development project that is not yet completed. [IAS 36 para 42].

18. 177 The estimate of cash flows expected to be received (or paid) for the disposal of assets or CGUs at the end of their useful lives should be the amount of the expected disposal proceeds in an arm's length transaction between knowledgeable, willing parties, reduced by the estimated costs of disposal. [IAS 36 para 52]. The estimates of cash flows from the disposal of assets are determined in a similar way to their fair value less costs to sell (see from para 18. 124 above) except that:

- The entity uses prices prevailing at the date of the estimate for similar assets or CGUs that have reached the end of their useful lives and that have operated under similar conditions to those in which the asset or CGU will be used.
- Those estimated selling prices are adjusted both for future inflation and for

18.175　与能够独立于其他资产产生现金流量的资产相关的现金流量不应当包括在预测中（这是因为这些资产也没有包括在 CGU 的账面价值中）。这样的例子包括金融资产，如应收款等。类似地，与已经确认为负债的义务相关的现金流出也不包括在内，这是因为相关负债也没有包括在 CGU 中。这样做确保了把同类与同类进行比较。此类负债的例子包括应付款、退休金或者预计负债［IAS 36 第 43 段］。但是，在实务中，如果某些现金流入和现金流出的项目（诸如应收账款和应付账款，它们能够产生与其账面价值相等的现金流量）很容易被分配到各个不同的 CGU 当中，则*可以*把它们纳入计算。如果这样，CGU 的账面价值中包括了这些资产和负债，同时其各自的收款和付款的金额也被包括在使用价值的计算中——这也是按照同类比较进行处理的。［IAS 36 第 79 段］。将余额包括在使用价值的计算中简化了营运资金预测的编制，并且不应当对减值计算产生任何差异。这一点在第 18.180.1 段及其下文中进行进一步探讨。

18.176　应当对资产或 CGU 达到使用或出售状态之前所发生的现金流量进行估计，并将其包括在预测之中，但前提是该项目已经处在进行当中。与在建的建筑物或者尚未完成的开发项目有关的未来现金流量可能就是这样的例子。［IAS 36 第 42 段］。

18.177　对在资产或者 CGU 使用寿命结束时将其处置而预期收到（或支付）现金流量的估计应当是在熟悉情况的交易各方之间自愿进行的公平交易中预期取得的处置收入，减去预期的处置费用后的金额。［IAS 36 第 52 段］。除了下列情况之外，对资产处置取得的现金流量的估计按照与估计其公允价值减去处置费用后的净额类似的方式进行确定（参见上文第 18.124 段）：

- 主体使用的价格是类似资产或者 CGU 在估计之日的现行价格，且这些资产或者 CGU 已经达到使用寿命终点，并且是在与未来使用所测试的资产或者 CGU 所处的类似环境下经营。
- 那些估计的销售价格对于未来的通货膨胀以及预期特殊的未来价格上涨进

expected specific future price increases. (However, if the effect of future inflation is excluded from the estimates of future cash flows and from the discount rate, it is also excluded from the estimate of net cash flows on disposal).

[IAS 36 para 53].

Transfer pricing

18.177.1 Internal transfer pricing directly affects the cash inflows and operating cash outflows relating to separate CGUs in, say, vertically integrated groups, for example, where one CGU transfers part of its output to another CGU in the same group at a price that is lower than the market price for its output. Whilst the product is sold internally an external market may exist for all the output of the CGUs. In such a situation, the cash inflows of the transferor CGU and the cash outflows of the transferee CGU that are used in the value in use calculations should be adjusted to reflect arm's length (usually market) prices rather than internal transfer prices (see also para 18.106 above). [IAS 36 para 71].

'Traditional' and 'expected cash flow' approaches to present value

18.178 In appendix A to the standard the IASB contrasts two approaches to estimating cash flows. These are what it terms the 'traditional' approach and the 'expected cash flow' approach. The appendix explains that either approach may be used to estimate an asset's value in use.

18.178.1 The traditional approach assumes that a single discount rate can incorporate all the expectations about the future cash flows and the appropriate risk premium. Therefore, this approach places most emphasis on the selection of the discount rate. The expected cash flow approach focuses more on the direct analysis of the cash flows. [IAS 36 App A paras A2, A4]. The appendix lists as one of the general principles that "*estimated cash flows or discount rates should reflect the range of possible outcomes rather than a single most likely, minimum or maximum*

行了调整。(然而，如果对未来的现金流量以及折现率的估计当中没有包括未来通货膨胀的影响，则其也不会包括在处置产生的净现金流量的估计当中)。

[IAS 36 第 53 段]。

转移定价

18.177.1　比如说在垂直一体化的集团中，内部转移定价直接影响着与各个单独的 CGU 相关的现金流入和现金流出，例如，一个 CGU 把其部分产品以低于该产品市场价格的价格转让给同一集团内的另一个 CGU。该产品在内部销售的同时，对于该 CGU 的所有产品可能也存在一个外部市场。在此类情况下，在计算使用价值时所使用的转让方 CGU 的现金流入和受让方 CGU 的现金流出应当调整为反映公平交易（通常是市场）的价格，而不是其内部转移价格（也可以参见上文第 18.106 段）。[IAS 36 第 71 段]。

计算现值的“传统法”和“预期现金流量法”

18.178　在该准则的附录 A 中，国际会计准则理事会（“IASB”）把估计现金流量的两种方法进行了对照。这两种方法被称为“传统”法和“预期现金流量”法。根据附录中的解释，任何一种方法都可以用于估计某项资产的使用价值。

18.178.1　传统法假定一个单一的折现率可以包括所有对未来现金流量和适当的风险溢价的预期。因此，这种方法最强调的是折现率的选择。预期现金流量法更关注的是对现金流量的直接分析。[IAS 36 附录 A 第 A2 段、A4 段]。该附录列举的总体原则之一是“*估计的现金流量或者折现率应当反映可能结果的范围，而不是一个单一的、最可能的最小金额或最大金额*”。[IAS 36 附录 A 第 A3 段]。

possible amount". [IAS 36 App A para A3].

18.178.2 The expected cash flow approach starts with cash flows that reflect the risk that management anticipate (for example, cash flows based on probability). Risk adjusted probability cash flow projections are not certain and, therefore, it is not appropriate to use a risk free rate to discount such cash flows. A risk-free rate will generally only be appropriate for discounting cash flows for a government bond in a mature economy.

18.179 The standard highlights some of the problems and difficulties with the traditional approach, which concentrates on encapsulating all of these variables into a single discount rate (this is, because it is not possible to use different discount rates for different risks and apply them to different 'slices' of cash flows). It then contrasts this with the expected cash flow approach, which breaks down the risks and uses all expectations about possible cash flows instead of the single most likely cash flow.

18.180 The expected cash flow approach has, amongst others, the following advantages in an environment of higher uncertainty:

- The sensitivity of the recoverable amount to uncertainties is explicit in the measurement compared with the 'traditional' approach where it is factored into the discount rate.
- It enables management to assess the uncertain assumptions that may have the most significant impacts on the recoverable amount.
- It calculates a range of expected cash flows instead of only considering the most likely case.
- It may be more aligned with the way management prepares forecasts.
- It lessens the impact of the judgemental exercise inherent in choosing a single specific risk premium, which may be difficult to quantify and document.

18.178.2 预期现金流量法的起点是反映管理层所期望的风险的现金流量(例如，以可能性为基础的现金流量)。按照风险可能性调整的现金流量预计是不确定的，因此，使用无风险折现率对这些现金流量进行折现是不合适的。一般情况下，只有在成熟经济中对政府债券的现金流量进行折现，使用无风险折现率才是合适的。

18.179 该准则强调了使用传统法会出现的一些问题和困难，即传统法注重把所有这些变量都囊括在一个单一的折现率中（这是因为，对不同的风险使用不同的折现率，然后再把这些折现率应用到不同的现金流的“份额”中是不可能的)。该准则进而把传统法与预期现金流量法进行对照，预期现金流量法把风险进行细分，并且使用有关各种可能的现金流量的所有预期，而不是一个单一的最可能性发生的现金流量。

18.180 在存在较高不确定性的环境中，预期现金流量法具有下列优点：

- 针对可收回金额对不确定性的敏感度，在预期现金流量法的计量中是很明显的，相比较之下，传统法只将其作为确定折现率的考虑因素。

- 预期现金流量法使管理层能够对不确定的假设作出评估，这些假设可能对可收回金额产生最重要的影响。
- 预期现金流量法计算预期现金流量的范围，而不是仅仅考虑最有可能出现的情况。
- 预期现金流量法可能与管理层编制预算的方式更加相符。
- 预期现金流量法减少了在选择某一单一的特殊风险溢价时所固有的因主观判断所产生的影响，这可能很难进行量化并进行记录。

Example – Modeling of uncertainty

Impairment test: modeling of uncertainty

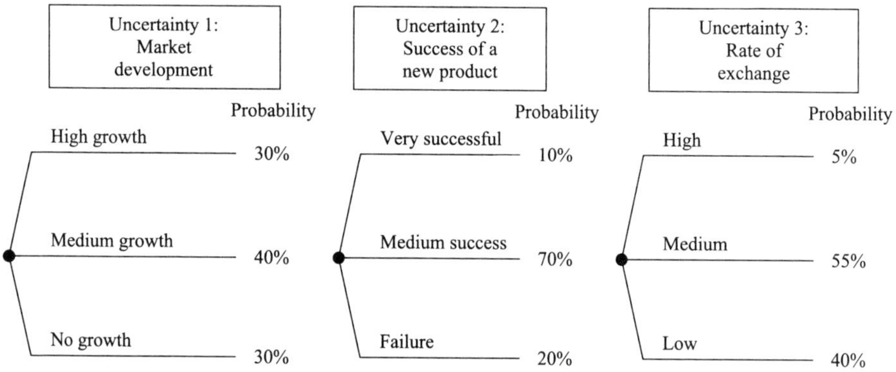

Management has identified three crucial uncertainties that might affect the forecast: market developments, the success of a new product and the exchange rate. For each uncertainty, three cash flow projections have been identified with the probability that they will occur. The recoverable amount will equal the expected value resulting from the combination of the 27 (3 × 3 × 3) possible scenarios.

Compare like with like

18. 180. 1 It is important, when entities are preparing their value in use calculations, that they ensure that the cash flows are prepared on a basis that is consistent with the calculation of the CGU's carrying amount. For example, if an entity includes the cash flows from trade debtors in the value in use calculation for a CGU then they should include the trade debtors as part of the carrying amount of the CGU.

18. 180. 1. 1 Following the principles of comparing like with like should ensure that the same answer is reached regardless of whether working capital receivables and payables are included or excluded from the calculation. This is illustrated in the example below.

示例——不确定性模型

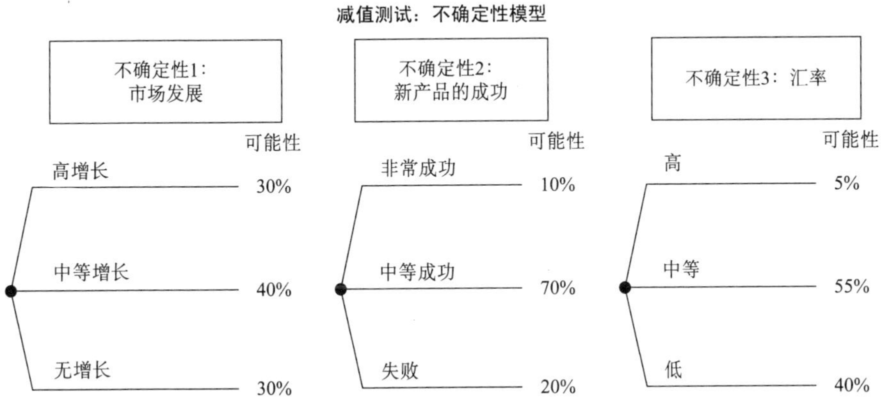

管理层已经识别出可能会对预测产生影响的三个关键不确定性：市场发展、新产品的成功以及汇率。对于每个不确定性而言，三个现金流量已经按照其发生的可能性进行识别。可收回金额将会和 27 个（3 ×3 ×3）可能情况组合而产生的期望值相等。

同类与同类比较

18.180.1　主体在编制其使用价值计算时，确保现金流量与 CGU 账面价值的计算按照一致的基础编制是很重要的。例如，如果主体将应收账款的现金流量包括在 CGU 的使用价值的计算中，则其也应当把应收账款作为 CGU 账面价值的一部分。

18.180.1.1　无论营运资金应收款项和应付款项是否包含在计算中，遵循同类与同类比较的原则应当确保所得到的答案是相同的。下文的示例将对此进行解释说明。

Example – Comparing like with like when including working capital balances

Entity A is performing a value in use test. The carrying value of assets excluding working capital balances is C180. The carrying value of working capital balances is C9. Entity A holds no inventory. The expected future cash flows and movements in working capital are given below.

	Year 1	Year 2	Year 3	Year 4	Total
	C	C	C	C	C
Cash flows before movement in working capita	100	120	130	140	490
Movements in working capital	(10)	(12)	(13)	(14)	(49)
Net cash flow	90	108	117	126	441

Method 1 – Excluding opening working capital

Under this method, the cash projections must include a one-off cash flow in year one as the entity 'buys' the working capital to perform its business. Year one also includes the normal working capital movement for that year.

Put another way, the cash flows included in Year one include the movement from nil to the closing working capital at the end of the year. In this case, closing working capital is C19 (being the opening position of (C9) plus the working capital movement during the year of C10) and, therefore, the total cash flows included in the model for Year one are C81; the C100 of cash flows prior to working capital movements less working capital movements of C19.

	Year 1	Year 2	Year 3	Year 4	Total
	C	C	C	C	C
Net cash flow as above	90	108	117	126	41
Opening working capital	(9)	–	–	–	(9)
Net cash flow	81	108	117	126	432

示例——包含营运资金余额时同类与同类比较

主体 A 在执行使用价值测试，未包含营运资金余额的资产的账面价值为 180 元。营运资金余额的账面价值为 9 元。主体 A 不持有存货。预期未来现金流量和营运资金的变动如下表所示。

	第一年 元	第二年 元	第三年 元	第四年 元	合计 元
未考虑营运资金变动的现金流量	100	120	130	140	490
营运资金变动	(10)	(12)	(13)	(14)	(49)
净现金流量	90	108	117	126	441

方法 1——不包含营运资金的期初余额

在这种方法下，在第一年，现金预计必须包含一笔一次性的现金流量，就如同该主体“购买”了营运资金以开展其业务。第一年也包含该年正常的营运资金变动。

换言之，第一年的现金流量包含从零到营运资金年末余额的变动。在这种情况下，营运资金的年末余额为 19 元（期初余额 9 元加上本年营运资金的变动 10 元），因此，在该模型中第一年的总现金流量为 81 元；即考虑营运资金变动之前的现金流量 100 元减去营运资金的变动 19 元。

	第一年 元	第二年 元	第三年 元	第四年 元	合计 元
上表中净现金流量	90	108	117	126	41
营运资金期初余额	(9)	–	–	–	(9)
净现金流量	81	108	117	126	432

The carrying value of assets excluding working capital (C180) is compared to the cash flow of C432 calculated above. The result is a surplus in the calculation of C252.

Method 2 – Including opening working capital

The cash flows are determined based upon actual cash movements for each year with no one-off adjustment to buy back the opening working capital. Total cash flows of C441 are compared to the carrying value of assets including the opening working capital (C189). This results in a surplus of C252.

The outcome is the same under both methods.

18.180.1.2 Entities should also consider the treatment of inventory in any value in use calculation. As with other working capital balances, it could be argued that inventory should be excluded from the value in use calculation by excluding it from the carrying amount and excluding the cash inflows from the sale of inventory already held. This is because impairment of inventory is considered by another standard (IAS 2, 'Inventories'). However, in practice, we would consider it acceptable to include inventory in the calculation provided that the calculation compares like with like. This means that cash receipts from the sale of inventory would be included in the discounted cash flows and the carrying value of the inventory would be included within the carrying value of the CGU. Unlike other working capital balances, the inclusion or exclusion of inventory could make a difference to the outcome of the impairment calculation. This is because inventory is held at cost on the balance sheet but associated future cash flows would include the expected margin to be made on sale. If margins are considerable, this could create a material discrepancy in the impairment calculation. In such a situation, an appropriate response might be to gross up the value of the inventory within the carrying value of the CGU to reflect the expected selling price.

18.180.2 The cash outflows associated with financing the CGU's operations (including interest-bearing debt, dividends and interest payable) are excluded from the value in use calculations. Therefore, the carrying amount of a CGU should exclude liabilities that relate to financing the CGU's operations. No distinction is

未包含营运资金的资产的账面价值（180 元）与上表计算的现金流量 432 元相比较，结果是盈余 252 元。

模式 2——包含营运资金的期初余额

现金流量基于每年实际的现金变动确定，而不包含对回购营运资金期初余额所做的一次性调整。总现金流量 441 元与包含营运资金期初余额的资产账面价值（189 元）相比较，结果为盈余 252 元。

两种方法的计算结果一致。

18.180.1.2　在任何使用价值的计算中，主体应当也要考虑存货的处理。正如其他的营运资金余额一样，可能有一种主张认为应该通过将存货从账面价值中排除以及排除已持有的存货销售产生的现金流量，而将存货排除在使用价值的计算之外。这是因为存货的减值是由另一项准则（《国际会计准则第 2 号——存货》（"IAS 2"））所规范的。然而，在实务中，在将同类与同类相比较的前提下，我们会认为将存货包含在计算中是可接受的做法。这意味着存货销售收得的现金流入将包含在折现现金流量中，而存货的账面价值也会包含在该 CGU 的账面价值中。与其他的营运资金余额不同，是否包含存货对于减值计算的结果可能会产生差异。这是因为在资产负债表中存货是以成本计量的，但是与之相关的未来现金流量将会包含销售产生的预期毛利。如果毛利较大，则可能会在减值计算中产生重大的差异。在这种情况下，适当的做法可能是将 CGU 账面价值中所包含的存货价值增加以反映预期的销售价格。

18.180.2　与为 CGU 的运营进行融资有关的现金流出（包括带息债务、股利和应付利息）不包括在使用价值的计算当中。因此，CGU 的账面价值不应当包括与为 CGU 的运营进行融资相关的负债。外部融资和公司内部融资之间没有区别。相关的现金流出（包括本金和利息）在确定可收回金额时都不会予

made between external and inter-company financing. The associated cash outflows, both principal and interest, are not considered in determining recoverable amount. Finance costs are indirectly considered in measuring recoverable amount by using the present value method to discount future cash flows.

18. 180. 3 As the cash flows in a value in use calculation are prepared on a pre-tax basis the cash flows associated with tax should not be included in the value in use calculation. (for further guidance see para 18. 219 onwards). Tax assets and liabilities are not included as part of the carrying value in a CGU. See paragraph 18. 225. 4. 1 onwards for more detail on what assets and liabilities should be allocated to a CGU.

Hedging instruments

18. 181 Management may use hedging instruments, such as swaps and collars, to hedge cash flows. The cash flows prepared for the VIU calculation should reflect management's best estimate of the future cash flows expected to be generated from the assets in the CGU. Management should use the contracted price for the relevant cash flows in its VIU calculation, unless the contract is already on the balance sheet at fair value.

18. 181. 2 Where the contract is on the balance sheet at fair value, it is accounted for under IAS 39, 'Financial instruments: Recognition and measurement'. Where this is the situation, the hedged cash flows are included in the VIU calculation at the spot price at the date of the impairment test. This is because the impairment of financial instruments that are within IAS 39's scope is addressed by IAS 39. In addition, including the contracted prices of a contract already on the balance sheet at fair value would double-count the effects of the contract.

18. 182 One approach to be applied is that working capital balances, including commodity contracts, recognised at fair value in accordance with IAS 39, are excluded from both the carrying amount of the CGU and the cash flows of the VIU calculation. Alternatively, following the principle of comparing like with like, the balances can be left in the CGU with their associated cash flows. (that is, the hedged cash flows at the hedged rates) being included in the VIU calculation.

[The next paragraph is 18. 186.]

以考虑。通过使用现值法对未来现金流量进行折现，融资成本在计量可收回金额时会被间接考虑。

18.180.3　因为使用价值计算中的现金流量是按照税前基础编制的，因此，与所得税有关的现金流量不应当包括在使用价值的计算当中（更多指引请参考第 18.219 段及其下文）。所得税资产和所得税负债不作为 CGU 使用价值的一部分而包括在内。有关应该把哪些资产和负债分配给 CGU 的更加详细的内容，请见第 18.225.4.1 段。

套期工具

18.181　管理层可以使用诸如互换和零成本双限期权等套期工具对现金流量进行套期。为使用价值计算编制的现金流量应当反映管理层对于预期从 CGU 中的资产所产生的未来现金流量的最佳估计。除非合同在资产负债表上已经以公允价值进行计量，否则在使用价值的计算中，管理层应当使用合同价格计算相关的现金流量。

18.181.2　在合同在资产负债表上以公允价值进行计量的情况下，则按照《国际会计准则第 39 号——金融工具：确认和计量》（“IAS 39”）对其进行会计处理。在这种情况下，被套期的现金流量按减值测试日的现行价格计量，并且包括在使用价值的计算中。这是因为在 IAS 39 的适用范围内的金融工具的减值是由 IAS 39 进行规范的。此外，将已经在资产负债表上以公允价值进行计量的合同的合同价格包括在内可能会对合同的影响进行重复计算。

18.182　一个可以被采用的方法是，把按照 IAS 39 以公允价值确认的营运资金余额（包括商品合同在内）排除在 CGU 的账面价值和使用价值计算的现金流量之外。或者，遵循同类与同类比较的原则，可以把该余额和相关的现金流量都予以保留（即，以套期比率计算的被套期的现金流量）包含在使用价值的计算中。

[下一段是第 18.186 段。]

Corporate overheads and day-to-day servicing

18.186 The inclusion in the cash flow forecasts of corporate overheads is mentioned only briefly in IAS 36, which notes that "Projections of cash outflows include those for the day-to-day servicing of the asset as well as future overheads that can be attributed directly, or allocated on a reasonable and consistent basis, to the use of the asset". [IAS 36 para 41]. It is reasonable to assume that the cash outflows attributable to a CGU should include sensible allocations of corporate overheads, in the same way that the carrying values of CGUs should, where practicable, include apportionments of corporate assets. The assets of a CGU could be considered to be impaired if, for example, its own cash flows did not make a contribution to corporate overheads that are incurred to support its activities.

18.187 It is important to ensure that corporate overheads are not omitted altogether in the value in use calculations. It is also important to ensure that corporate assets and overheads are not double-counted in the impairment review. For example, if part of the carrying value of head office property is allocated to CGUs for the purpose of impairment reviews, any internal management charges that are rendered to CGUs relating to the use of that property should be excluded from their cash outflows — otherwise, the carrying value of the CGU would be increased and its value in use decreased by elements relating to the same item.

18.188 Estimates of future cash flows include those cash flows that are necessary to maintain the current level of economic benefits expected to arise from the asset in its current condition. An asset will usually deteriorate through use or component parts will wear out. The standard makes clear that the cash outflows for servicing the asset to maintain its current capability are taken into account in the estimates.

18.188.1 In addition, where a CGU consists of assets with different useful lives, all of which are essential to the ongoing operation of the CGU, the replacement of assets with shorter useful lives is considered to be part of the day-

总部费用与日常服务

18.186　在 IAS 36 中仅是简要提及将总部费用包含在现金流量预测中，其谈到“现金流出预计包括那些为资产的日常服务以及可以直接归属于、或者按照某一合理且一致的基础分配给资产的使用的未来费用而发生的现金流出”。[IAS 36 第 41 段]。合理的假设是可归属于某一 CGU 的现金流出应当包括合理分配的总部费用，同样地，在切实可行的情况下，CGU 的账面价值也应当包括对总部资产的分摊。例如，如果某个 CGU 自身的现金流量没有为支持其活动而发生的总部费用作出贡献，则可能认为该 CGU 的资产发生了减值。

18.187　确保在使用价值的计算中没有把总部费用全部遗漏是很重要的。确保总部资产和费用在减值复核中没有被重复计算也是很重要的。例如，如果为作减值复核而将总部大楼账面价值的一部分分配给了多个 CGU，则向这些 CGU 收取的任何与使用该大楼有关的内部管理费用都不应当包括在它们的现金流出中——否则，与同一项目有关的因素将会导致 CGU 的账面价值增加而使用价值下降。

18.188　对未来现金流量的估计包括那些为维持资产在其现有的状况下预期产生的经济利益的现有水平所必需的现金流量。通常情况下，资产由于使用或者零件磨损而慢慢失去功能。该准则对此作出解释，即对资产进行维修以保持其现有的能力而发生的现金流出应当在估计中予以考虑。

18.188.1　此外，在某一 CGU 是由使用寿命各不相同资产所组成、且所有这些资产对于该 CGU 的持续运营都是必要的情况下，在估计可归属于该 CGU 的现金流量时，对那些使用寿命较短的资产进行重置被认为是对该 CGU 进行

to-day servicing of the CGU when the future cash flows attributable to the CGU are estimated. This means the replacement costs will be regarded as maintenance and included in the future cashflows attributable to the CGU. The same principle applies to a single asset consisting of components with different useful lives. [IAS 36 para 49]. Examples of assets with components that have different useful lives are given in IAS 16, 'Property, plant and equipment'. Such components include for example the lining of a furnace that has to be replaced several times during the furnace's life or aircraft seating that is similarly replaced several times during the aircraft's life. Another example that is treated as a separate component in some situations is the cost of major inspection or overhaul, such as the dry docking of a ship.

Inflation

18.189 Assumptions about inflation can be dealt with in one of two ways. One method is to forecast cash flows in current prices — that is, not to forecast future inflation. The cash flows are then discounted at a real discount rate (that is, a rate of return that excludes inflation). The second method is to forecast cash flows to include estimates of inflation in revenues and costs. The cash flows are then discounted at a nominal discount rate (that is, a rate of return that includes inflation). It is important that inflation is treated consistently in the cash flow projections and the choice of discount rate. [IAS 36 para 40]. The preferred method is to use nominal cash flows and a nominal discount rate. This is because the components of the discount rate are obtained from market data which reflect expectations of future inflation rates. It is difficult to remove the impact of inflation other than in a crude and thus unreliable fashion.

Foreign currency cash flows

18.190 Where future cash flows are expected to be denominated in a foreign currency, they should be estimated in that currency and then discounted at a rate appropriate for that currency. The entity then translates the present value (expressed in the foreign currency) at the spot rate of exchange at the date of the value in use calculation. [IAS 36 para 54]. IAS 36 specifically prohibits use of

日常维修的一部分。这就是说，重置成本将被视为维护费用，并且会包括在可归属于该CGU的未来现金流量中。同样的原则也适用于由使用寿命不同的组成部分所组成的单项资产。[IAS 36第49段]。《国际会计准则第16号——不动产、厂场和设备》给出了由使用寿命不同的组成部分组成的资产的例子。例如，这些组成部分包括锅炉的炉衬（其在锅炉的使用寿命内必须要被更换数次）或者飞机座椅（其在飞机的使用寿命内同样也必须被更换数次）。在某些情况下，大检查或大修理的费用例如船舶坞修费用，会是将其作为一个单独的组成部分进行处理的另一个例子。

通货膨胀

18.189 对通货膨胀的假设可以采用两种方法进行处理。一种方法是按当前价格对现金流量进行预测——也就是说，不预测未来的通货膨胀，则现金流量按照真实的折现率（即不包括通货膨胀的回报率）进行折现。第二种方法是对现金流量进行预测，以包括对收入和费用中的通货膨胀的估计。这种情况下，现金流量会按照名义折现率（即包括了通货膨胀的回报率）进行折现。很重要的一点是，在现金流量预计和折现率的选择中对于通货膨胀的处理要保持一致。[IAS 36第40段]。使用名义现金流量和名义折现率是更倾向采用的方法。这是因为，折现率的组成部分是从市场数据获得的，而这些市场数据反映了未来通货膨胀率的预期。除了在原始资料中，人们很难消除通货膨胀的影响，这样作出的数字是不可靠的。

外币现金流量

18.190 在未来现金流量预期以外币计价的情况下，这些现金流量应当按该种货币进行估计，并且按照该种货币的适当的折现率进行折现。进而，主体采用计算使用价值当天的即期汇率对该现值（用外币表示）进行折算。[IAS 36第54段]。IAS 36专门规定，禁止使用在对使用价值减值测试进行减值复核日存在的远期汇率。远期差额考虑的是利率，由于要对现金流量进行折现，

the forward rate existing at the date of the impairment review for value in use impairment tests. Forward differentials take into account interest rates and as the cash flows are to be discounted, the time value of money has already been taken into account. It also does not permit the forecasting of future foreign cash flows and converting them at estimated spot exchange rates at future dates as such estimates cannot be reliably made. [IAS 36 paras BCZ49 to BCZ50].

Future restructuring and expenditure to improve or enhance an asset's performance

18.191 A key constraint concerning the assumptions in the cash flow forecasts relates to future restructuring or reorganisation and capital investment. In calculating value in use, future cash flows should be estimated for assets and goodwill in their current condition. The future costs and benefits of a future restructuring should not be recognised in the cash flow forecasts, unless the entity is committed to the restructuring and related provisions have been made. The costs and benefits of future expenditure that is intended to improve or enhance the assets or business should not be taken into account in the cash flow forecasts. [IAS 36 paras 44, 45].

Example – Cash flows from replacement assets

An entity's management has decided to redevelop its main offices to improve the environment in which its employees work and to provide better facilities to receive clients. The office building is subject to depreciation, but the land is not. The building and the land are carried at re-valued amounts.

The main office building will be demolished and replaced by a new building. The re-valued carrying amount of the building is C100,000. Management argue that the redevelopment's plans increase the total value of the property (land and building). Management does not wish to recognise an impairment loss on the existing building in spite of its commitment to the property's demolition and replacement.

The cash flow from a replacement asset cannot be considered when estimating future cash flows for an existing asset. The recoverable amount of the old

因此已经把货币的时间价值考虑进去了。预测未来的外币现金流量，并且将其按照估计在未来某天的即期汇率进行转换也是不被允许的，这是因为无法可靠作出这样的估计。[IAS 36 BC 第 Z49—Z50 段]。

为改进或提高资产绩效进行的未来重组以及发生的支出

18.191　一项对于在现金流量预测中采用的假设的关键限制与未来的重组或者改组以及资本性投资有关。在计算使用价值时，应当以资产和商誉的当前状况估计其未来的现金流量。除非主体已经承诺进行重组并且已经计提了相关负债，否则未来重组的成本和收益不应当在现金流量预测中进行确认。旨在改进或提高资产或者业务发生的未来支出产生的成本和收益，在现金流量预测中也不应当被考虑。[IAS 36 第 44 段、第 45 段]。

示例——重置资产产生的现金流量

某一主体的管理层已经决定重建其主要的办公楼，以改善其员工的工作环境，并且为接待客户提供更好的设施。该办公楼需要计提折旧，而土地并不需要。该办公楼和土地都是按照重估价金额计量的。

该主办公楼将会被拆除，并以一栋新楼取而代之。该办公楼的重估价账面价值为 100,000 元。管理层认为，该重建计划增加了该房地产（土地和办公楼）的总价值。尽管管理层已经承诺对该房地产进行拆除并重建，但是其不希望对现有建筑物确认减值损失。

估计现有资产的未来现金流量时，不能考虑重置资产的现金流量。旧办公楼的可收回金额为零。拆除旧办公楼的费用是建造新办公楼的成本

building is zero. The cost of demolishing the old building is part of the costs of constructing the new building, as it represents site preparation costs. [IAS 16 para 17].

The impairment loss should be recognised first against the revaluation surplus for the asset. To the extent that the impairment exceeds the revaluation surplus for that building, it should be recognised in profit or loss.

18.192 The restrictions on taking account of the costs and benefits of future restructuring and enhancement capital expenditure in value in use calculations are severe constraints. Impairment reviews should be based on the most recent budgets and forecasts that have been formally approved by management. [IAS 36 para 33]. Where management has approved restructuring and capital investment plans, however, the most recent formally approved budgets and forecasts would typically include both the costs and benefits (such as lower production costs or extra revenues from higher quality output) of the planned restructuring and capital expenditure. Provisions for restructuring costs might, however, be recognised in financial statements later than their inclusion in formal budgets and plans—say, after the balance sheet date at which assets are being reviewed for impairment. If this is the case, forecasts must be adjusted to remove the related costs and benefits.

18.193 A restructuring is a programme that is planned and controlled by management and that materially changes either the scope of the business undertaken by the entity or the manner in which the business is conducted. [IAS 36 para 46]. IAS 37, 'Provisions, contingent liabilities and contingent assets', sets out in some detail the conditions that must be complied with before provisions for restructurings may be recognised in financial statements. In particular, IAS 37 states that a management or board decision to restructure that is taken before the balance sheet date does not give rise to a constructive obligation (the trigger for recognising a provision), unless the entity has before the balance sheet date:

- started to implement the restructuring plan, or
- announced its main features to those affected by it in a sufficiently specific manner to raise a valid expectation in them that the entity will carry out the

组成部分，这是因为其属于场地整理费。［IAS 16 第 17 段］。

减值损失首先应当冲减资产的重估价盈余。减值超过该办公楼的重估价盈余的部分，应当确认为当期损益。

18.192　计算使用价值时，对于考虑未来重组和对资产进行改进发生的资本支出产生的成本和收益所作的限制是非常严格的约束条件。减值复核应该以管理层正式批准的最新的预算和预测为基础。［IAS 36 第 33 段］。然而，在管理层已经批准了重组和资本投资计划的情况下，其正式批准的最新的预算和预测通常可能已经包括了计划的重组和资本支出的成本和收益（诸如较低的生产成本或者由于更高质量的产品所带来的额外收入等）。然而，为重组成本计提的预计负债在财务报表中确认的时间可能会晚于其纳入正式预算和计划的时间——也就是说，在资产负债表日（对资产作减值复核的日期）之后。如果是这种情况，必须调整预测，以扣除相关成本和收益。

18.193　重组是由管理层作出计划并进行控制会重大地改变主体的业务范围或业务开展方式的方案。［IAS 36 第 46 段］。《IAS 37——准备、或有负债和或有资产》较详细地规定了在财务报表中确认重组准备前必须符合的条件。IAS 37 特别规定，资产负债表日前管理层或董事会作出的重组决定并不产生推定义务（它是确认准备的触发事件），除非主体在资产负债表日前已经有下列活动：

- 开始实施重组计划；或者
- 以足够具体的方式向受到重组计划影响的人员宣布重组计划的主要特征，让人们可以有效地预期：主体将进行重组。

restructuring.

[IAS 37 para 75].

18.194 If those criteria are met by the balance sheet date and the costs have been provided for in the financial statements, the expenditure and the related benefits (such as savings from lower staff costs) of the restructuring should also be included in the cash flow forecasts in the appropriate period for determining value in use. [IAS 36 para 47].

18.195 If, however, those criteria are not met by the balance sheet date and, therefore, no provisions for restructuring costs have been booked, the costs and benefits of the reorganisation should not be taken into account in calculating value in use either. It is necessary to strip out the planned expenditure on restructuring and the related benefits from the formally approved budgets and plans to comply with the standard. [IAS 36 para 48].

18.196 Stripping out the cash inflows and outflows relating to a planned restructuring or improvement-type capital expenditure may not be straightforward. For example, it is hypothetical to forecast what future revenues would be if the business remained static rather than being developed in the way that is envisaged. It may, therefore, be difficult to adjust a budget to show what the cash flows would be estimated to be if a planned restructuring or capital expenditure did not take place.

18.196.1 In practice, these restrictions on value in use could lead to entities using a fair value less costs to sell basis for the calculation of recoverable amount, as it will, in many cases, be higher. In cases where a restructuring is foreseen but not yet provided for, and it is reasonable to assume market participants would also restructure, in the absence of other factors that might influence fair value less cost to sell, then a calculation on that basis is likely to produce a higher amount.

Future restructuring-example

18.197 The following example illustrates the treatment of a future restructuring and the interaction of the impairment calculations with the recognition of

[IAS 37 第 75 段]。

18. 194　如果资产负债表日满足确认重组准备的条件并且已于财务报表中计提了费用，则重组的支出和相关利益（如减少员工费用所产生的成本节约）也应包括在为确定使用价值而进行的现金流预测的适当期间。[IAS 36 第 47 段]。

18. 195　但是，如果资产负债表日尚未满足确认重组准备的条件，因此尚未记录为重组费用所计提的准备，那么在计算使用价值的过程中，即不应考虑重组的费用，也不应考虑重组的利益。为与准则相符，有必要从正式批准的预算和计划中剔除为重组所作的计划性支出和相关利益。[IAS 36 第 48 段]。

18. 196　剔除与计划中的重组或改良型资本性支出相关的现金流入和流出可能并不容易。例如，预测业务依然处于现有状态、而非按照设想地去开展时的未来收入是一件凭空想象的事情。因此，调整预算以反映如果不发生所计划的重组或资本性支出时的预计现金流，可能非常困难。

18. 196. 1　在实务中，这些对使用价值的限制可能使得主体采用公允价值减去处置费用来计算可收回金额，因为在很多情况下，公允价值减去处置费用的金额要高些。预见到重组但是还没有计提准备的，且能合理假设市场参与者也会进行重组的，在不考虑可能影响公允价值减去处置费用的其他因素时，以公允价值减去处置费用为基础的计算很可能会产生较高的金额。

未来重组——示例

18. 197　下面示例说明的是对未来重组的会计处理，及减值计算与确认重组准备之间的相互关系。这个例子把减值损失的时点和重组费用进行对比，区

restructuring provisions. The example contrasts the timing of impairment losses and restructuring costs, which differ according to whether or not the restructuring is sufficiently advanced in its execution for provisions to be recognised in the financial statements. It also shows how an impairment loss calculated only by reference to value in use may give rise to the recognition of impairment losses in earlier periods, even though management may expect to avoid impairment by restructuring and the reversal of such impairment losses in later periods when the restructuring is implemented. An impairment calculation on a fair value less costs to sell in these circumstances would be likely to lead to no impairment charge.

Example – Future restructuring planned

At 31 December 20X1, the assets of a cash-generating unit are being reviewed for impairment. The carrying value of the CGU's net assets is C6.5m (excluding any restructuring provision) and the remaining useful economic life of the recognised assets is 8 years.

Management's approved budgets at 31 December 20X1 include restructuring costs of C350,000 to be incurred in 20X2; the restructuring is expected to generate cost savings of C100,000 per annum from 20X3 onwards. Formal budgets have been prepared for the 3 years to 31 December 20X4; thereafter, for the purpose of the impairment review, a zero growth rate is assumed, because market conditions are extremely competitive and this is expected to continue for the foreseeable future. The future cash flow estimates are set out below, along with figures that exclude from those estimates the cost and benefits of the planned restructuring. Thus in 20X2 the net cash flows without restructuring (C870,000) exceed the net cash flows with restructuring (C520,000) by the amount of the restructuring costs (C350,000).

The future cash flows (which exclude inflation) have been discounted at a rate of 4%. For simplicity, it has been assumed that the cash flows arise at the end of each year; therefore, the figures in the 'present value' columns for the cash flows (CF) in 'n' years time from 31 December 20X1 are derived from the formula $CF^n/(1+i)^n$, where i (the discount rate) is 0.04.

分重组是否已足够提前以便在财务报表中确认重组准备。它还列示了仅以使用价值为基础计算出来的减值损失如何导致可能在较早期间确认减值损失，尽管管理层可能已预期能够通过重组避免减值，且预期重组实施后这些减值损失会在较晚期间转回。在这些情况下，基于公允价值减去处置费用的减值计算可能不会产生减值费用。

示例——计划的未来重组

20X1 年 12 月 31 日，主体正在对一个现金产出单元的资产进行减值复核。该 CGU 净资产的账面价值为 6.5 百万元（不包括任何重组准备），所确认的资产的剩余使用经济寿命为 8 年。

管理层批准了的于 20X1 年 12 月 31 日的预算包括将于 20X2 年发生的重组费用，金额为 350,000 元；预计该重组自 20X3 年开始，每年可以节省成本 100,000 元。正式预算编制了三年，截止到 20X4 年；之后，为了减值复核的目的，假定增长率为零，这是因为市场竞争特别激烈，并且在可以预见的未来仍然如此。未来现金流的估计在下文给出，同时下文还给出了不包括在该估计中的计划的重组费用和利益的金额。这样，20X2 年，不包含重组的净现金流（870,000 元）超出包含重组的净现金流（520,000 元）的部分，是重组费用(350,000 元)。

未来现金流（不包括通货膨胀）已经按 4% 的折现率进行了折现。为了简化起见，假定现金流在年底产生；因此，自 20X1 年 12 月 31 日起的第“n”年的现金流（CF）的“现值”栏里的金额是根据公式 $CF^n/(1+i)^n$ 计算出来的，其中 i（折现率）为 0.04。

	With re-organisation		Without re-organisation	
	Future net cash flows	Present value	Future net cash flows	Present value
	C000	C000	C000	C000
20X2	520	500	870	836
20X3	1,000	925	900	832
20X4	1,050	933	950	845
20X5	1,050	898	950	812
20X6	1,050	863	950	781
20X7	1,050	830	950	751
20X8	1,050	798	950	722
20X9	1,050	767	950	694
Value in use		6,514		6,273

The impairment calculations at 31 December 20X1 differ according to whether or not provision for the restructuring costs is recognised in the financial statements. This will depend on whether the requirements of IAS 37 have been met for recognition – see paragraph 18. 193 above.

A — Provision for restructuring costs recognised at 31 December 20X1

If provision has been made for restructuring costs, the costs and benefits of the restructuring are taken into account in determining the CGU's value in use. In this example, the post-restructuring value in use (C6,514,000) exceeds the CGU's carrying value (C6,500,000 less restructuring provision C350,000). Hence, there is no impairment of the CGU's assets.

In the year to 31 December 20X1, the financial statements reflect the following charges:

Restructuring provision	C350,000
Impairment loss	Nil

	考虑重组		不考虑重组	
	未来净现金流	现值	未来净现金流	现值
	千元	千元	千元	千元
20X2	520	500	870	836
20X3	1,000	925	900	832
20X4	1,050	933	950	845
20X5	1,050	898	950	812
20X6	1,050	863	950	781
20X7	1,050	830	950	751
20X8	1,050	798	950	722
20X9	1,050	767	950	694
使用价值		6,514		6,273

20X1 年 12 月 31 日的减值计算根据财务报表中是否为重组费用确认了准备而有所不同。这取决于是否符合 IAS 37 中确认的规定——见上文第 18.193 段。

A——20X1 年 12 月 31 日确认了重组费用准备

如果已经为重组费用计提了准备，在确定 CGU 的使用价值时，需要考虑重组费用和利益。本例中，重组后使用价值（6,514,000 元）超过了 CGU 的账面价值（6,500,000 元减去重组准备 350,000 元）。因此，CGU 资产没有发生减值。

在截止日为 20X1 年 12 月 31 日的财务年度，财务报表所反映的费用如下：

重组准备	350,000 元
减值损失	无

B — No provision for restructuring costs recognised at 31 December 20X1

If no provision for restructuring costs is permitted by IAS 37, the costs and benefits of the restructuring have to be stripped out of the projections in determining the CGU's value in use. In this example, the CGU's carrying value (C6,500,000) exceeds its pre-restructuring value in use (C6,273,000). Therefore, there is an impairment loss of C227,000.

In the year to 31 December 20X1, the financial statements reflect the following charges:

Impairment loss	C227,000
Restructuring provision	Nil

In the year to 31 December 20X2, the restructuring is carried out. Assuming that the cash flow projections at 31 December 20X2 are the same as those previously estimated at 31 December 20X1 (including the benefits of the restructuring), the calculation of the CGU's value in use at 31 December 20X2 is as follows. Note that the present values of each year's cash flows have increased from the previous table because they are one year closer.

	Future net cash flows	**Present value**
Year	**C000**	**C000**
20X3	1,000	961
20X4	1,050	971
20X5	1,050	933
20X6	1,050	898
20X7	1,050	863
20X8	1,050	830
20X9	1,050	798
Value in use		6,254

As a result of the restructuring, the CGU's value in use at 31 December 20X2 (C6,254,000) will exceed its impaired carrying value (C6,273,000 less depreciation charged in the year). For example, assume the carrying value of

B——20X1 年 12 月 31 日未确认重组费用准备

如果重组费用准备尚未满足 IAS 37 的要求，应该把重组费用和利益从确定 CGU 使用价值的预期中剔除。本例中，CGU 的账面价值（6,500,000 元）超过了它重组前的使用价值（6,273,000 元）。因此，发生了减值损失，金额为 227,000 元。

在截止日为 20X1 年 12 月 31 日的财务年度，财务报表所反映的费用如下：

减值损失	227,000 元
重组准备	无

在截止日为 20X2 年 12 月 31 日的财务年度，进行了重组。假定 20X2 年 12 月 31 日的现金流预测和之前于 20X1 年 12 月 31 日（包括重组利益）所估计的一致，20X2 年 12 月 31 日，对 CGU 使用价值的计算如下。请注意每年现金流的现值比前表中的增加了，原因在于它们少折算了一年。

年份	**未来净现金流** **千元**	**现值** **千元**
20X3	1,000	961
20X4	1,050	971
20X5	1,050	933
20X6	1,050	898
20X7	1,050	863
20X8	1,050	830
20X9	1,050	798
使用价值		6,254

重组的结果是，20X2 年 12 月 31 日，该 CGU 的使用价值（6,254,000 元）将超过其减值后的账面价值（6,273,000 元减去当年的折旧费用）。例如，假定 CGU 的账面价值由下列固定资产组成，这些固定资产在剩余

the CGU comprises fixed assets as follows, which are depreciated uniformly over their remaining useful life of eight years.

	Depreciated historical cost before impairment	**Carrying value after impairment**
	C000	**C000**
31 December X1	6,500	6,273
Depreciation	812	784
31 December X2	5,688	5,489
Value in use		6,254

The CGU's value in use at 31 December 20X2 exceeds the impaired carrying value by C765,000. Therefore, the impairment loss of C227,000 should be reversed insofar as permitted by IAS 36. Impairment losses should be reversed in situations where the recoverable amount increases as a result of a restructuring, the benefits of which had been excluded from the original measurement of value in use. [IAS 36 para 111]. In this case, the impairment loss should be reversed by increasing the carrying value of the fixed assets to what it would have been had no impairment loss been recognised in the previous year, that is, from C5,489,000 to C5,688,000 — a reversal of C199,000. [IAS 36 para 117].

In the year to 31 December 20X2, the financial statements reflect the following charges and credits:

Restructuring provision	C350,000
Reversal of impairment loss	C199,000 CR

Note: In this example it has been assumed that there is no goodwill in the CGU. Had there been goodwill the impairment loss in 20X1 would first have been set against the carrying amount of goodwill and then *pro rata* to the other assets. When the impairment loss reverses in 20X2 only that amount of the impairment loss that relates to the assets other than goodwill may be reversed. The portion of the impairment loss that related to goodwill may not be reversed. [IAS 36 para 124].

使用寿命八年的期间内统一折旧：

	减值前折旧后的历史成本	减值后账面价值
	千元	千元
X1 年 12 月 31 日	6,500	6,273
折旧	812	784
X2 年 12 月 31 日	5,688	5,489
使用价值		6,254

20X2 年 12 月 31 日，CGU 的使用价值超出减值后的账面价值 765,000 元。因此，应该在 IAS 36 允许的范围内转回 227,000 元的减值损失。减值损失应在重组使可收回金额增加时转回，重组的利益在原使用价值的计量中未予考虑。[IAS 36 第 111 段]。这种情况下，应通过增加固定资产的账面价值的方法将减值损失转回，转回的金额以把该固定资产的账面价值增加到如果前一年没有确认减值损失的话该固定资产现在应有的账面金额为限，即，从 5,489,000 元增加到 5,688,000 元— 转回金额为 199,000 元。[IAS 36 第 117 段]。

在截止日为 20X2 年 12 月 31 日的财务年度，财务报表所反映的费用和转回数如下：

重组准备	350,000 元	
减值损失的转回	199,000 元	贷方

注：本例假设 CGU 中没有商誉。如果存在商誉，则 20X1 年的减值损失首先应该冲减商誉的账面价值，然后按比例分配给其他资产。当减值损失在 20X2 年转回时，则只可以转回除了商誉以外资产的减值损失。商誉减值损失的部分不能转回。[IAS 36 第 124 段]。

Example – Restriction on reversal of impairment loss

Assume that the carrying amount at 31 December 20X1 of C6, 500, 000 included C100, 000 of goodwill that, in accordance with IFRS 3 is not amortised. The impairment loss of C227,000 would be allocated first against the goodwill, eliminating it completely, and then against the other assets *pro rata*. The carrying amount of the CGU at 31 December 20X2 would be C5,401,000 to the nearest thousand. ((C6, 273, 000 - C100,000) ×7/8 years remaining useful life). The recoverable amount is C6, 253, 000 as above. The amount of the original reversal loss that may be recognised is calculated as follows:

	C	C
Original impairment		227,000
Goodwill impairment that cannot be reversed		(100,000)
Balance		127,000
Net carrying amount of assets other than goodwill assuming no impairment		
((C6,500,000 – 100,000) ×7/8)	5,600,000	
Less carrying amount of assets other than goodwill after impairment	5,401,000	
Potential reversal	199,000	
Reduced to actual remaining reversal	(72,000)	127,000

As can be seen from the above in this situation only C127,000 of the reversal may be made. In fact only C127,000 of the original impairment was allocated to assets other than goodwill so that impairment is reversed in full, but because the goodwill impairment cannot be reversed the overall reversal of impairment on the CGU is C72, 000 less than if there had been no goodwill. The difference of C72,000 is effectively the difference between the impairment amount that cannot be reversed of C100, 000, reduced by the C28, 000 restriction (C227, 000 – C199,000) that does not apply here because none of the goodwill impairment is

示例——对减值损失转回的限制

假定20X1年12月31日的账面价值为6,500,000元，其中包括按照IFRS 3不允许摊销的商誉100,000元。227,000元的减值损失首先分配给商誉，把商誉金额全部冲减完后，然后按*比例*分配给其他资产。20X2年12月31日，CGU的账面价值将为5,401,000元（精确到千位）((6,273,000－100,000元)×7/8年的剩余使用寿命)。可收回金额为上文中的6,253,000元。可以确认的原损失的转回金额计算如下：

	元	元
原减值		227,000
不能转回的商誉减值		(100,000)
余额		127,000
假定没有发生减值,除商誉外的资产的净账面价值		
[(6,500,000元－100,000元)×7/8]	5,600,000	
减:减值后除商誉外资产的账面价值	5,401,000	
可能的转回金额	199,000	
减至实际剩余转回金额	(72,000)	127,000

从上表可以看出，这种情况下，可以转回的金额只有127,000元。实际上，原减值金额中，只有127,000元分配给了除商誉外的资产，此减值可以全额转回；但是，因为商誉减值不能转回，所以，CGU的整体减值转回金额为72,000元，这个金额小于如果没有商誉的情形。72,000元的差额实际上是用不能转回的减值损失100,000元减去28,000元后的差值，28,000元(227,000－199,000)是不能转回的部分，在此例中不受限制，因为商誉减值没有转回。

reversed.

Note also that, had there been goodwill in the CGU, assuming an ongoing business at the end of the eight year life of the assets currently held, the impairment test would have been carried out using cash flows (comprising revenues and costs including replacement capital expenditure) into perpetuity. Any impairment recognised in relation to the goodwill could not subsequently be reversed.

Future expenditure to improve or enhance an asset's performance

18.198 Future expenditure and the related benefits should also be excluded from the calculation of value in use to the extent that the expenditure will improve or enhance the asset's performance. [IAS 36 para 44]. Improvement-type capital expenditure should be excluded; that which is necessary to maintain the asset or CGU at its current standard of performance should be included. [IAS 36 para 49].

18.199 This treatment of future expenditure to improve or enhance performance, referred to below as capital expenditure, needs to be considered carefully. For an individual fixed asset that is being reviewed for impairment, the treatment is relatively straightforward. The value in use takes into account the expenditure that is necessary to maintain the asset for its estimated useful economic life, but it does not anticipate the asset's enhancement or replacement. When those events occur, they result in new capital expenditure being recognised—until then, only the old asset exists.

18.201 Under IAS 36, the costs and benefits of enhancing assets in excess of their current standard of performance should be excluded from the impairment calculations. An example would be expenditure that results in the useful life of an asset being extended from five years to eight years.

18.202 A situation where expenditure is *not* excluded from the cash flows is expenditure that replaces or restores separate components of a single fixed asset that have different useful lives from the rest of the asset, for example the lining of a furnace. It is unlikely that the component would be tested individually for impairment, since it forms part of a larger asset. Under IAS 16 the cost of

也要注意，如果 CGU 有商誉，假设 CGU 在目前持有的资产 8 年使用寿命结束后仍能持续经营，减值测试应使用永续现金流量（包括收入和考量重置资本支出后的成本）。确认的与商誉相关的任何减值均不能在以后期间转回。

改进或提高资产绩效的未来支出

18.198　改良或提高资产绩效的未来支出及相关利益应从使用价值的计算中剔除。[IAS 36 第 44 段]。改良型的资本支出不应该包括在内；但维持资产或 CGU 当前绩效标准的未来支出应该包括在内。[IAS 36 第 49 段]。

18.199　需要认真考虑改良或提高绩效的未来支出（以下称为资本性支出）的处理。对正在作减值复核的单项固定资产来说，处理相对简单。使用价值中考虑为维持资产预计使用经济寿命而必要的支出，但是不预计资产的改良或重置。当改良或重置事项发生时，它们导致确认新的资本性支出资产——到那时之前，就只有老资产存在。

18.201　根据 IAS 36 的规定，减值计算中不包括能提高资产当前绩效水平的资本性支出及其利益。例如，将资产的使用寿命期限从 5 年延长至 8 年的支出。

18.202　支出不从现金流中剔除的情况之一是重置或恢复单项固定资产的与该资产其他部分具有不同使用寿命的组成部分的支出，比如锅炉的内衬。不大可能对组成部分分别做减值测试，因为它们是一项较大资产的组成部分。按照 IAS 16 的规定，对重置组成部分的成本作资本化处理，被替换的组成部分的账面价值（如有）则被转销。但是，根据 IAS 36 的规定，组成部分的预

replacing the component would be capitalised and the carrying amount, if any, of the replaced component is eliminated. However, under IAS 36 the expected future cost of replacement or restoration expenditure for the component is treated as if it were part of the day to day servicing of the larger asset and is included in the cash flows used to assess the recoverable amount of the larger asset.

Example – Treatment of costs that maintain the current standard of performance

The carrying value of a furnace is being reviewed for impairment. The furnace has a useful life of 20 years and requires relining every 5 years. The lining is treated as a separate asset component under IAS 16. Thus the cost of the lining is depreciated over 5 years; the remainder of the furnace is depreciated over 20 years.

For calculating the furnace's value in use, the net cash flows forecast for the remainder of the furnace's 20-year useful life would include the costs relating to relining the furnace every 5 years, because that expenditure is necessary to maintain the current standard of performance.

18.203 The same principle applies to assets of a CGU that have different estimated useful lives from the rest of the assets in the CGU. Under IAS 16 the costs of replacement or restoration of such assets would be capitalised if they met the recognition criteria in IAS 16. Under IAS 36, despite the fact that they are capital expenditure, the estimated cash flows relating to the replacement or restoration are not excluded from the impairment calculation for the CGU. This is because they are regarded for the purpose of the impairment calculation as day-to-day servicing costs of the CGU. They maintain, but do not enhance, the current performance of the CGU.

18.204 Another situation where expenditure is included in cash flows is expenditure that relates to a major inspection for faults of a fixed asset that restores the asset's economic benefits that have been consumed. Under IAS 16, such expenditure is recognised as part of the cost of the fixed asset if it meets the recognition criteria in that standard. However, under IAS 36 the estimated future

期重置或恢复支出的未来成本作为服务于较大资产的日常支出的一部分进行处理，包括在用来评估较大资产可收回金额的现金流中。

示例——维持当期绩效水平的成本的处理

主体正在对锅炉的账面价值作减值复核。锅炉的使用寿命为20年，要求每5年更换一次内衬。根据IAS 16的规定，把内衬作为一项单独资产组成部分处理。这样，内衬的成本分5年进行折旧；锅炉的其余部分分20年进行折旧。

为了计算锅炉的使用价值，锅炉其余部分20年使用寿命的净现金流预测包括每5年更换锅炉内衬的相关成本，因为这些支出是为了维持当前绩效水平所必要的支出。

18.203 同样的原则也适用于CGU内预计使用寿命与该CGU内其余资产不一样的资产。根据IAS 16的规定，如果重置或恢复这些资产的成本符合IAS 16的确认条件，则把它们作资本化处理。按照IAS 36的规定，尽管这些成本实际上是资本性支出，但是与重置或恢复有关的预计现金流并不在CGU的减值计算中剔除。这是因为，为了减值计算的目的，这些支出视同CGU的日常服务费。它们维持但并不提高CGU的当前绩效。

18.204 现金流中包括支出的另一个情形是，为恢复资产已消耗的经济利益而发生与固定资产大修检查相关的支出。按照IAS 16的规定，如果这样的支出符合准则中的确认条件，把它们作为固定资产成本的一部分进行确认。但是，根据IAS 36的规定，与大修或检查相关的预计未来现金流包括在资产的减值计算内。这是因为，检查费用的处理方法与上述对资产或CGU单独组成

cash flows related to such overhauls or inspections would not be excluded from the impairment calculations for the asset. This is because the inspections would be treated in the same way as separate components of the asset or CGU, as described above.

18.205 The following example illustrates the value in use calculations for an asset where future improvement-type expenditure is planned.

Example – Improvement-type expenditure

A cruise ship is being reviewed for impairment at 31 December 20X1. The ship is a CGU. Its carrying value is C72m and its estimated remaining useful life is 10 years, with a residual value estimated at C6m.

Management has approved a major investment plan to increase the ship's passenger capacity. The work will be carried out in 20X4 and is expected to result in a significant increase in passenger revenues and a decrease in running costs. The remaining useful life is expected to be extended by two years. The estimated cost of the new investment is C8m. There is also a period of inactivity for the ship while the upgrade is being carried out, resulting in a net cash outflow in 20X4.

Management assess the recoverable amount by determining the ship's value in use. (In order to comply with IAS 36, management would also need to calculate the fair value less costs to sell. The FVLCS is not relevant to this illustration and is, therefore, not considered here). The future cash flow estimates for the VIU calculation are set out below, along with figures that exclude from those estimates the cost and benefits of the planned C8m of future expenditure to enhance the asset's current level of performance (referred to below as 'capex'). The future cash flows (which exclude inflation) have been discounted at a rate of 6%. For simplicity, it has been assumed that the cash flows arise at the end of each year; therefore, the figures in the 'present value' columns for the cash flows (CF) in 'n' years time from 31 December 20X1 are derived from the formula $CF^n/(1+i)^n$, where i (the discount rate) is 0.06.

部分的处理方法一致。

18.205　下面的例子说明，当计划了未来改良型支出时，如何计算资产的使用价值。

示例——改良型支出

20X1 年 12 月 31 日，主体正在对一艘游轮做减值复核。这艘游轮是一个 CGU。它的账面价值是 72 百万元，预计剩余使用寿命为 10 年，残余价值预计为 6 百万元。

为增加游轮的载客量，管理层批准了一项重大投资计划。这项工作将于 20X4 年开展，预期游客收入将大幅增长，经营费用将大幅下降。预期剩余使用寿命将延长两年。新投资的预计成本为 8 百万元。改造期间，游轮将有一段时间不能运营，导致 20X4 年产生现金净流出。

管理层通过确定游轮的使用价值来评估其可收回金额。（为遵守 IAS 36 的规定，管理层也需要计算公允价值减去处置费用的金额。FVLCS 与这段说明不相关，因此这里不予考虑）。VIU 计算所需的未来现金流的估计如下表所示，同时给出的还有剔除在估计外的为了提高资产的当前绩效水平而计划的未来支出（以下简称为“capex”）8 百万元的成本和利益。未来现金流（不包括通货膨胀）已经按 6% 的折现率进行了折现。为了简单起见，假定现金流在年底产生；因此，自 20X1 年 12 月 31 日起的第“n”年的现金流（CF）的“现值”栏里的金额是根据公式 $CF^n/(1+i)^n$ 计算出来的，其中 i（折现率）为 0.06。

Year	Including new capex		Excluding new capex	
	Future net cash flows	Present value	Future net cash flows	Present value
	C000	C000	C000	C000
20X2	8,300	7,830	8,300	7,830
20X3	8,500	7,565	8,500	7,565
20X4	(4,000)	(3,358)	8,500	7,137
20X5	10,500	8,317	8,500	6,732
20X6	10,800	8,070	8,285	6,191
20X7	11,050	7,790	8,078	5,695
20X8	11,250	7,482	7,876	5,238
20X9	11,450	7,184	7,679	4,818
20Y0	10,990	6,505	7,487	4,431
20Y1	10,550	5,891	13,300	7,427
20Y2	10,130	5,336		
20Y3	15,725	7,815		
Value in use		76,427		63,064

For the purpose of the impairment review at 31 December 20X1, the future expenditure and the related benefits should be excluded from the calculation of value in use so the ship is tested for impairment in its present form and condition. On this basis, the estimated value in use of the ship in its existing state (C63,064,000) is lower than its carrying value (C72,000,000) and so an impairment loss of C8,936,000 should be recognised.

The improvement work is carried out in the year to 31 December 20X4. Assuming that the cash flow projections at 31 December 20X4 are the same as those previously estimated at 31 December 20X1, the calculation of the ship's value in use at 31 December 20X4 is as follows.

年份	包括新 capex		不包括新 capex	
	未来净现金流	现值	未来净现金流	现值
	千元	千元	千元	千元
20X2	8,300	7,830	8,300	7,830
20X3	8,500	7,565	8,500	7,565
20X4	(4,000)	(3,358)	8,500	7,137
20X5	10,500	8,317	8,500	6,732
20X6	10,800	8,070	8,285	6,191
20X7	11,050	7,790	8,078	5,695
20X8	11,250	7,482	7,876	5,238
20X9	11,450	7,184	7,679	4,818
20Y0	10,990	6,505	7,487	4,431
20Y1	10,550	5,891	13,300	7,427
20Y2	10,130	5,336		
20Y3	15,725	7,815		
使用价值		76,427		63,064

为了20X1 年 12 月 31 日减值复核之目的，使用价值的计算不应该包括未来支出和相关利益，这样，对游轮的减值测试则是基于其现有形态和条件进行的。以此为基础，游轮目前状态下的预计使用价值（63,064,000 元）小于它的账面价值（72,000,000 元），因此，应该确认 8,936,000 元的减值损失。

改良工作于 20X4 年 12 月 31 日年度内完成。假定在截止日为 20X4 年 12 月 31 日的财务年度所做的现金流预测和之前在 20X1 年 12 月 31 日所做的估计一样，20X4 年 12 月 31 日，对游轮使用价值的计算结果如下：

Year	Future net cash flows C000	Present value C000
20X5	10,500	9,906
20X6	10,800	9,612
20X7	11,050	9,278
20X8	11,250	8,911
20X9	11,450	8,556
20Y0	10,990	7,748
20Y1	10,550	7,016
20Y2	10,130	6,356
20Y3	15,725	9,307
Value in use		76,690

The ship's carrying value at 31 December 20X4 is as follows (straight-line depreciation at 10% per annum to the estimated residual value of C6m has been assumed).

	Carrying value C000
31 December 20X1	63,064
Depreciation 20X2 to 20X4((63,064,000 – 6,000,000) × 10% ×3)	(17,119)
Capital expenditure in 20X4	8,000
31 December 20X4	53,945

The ship's value in use following the improvement exceeds its impaired carrying value. In accordance with paragraphs 111 and 114 of IAS 36, an increase in the recoverable amount as a result of further improvement expenditure (the benefits of which had been excluded from the original measurement of value in use) should result in a reversal of the original impairment loss at 31 December 20X4. The amount of the reversal is restricted to the extent that the ship's carrying value is increased to what it would have been had the original impairment not occurred. [IAS 36 para 117]. This is calculated as follows, resulting in a reversal of C6,255,000 (C60,200,000 – C53,945,000).

年份	未来净现金流 千元	现值 千元
20X5	10,500	9,906
20X6	10,800	9,612
20X7	11,050	9,278
20X8	11,250	8,911
20X9	11,450	8,556
20Y0	10,990	7,748
20Y1	10,550	7,016
20Y2	10,130	6,356
20Y3	15,725	9,307
使用价值		76,690

20X4 年 12 月 31 日，游轮的账面价值如下（假设按照 6 百万元的预计残余价值，使用 10% 的年度折旧率，按直线法折旧）。

	账面价值 千元
20X1 年 12 月 31 日	63,064
20X2 年至 20X4 年的折旧[(63,064,000 - 6,000,000) × 10% ×3]	(17,119)
20X4 年的资本性支出	8,000
20X4 年 12 月 31 日	53,945

改良后，游轮的使用价值大于其减值后的账面价值。根据 IAS 36 第 111 段和第 114 段的规定，由于进一步的改良支出（原使用价值的计量中未考虑支出所带来的利益）导致可收回金额增加的，应该考虑于 20X4 年 12 月 31 日将原减值损失转回。转回金额限制在把游轮的账面价值增加到假如没有发生原减值，其应有的账面金额的范围内。[IAS 36 第 117 段]。计算如下，产生的转回金额为 6,255,000 元(60,200,000 - 53,945,000)。

	Carrying value C000
31 December 20X1	72,000
Depreciation 20X2 to 20X4 ((72,000,000 – 6,000,000) × 10% × 3)	(19,800)
Capital expenditure in 20X4	8,000
31 December 20X4	60,200

18.206 In practice, the dividing line between maintenance-type and improvement-type capital expenditure is rarely clear-cut, since businesses are not static and judgement must be applied.

Assets under construction

18.206.1 Assets under construction also need to be considered when looking at the cash flows to include in a value in use calculation. Where the carrying amount of an asset does not yet include all the cash outflows that must be incurred before it is ready for use, for example a building under construction or an incomplete development project, then IAS 36 gives some specific guidance on what to include in the estimates of future cash flows; the future cash flows should include an estimate of the future cash flows expected to be incurred before the asset is ready for use or sale. [IAS 36 para 39(b)]. For consistency, the expected cash inflows once the asset is complete should also be included.

18.206.2 If the value in use cannot be determined for an individual asset under construction and the fair value less costs to sell of the asset is lower than the carrying amount then the CGU to which the asset belongs will need to be tested for impairment.

Discount rate

18.207 Investment decisions take account of the time value of money and the risks associated with expected future cash flows. These are also reflected in the measurement of an asset's value in use.

	账面价值 千元
20X1 年 12 月 31 日	72,000
20X2 年至 20X4 年的折旧[(72,000,000 - 6,000,000) × 10% ×3]	(19,800)
20X4 年的资本性支出	8,000
20X4 年 12 月 31 日	60,200

18.206　在实务中，维持型资本支出和改良型资本支出的分界线很少是非常清楚的，因为业务不是静止的，因此必须运用判断才行。

在建资产

18.206.1　检查包括在使用价值计算过程中的现金流时，也需要对在建资产予以考虑。如果资产的账面价值尚未包括使其达到可使用状态前必须发生的所有现金流出（比如一栋在建建筑物或者一个尚未完成的开发项目），IAS 36 对这种情况下预计未来现金流时应包括哪些内容给出了一些具体指南；未来现金流应该包括使资产达到可使用或可销售状态前所发生的预计未来现金流。[IAS 36 第 39（b）段]。为了保持一致，资产完工后的预期现金流入也应该包括在内。

18.206.2　如果不能确定个别在建资产的使用价值，并且该资产的公允价值减去处置费用低于其账面价值的情况下，那么需要对该资产所属的 CGU 作减值测试。

折现率

18.207　投资决策考虑货币的时间价值以及与预期未来现金流相关的风险。这些也反映在资产使用价值的计量中。

18.208 Projected future cash flows are discounted at a pre-tax rate that reflects both current market assessments of the time value of money and the risks specific to the asset for which the future cash flow estimates have not been adjusted. [IAS 36 para 55]. This means that (unless fair value less costs to sell is higher) an asset is regarded as impaired if it is not expected to earn a current market-related rate of return on its carrying value.

18.209 The rate of return expected by the market is the return that investors would require if they chose an investment that would generate cash flows of the same amounts, timing and risk profile as those that the entity expects from the asset or CGU under review. The rate is independent of the way the asset is financed. It is estimated from current market transactions for similar assets or from the 'weighted average cost of capital' (WACC) of a listed entity that has a single asset or portfolio of assets that are similar in terms of service potential and risks to the asset under review. [IAS 36 para 56].

18.210 If an asset specific rate is not available directly from the market an entity should estimate an appropriate discount rate that reflects as far as possible a market assessment of:

- The time value of money to the end of the asset's useful life.
- The risks that the future cash flows will differ in amount or timing from estimates.
- The price for bearing the uncertainty inherent in the asset.
- Other factors that market participants would reflect in the rate such as illiquidity.

[IAS 36 para 57, App A para A16].

18.211 The entity may take into account the following factors in determining this rate:

- The WACC for the entity (adjusted as explained in the next paragraph), determined using techniques such as the capital asset pricing model.
- The entity's incremental borrowing rate.
- Other market borrowing rates.

[IAS 36 App A para A17].

18.208 预期未来现金流按税前折现率折现，该折现率既要反映对货币时间价值的当前市场评估，也要反映尚未在未来现金流预计中调整的资产的特定风险。[IAS 36 第55 段]。这意味着，（除非公允价值减去处置费用后的金额较高），如果预期一项资产，基于其账面价值，不能为主体带来和当前市场有关的报酬率，则认为该资产发生了减值。

18.209 市场预期报酬率是，如果投资者选择一项能产生与主体预期从正被检查的资产或 CGU 中产生相同金额、时点和风险预测的现金流的投资，投资者所要求的报酬。报酬率与资产的融资方式无关。报酬率根据当前类似资产的市场交易或拥有与正被检查资产相似的服务潜能和风险的单项资产或资产组合的上市主体的“加权平均资本成本”（WACC）来预计。[IAS 36 第 56 段]。

18.210 如果不能直接从市场上得到资产的特定折现率，主体应该估计一个尽可能反映了市场评估了下列内容后的适当的折现率：

- 直至资产使用寿命到期日的货币时间价值。
- 未来现金流在金额或时点上和预计的不一样的风险。
- 承担资产固有不确定性的价格。
- 市场参与者在折现率中所反映的其他因素，如非流动性。

[IAS 36 第 57 段、附录 A 第 A16 段]。

18.211 确定折现率时，主体可以考虑下列因素：

- 使用资本资产定价模型等技术所确定的（按下段的说明进行调整之后的）主体的 WACC。
- 主体的增量借款利率。
- 其他市场借款利率。

[IAS 36 附录 A 第 A17 段]。

18.212 The rates are adjusted to take account of the way in which the market would assess the specific risks associated with the estimated cash flows and to exclude risks that are not relevant to the estimated cash flows or for which the estimated cash flows have been adjusted. Factors to consider might include:

- Country risk, for example the risk of political unrest.
- Currency risk, for example the risk of devaluation.
- The nature of the asset being tested; intangible assets are higher risk.
- Whether the cash flows are optimistic or stretch targets.
- Price risk, for example the risk that prices may be forced down by competitive pressures.

[IAS 36 App A para A18].

Example – Impact of country and currency risk on discount rate

A Venezuelan entity carries significant goodwill and indefinite lived intangible asset balances in its consolidated balance sheet. These arise from multiple acquisitions in recent years. The entity manufactures goods in Venezuela that are sold locally and exported to Europe. The entity's functional currency is the Bolivar and its financial statements are presented in Bolivars.

In carrying out their first impairment review under IAS 36, management propose to use a discount rate based on the local Bolivar risk free rate, the local market risk premium and a country risk premium. This discount rate will be applied to the Bolivar denominated cash flow projections for each CGU.

Management's approach is incorrect. The Bolivar risk free rate will include the perceived risks associated with investing in the country and in the local currency. To add a country risk premium is, therefore, double-counting. A separate country risk premium is only usually relevant when cash flow projections are prepared in a different currency such as the euro.

It is always important to ensure consistency between the assumptions underlying the projected cash flows and the discount rate.

18.212　应对折现率进行调整，考虑市场评估和预计现金流有关的特定风险时所采用的方法，剔除和预计现金流无关的风险，或者已经在预计现金流中作了调整的风险。需要考虑的因素可能包括：

- 国家风险，例如政治动荡的风险。
- 货币风险，例如贬值的风险。
- 被测试资产的性质；无形资产的风险较高。
- 现金流是乐观的估计还是保守的估计。
- 价格风险，例如，由于竞争压力，可能被迫降价的风险。

[IAS 36 附录 A 第 A18 段]。

示例——国家风险和货币风险对折现率的影响

一家委内瑞拉主体在合并资产负债表中记录有一项重大商誉和一项使用寿命不确定的无形资产。这些商誉和无形资产产生于近几年来的多次收购。该主体在委内瑞拉制造商品，商品在当地出售，同时出口到欧洲。该主体的功能货币是波利瓦尔，财务报表以波利瓦尔列报。

按照 IAS 36 进行第一次减值测试时，管理层计划使用以当地波利瓦尔无风险报酬率、当地市场风险溢价及国家风险溢价为基础而确定的折现率。该折现率将被用于每个以波利瓦尔计价的 CGU 的现金流预测上。

管理层的方法不正确。波利瓦尔无风险报酬率已包括本国投资及使用本地货币投资有关的已知风险。因此，加上国家风险溢价则会导致双重计算。通常情况下，只有按不同货币（如欧元）编制现金流预测时，才会单独考虑国家风险溢价。

保证预计现金流所使用的假设和预计折现率所使用的假设之间的一致性，这始终都是非常重要的。

18. 213 Rates applicable to different business units within a group may vary to reflect any risk factors that are specific to those units. Trading activities and investments in different countries are likely to have different risks, for example, currency and political risks. The rate should be appropriate to the country in which the CGU operates (or in whose currency it derives its major cash flows) rather than the country in which the finance is sourced. Different business sectors also attract different risks — for example, a biotechnology entity will carry a greater market risk than a regulated utility. In general, the more uncertain the cash flows are, the more risky the investment is, and the greater the risk adjustment is to increase the discount rate. The rate is independent of the entity's capital structure and the way in which purchase of the asset or CGU was financed. This is because the future cash flows from the asset do not depend on how the asset was purchased. [IAS 36 App A para A19].

18. 214 For some companies, the WACC will be an observable rate that they are familiar with and will often be the starting point for determining a suitable discount rate before adjustment for the risks specific to the CGU being tested. IAS 36 refers to using techniques such as the capital asset pricing model, which is commonly used in assessing the cost of equity.

18. 215 The discount rate should not reflect risks for which the estimates of future cash flows have already been adjusted, to avoid double counting. [IAS 36 para 56, App A para A15]. Discount rates should reflect assumptions that are consistent with those inherent in the estimated cash flows. For example a discount rate of 12 per cent might be applied to contractual cash flows from a loan receivable. That rate reflects expectations about future defaults. However, if the cash flows are based on expected rather than contractual cash flows, the same 12 per cent rate should not be used, because the cash flows themselves will have been adjusted for default risk in arriving at the expected (as opposed to contractual) cash flows. [IAS 36 App A para A3].

18. 216 An entity normally uses a single discount rate for estimating an asset's value in use. However, if the value in use is sensitive to risks for different periods or to the structure of interest rates over the asset's life separate discount rates are used for different future periods. [IAS 36 App A para A21].

18.213 为反映集团内不同业务单位的特定风险因素，适用于不同业务单位的折现率可能不一样。在不同国家从事贸易活动、进行投资可能会有不同的风险，例如，不同的货币风险和政治风险。使用 CGU 运营所在的国家（或者产生主要现金流的货币所属的国家）而非资金来源国的折现率应该是恰当的。不同业务部门也会带来不同的风险——例如，一家生物技术主体要比受管制的公用公司承担更大的风险。总的来说，现金流的不确定性越大，投资的风险也越大，对风险进行调整、增加折现率的可能性也越大。折现率与主体的资本结构及购买资产或 CGU 的融资方式无关。这是因为，资产的未来现金流并不取决于资产的购买方式。[IAS 36 附录 A 第 A19 段]。

18.214 对一些公司来说，WACC 是一个他们熟悉并且可以观察得到的折现率，通常它是确定被测试 CGU 特定风险调整前合适折现率的起始点。IAS 36 提到使用估值技术，如评估所有者权益成本常用的资本资产定价模型，来确定折现率。

18.215 为避免重复计算，折现率不应该反映已经对未来现金流预计做了调整的风险。[IAS 36 第 56 段、附录 A 第 A15 段]。折现率应该使用和预计现金流一致的假设。例如，12% 的折现率可以适用于应收贷款的合同现金流。这个折现率反映了对未来违约的预期。但是，如果现金流是基于预期现金流而非合同现金流的情况下，那么不应该使用相同的 12% 的折现率，因为为了得出预期现金流（而非合同现金流），现金流本身已经对违约风险作出了调整。[IAS 36 附录 A 第 A3 段]。

18.216 一般情况下，主体在估计资产的使用价值时采用单一折现率。但是，如果使用价值对不同期间的风险或对资产使用寿命中的利率结构敏感化，则不同的未来期间应使用不同的折现率。[IAS 36 附录 A 第 A21 段]。

18.217 If an impairment loss is recognised and is measured by reference to a discounted cash flow for a fixed asset or CGU, IAS 36 also requires the discount rate to be disclosed in the financial statements. [IAS 36 para 130 (g)]. As an alternative to using a risk-adjusted discount rate, an entity may adjust the expected cash flows (downwards) for risk and discount those risk-adjusted cash flows at a lower discount rate. In practice, risk-free cash flows are almost impossible to obtain, because risk-free means certain, but where this is done, it would be useful to give some indication of the risk-adjustments made to the cash flows. This is because IAS 36 encourages entities to disclose key assumptions used to determine the recoverable amount of assets and CGUs. [IAS 36 para 132]. The standard also requires disclosure of information about the estimates used where a CGU includes goodwill or an intangible asset with an indefinite life. [IAS 36 para 134(d)]. It is important that risk is not double-counted in the calculations; that is, the discount rate should not include a risk weighting if the underlying cash flows have already been adjusted for risk.

18.218 Inflation should also be treated consistently in the present value calculations. If the future cash flows are estimated at current values, the discount rate is a real rate – that is, inflation should be excluded. If the estimated future cash flows include inflation, the discount rate is a nominal rate, that is, including inflation.

Discount rate-pre-tax rate

18.219 IAS 36 requires the discount rate for value in use calculations to be calculated on a pre-tax basis. [IAS 36 para 55]. Thus a CGU's pre-tax cash flows should be discounted at the pre-tax discount rate.

18.220 Where a pre-tax discount rate is available this presents no issues. However, IAS 36 recognises that in many cases the only observable market rate of return is a post-tax rate. This is the case, for example, where the discount rate is derived from an entity's WACC, which many companies would look towards when estimating the appropriate discount rate for a business unit. The IAS 36 requires the post-tax rate to be adjusted to a pre-tax basis. [IAS 36 App A para A20].

18.217　如果已经对固定资产或 CGU 确认了减值损失，并且该减值损失是参照折现后现金流进行的计量，IAS 36 还要求在财务报表中披露折现率。[IAS 36 第 130（g）段]。作为使用风险调整后折现率的替代方法是，主体可以将风险调整在预期现金流中，调减预期现金流，然后以较低的折现率把这些经过风险调整的现金流进行折现。在实务中，几乎不可能获得无风险的现金流，因为无风险意味着确定，但是如果对现金流作了风险调整，给出一些指示作了哪些调整可能是有用的。这是因为，IAS 36 鼓励主体披露确定资产和 CGU 可收回金额所使用的主要假设。[IAS 36 第 132 段]。当 CGU 包含商誉或使用寿命不确定的无形资产时，准则还要求披露所使用的估计信息。[IAS 36 第 134（d）段]。重要的是，计算中不能对风险作重复计算，即如果已经对现金流作了某种风险调整，那么折现率中就不应该包括该风险因素。

18.218　现值计算中，通货膨胀的处理也应一致。如果未来现金流根据现在的价值进行估计，那么折现率应使用实际折现率——也就是说，不包括通货膨胀的折现率。如果预计的现金流包括通货膨胀，那么折现率应为名义折现率，即包括通货膨胀的折现率。

折现率——税前折现率

18.219　IAS 36 要求使用价值计算中所使用的折现率为税前折现率。[IAS 36 第 55 段]。这样，CGU 的税前现金流应该按照税前折现率进行折现。

18.220　如果税前折现率可以获得，那就没有什么问题。但是，IAS 36 承认，许多情况下，唯一可以观察得到的市场报酬率是税后折现率。比如，许多公司在估计业务单位的合适折现率时普遍先看自己的 WACC，在折现率来自于主体的 WACC 的情况下确实如此。IAS 36 要求把税后折现率调整到税前折现率。[IAS 36 附录 A 第 A20 段]。

18. 221 When only the post-tax discount rate is known, management should adjust the post-tax rate to estimate a pre-tax rate. Value in use calculated using post-tax cash flows and a post-tax discount rate would not necessarily give the same result as if the pre-tax rate had been applied to pre-tax cash flows. They would be equal only if there is no deferred tax to consider, that is, the current tax base of all the assets/liabilities is equal to the carrying amount of those assets/liabilities. This is illustrated in paragraphs that follow.

18. 222 How to calculate the appropriate pre-tax rate from a post-tax starting point is a key practical issue. It is not simply a matter of grossing up the required post-tax rate of return at the standard or effective rate of tax and discounting the pre-tax cash flows at that grossed up rate. This would only give the correct result if there is no growth in cash flows and no deferred tax. This situation rarely, if ever, arises. It is necessary to adjust the post-tax rate much more carefully, to reflect the specific amount and timing of the future cash flows.

18. 222. 1 The pre-tax discount rate can be derived using the post-tax discount rates that are directly observable from capital markets by using a two-step iterative calculation process to convert the post-tax discount rate into an implicit pre-tax rate. This is based on: first, discounting the post-tax cash flows using a post-tax discount rate; then determining the implicit pre-tax rate that needs to be applied to pre-tax cash flows to arrive at the same result. Post-tax cash flows should reflect the specific amount and timing of the future tax cash flows. Where deferred tax exists, this can complicate the situation; see further from paragraph 18. 222. 5. 1.

18. 222. 2 In theory, discounting post-tax cash flows at a post-tax discount rate should lead to the same result as discounting pre-tax cash flows with a pre-tax discount rate, as long as the pre-tax discount rate is the post-tax discount rate adjusted to reflect the specific amount and timing of the future tax cash flows. [IAS 36 para BCZ 85]. An example illustrating how this can be done is given in paragraph BCZ85 of IAS 36.

18. 222. 3 A two-step approach can be applied to derive iteratively the implicit pre-tax discount rate from post-tax data. In step 1, the expected actual tax cash payments are calculated to arrive at post-tax cash flows from pre-tax cash flow projections. These post-tax cash flows are discounted at an appropriate post-tax

18.221　只有税后折现率已知的情况下，管理层应该通过调整税后折现率来预计税前折现率。使用税后现金流和税后折现率计算的使用价值不一定与使用税前折现率将税前现金流折现得出的结果相同。只有在无递延所得税的情况下，也就是说，所有资产/负债的当前税务基础等于这些资产/负债的账面价值时，它们的计算结果才会相同，这一点将在以下段落进行说明。

18.222　如何根据税后折现率计算出合适的税前折现率是一个重要的实务问题。它不是把所要求的税后报酬率按法定或实际税率还原、然后用还原后的报酬率对税前现金流进行折现这么简单的事情。只有在现金流没有增长，并且没有递延所得税的情况下，还原才有可能得出正确结果。即便过去出现过，这种情况也很少见。有必要更加认真地调整税后折现率以便反映未来现金流的具体金额和时点。

18.222.1　可以应用两步迭代计算法把能直接从资本市场获得的税后折现率转换成内含税前折现率。具体操作如下：首先，用税后折现率对税后现金流进行折现；然后确定应用于税前现金流能够得出相同结果而需要采用的内含税前折现率。税后现金流应该反映未来所得税现金流的具体金额和时点。如果存在递延所得税，情况会变得复杂；进一步解释请参见第 18.222.5.1 段。

18.222.2　从理论上讲，只要税前折现率是将未来所得税现金流的具体金额和时点的影响从税后折现率中调整后所得出的，用税后折现率对税后现金流进行折现所得出的结果应该和使用税前折现率对税前现金流进行折现所得出的结果一样。[IAS 36 第 BCZ 85 段]。IAS 36 第 BCZ 85 段给出了一个例子列示具体应用。

18.222.3　可以采用两步迭代法，根据税后折现率计算出内含税前折现率。第一步，计算预期实际所得税的现金支付，根据税前现金流预测得出税后现金流。用资本市场可以得到的信息，计算出合适的税后折现率，然后用它对这些税后现金流进行折现。

discount rate derived using information observable on the capital markets.

18.222.4 As a starting point for the derivation of the post-tax discount rate, the entity's weighted average cost of capital (WACC) could be taken into account (as opposed to entity's incremental borrowing rate or other market borrowing rates). This is because the WACC is usually a good reflection of the risk specific to the asset/CGU (as required by IAS 36) provided that it is similar to the rate a market participant would use. [IAS 36 para A17]. This WACC should be adjusted for specific risks associated with the asset/CGU's estimated cash flows (for example, country/currency/price risk). If such a WACC for the entity is not available, it may be necessary to estimate a WACC using peer group data.

18.222.5 In step 2, the pre-tax discount rate is derived by determining the rate required to be applied to the pre-tax cash flows to arrive at the result obtained in step 1. In practice, the rate is calculated using the same methodology as for the calculation of an internal rate of return.

18.222.5.1 The situation is more complicated when deferred tax exists upfront; that is where there is a difference between the carrying value of the asset and the tax base at the date of the impairment test.

18.222.5.2 Upfront deferred tax causes a double-counting issue. Deferred tax is the way in which the future tax consequences of recovering assets are recorded on the balance sheet. Therefore, if more tax will be payable in the future in relation to a CGU (say, because all available tax deductions have already been taken), this future tax payable will be recognised as a deferred tax liability. If VIU is calculated with reference to post tax cash flows, the higher future tax payments will be included as cash outflows in the VIU measure, reducing the VIU. By excluding the deferred tax liabilities from the carrying amount of the CGU (as mandated by para 76 of IAS 36), the carrying value of the CGU will be higher. This means that the test no longer compares like with like. If the higher CGU carrying value is compared to a VIU measure that is depressed by tax cash outflows, the result may show an impairment. Any such impairment would include the (discounted) impact of the future tax outflows. It would not seem appropriate to book this element of the impairment as the future tax outflows have already been accounted for (on an undiscounted basis) as deferred tax. Paragraph BCZ82 of IAS 36 acknowledges

18.222.4　作为计算税后折现率的起点，可能考虑的是主体的加权平均资本成本（WACC）（而非主体的增量借款费率或其他的市场借款费率）。这是因为，假如主体的 WACC 和市场参与者所使用的折现率相似的话，通常它很好地反映了资产/CGU 的特定风险（如 IAS 36 所要求的）。[IAS 36 第 A17 段]。与资产/CGU 预计现金流相关的特定风险（例如，国家风险、货币风险、价格风险），应该在 WACC 中进行调整。如果不能得到主体的这个 WACC，使用同类型公司的数据估计得出一个 WACC，可能是有必要的。

18.222.5　第二步，找出应用于税前现金流能够得出与第一步相同结果的税前折现率。在实务中，税前折现率使用和内部报酬率计算相同的方法计算得出。

18.222.5.1　当前期存在递延所得税时，即，减值测试执行日，资产的账面价值和税务基础存在差异时，情况会更复杂。

18.222.5.2　前期递延所得税会造成双重计算的问题。递延所得税是将收回资产成本所带来的未来税务影响记录于资产负债表的方法。因此，如果一个 CGU 未来需要支付较多的税款（比如因为已无所得税抵扣可用），该未来的应交税金将被确认为一项递延所得税负债。如果 VIU 参照税后现金流量计算，则 VIU 计量时现金流出中将包含较高的未来所得税支出，从而导致 VIU 降低。而通过将递延所得税负债排除在 CGU 的账面价值之外（IAS 36 第 76 段规定），CGU 的账面价值将会增加。这则意味着减值测试时比较的内容不一致。如果将 CGU 较高的账面价值与被所得税现金流出压低后的 VIU 计量相比较，结果可能显示为减值。这种情况下减值将包括未来所得税流出（折现后）的影响。将所得税产生的减值因素考虑在内显然不够恰当，因为未来所得税流出已经作为递延所得税（在非折现基础上）予以核算。IAS 36 第 BCZ82 段承认这个问题并指出，为了避免双重计算，当确定可收回金额时，不应考虑前期递延所得税，但准则并未明确如何排除这种影响。

this issue and notes that, to avoid double-counting, the impact of upfront deferred tax should be eliminated when determining the recoverable amount. It does not clarify however how the impact should be eliminated.

18.222.5.3 Due to this double-counting issue, in situations where there is significant deferred tax upfront, an IAS 36 value in use test may not be the most appropriate method to determine the recoverable amount of a CGU. For information, we illustrate below how the IAS 36 VIU and the pre-tax discount rate can be derived by using post-tax information. In practice, if faced with this situation, it may be practical for entities to consider how the VIU test can be adjusted to avoid any double-counting or to consider using a FVLCS test.

Example – Calculating a pre-tax discount rate

Entity A has calculated a WACC of 8% based on market assumptions. Management is aware that this is a post-tax rate and, therefore, wants to determine a pre-tax discount rate by grossing up the 8% by the statutory tax rate in entity A's country, which is 35%. The result is 12.3% (8%/0.65).

The 12.3% is only the correct pre-tax discount rate if the specific amount and timing of the future tax cash flows are reflected by this rate. [IAS 36 BC para Z85]. So a grossed up discount rate works only if there is no deferred tax.

As soon as there is deferred tax an iterative calculation needs to be done that considers the fact that a carrying amount after impairment would trigger new deferred taxes and this would again change the carrying amount.

The required pre-tax rate is the rate of return that will, after tax has been deducted, give the required post-tax rate of return. The following calculation illustrates how the pre-tax rate could correctly be derived from the post-tax rate.

A CGU is being tested for impairment at the end of 20X0. The CGU comprises a specific asset, which was purchased two years ago for C2,400. The asset has a ten year useful life for accounting purposes. Tax relief on the asset is available on a straight line basis over the asset's first three years of the life. The tax rate is 35%.

18.222.5.3　因为双重计算的问题，当存在金额重大的前期递延所得税时，IAS 36 的使用价值测试可能不是确定 CGU 可收回金额的最合适的方法。我们在下文描述了如何得出 IAS 36 的 VIU 和如何从税后信息计算得出税前折现率以供参考。在实务中，遇到这种情况时，可行的方法可能是主体考虑如何调整 VIU 测试以避免双重计算，或者考虑使用 FVLCS 测试。

示例——计算税前折现率

主体 A 根据市场假设，计算出 WACC 为 8%。管理层知道，这是一个税后折现率，因此，想根据主体 A 所在国的法定税率 35%，将 8% 还原为税前折现率。结果为 12.3%（8%/0.65）。

只有当 12.3% 反映了未来所得税现金流的具体金额和时点时，该折现率才是正确的税前折现率。[IAS 36 BC 第 Z85 段]。所以，还原后的折现率仅适用于没有递延所得税的情况。

一旦出现了递延所得税，需要进行迭代计算，迭代计算考虑减值后的账面价值将产生新的递延所得税的事实，并且这将再次改变账面价值。

所要求的税前折现率是扣除所得税后将得出所要求的税后报酬率的报酬率。下面的计算说明了如何根据税后折现率正确计算得出税前折现率。

20X0 年年底，某个 CGU 正在作减值测试。该 CGU 由一个特定资产组成，该特定资产于两年前以 2,400 元的价格购买取得。会计上，该资产的使用寿命为十年。税务上，该资产在使用的前三年，采用直线法进行所得税抵扣。税率为 35%。

Hence the carrying value for tax purposes at the end of 20X0 is C800 (C2,400 × 1/3 years) and the carrying value for accounting purposes is C1,920 (C2,400 × 8/10 years). Applying the tax rate of 35% to the difference gives a deferred tax liability with a carrying value of C392 (C1,920 – C800) × 35%). The post-tax discount rate, determined from the WACC of the entity, is 8%.

There are two potential applications of the requirements of IAS 36 that are commonly seen. Neither of these gives the correct value in use per the requirements of IAS 36.

Common error 1: Discount a imputed 'post-tax cash flow' at post-tax discount rate of 8%. The 'post cash flow' is determined by assuming that cash outflow for tax will be equal to the pre-tax profit at the standard tax rate. This is illustrated in the table below.

Pre-tax profits from the asset are expected to be C125 at the end of 20X1, increasing by 5 for each of the following seven years. The appropriateness of such an increasing rate has been considered and determined reasonable. The results for the seven years in question are therefore as follows:

Currency (C)	**20X1**	**20X2**	**20X3**	**20X4**	**20X5**	**20X6**	**20X7**	**20X8**
Pre-tax profit	125	130	135	140	145	150	155	160
Add back depreciation	240	240	240	240	240	240	240	240
Pre-tax cash flow	**365**	**370**	**375**	**380**	**385**	**390**	**395**	**400**
Tax on profit (@35%)	(44)	(46)	(47)	(49)	(51)	(53)	(54)	(56)
Post-tax cash flow	**321**	**325**	**328**	**331**	**334**	**338**	**341**	**344**

Applying the post tax discount rate to the estimated cash flows above gives a value in use of C1,904.

Common error 2: Discount pre-tax cash flow at post-tax discount rate grossed up for the tax rate. This rate would be 8%/(1 – 0.35) = 12.3%. This gives a value in use of C1,866.

These applications fail to achieve the correct result, either by not accounting for varying period-on-period cash flows or by ignoring deferred tax. The

因此，为了税务的目的，20X0 年年底，账面价值为 800 元（2,400 元 × 1/3 年），为了会计的目的，账面价值为 1,920 元(2,400 元 ×8/10 年)。把 35% 的税率应用在上面两个账面价值差额之上，得出账面价值为 392 元（(1,920 − 800) ×35%）的递延所得税负债。根据主体的 WACC 所确定的税后折现率为 8%。

对 IAS 36 的要求，有两种可能的误用非常常见。任何一种误用都不会得出 IAS 36 要求下的正确的使用价值。

常见错误一：使用税后折现率 8% 对估算的“税后现金流量”进行折现。“税后现金流量”的确定是假设所得税现金流出等于税前利润乘以法定税率得出的。这将在下表中进行说明。

20X1 年年底，资产的税前利润预期为 125 元，之后的 7 年中，每年增长 5 元。已经考虑了这样的增长速度是否合适，确定这样的增长速度是合理的。因此，对现在正在考虑的 7 年的结果列示如下：

币种(元)	**20X1**	**20X2**	**20X3**	**20X4**	**20X5**	**20X6**	**20X7**	**20X8**
税前利润	125	130	135	140	145	150	155	160
加回折旧	240	240	240	240	240	240	240	240
税前现金流	**365**	**370**	**375**	**380**	**385**	**390**	**395**	**400**
所得税(税率 35%)	(44)	(46)	(47)	(49)	(51)	(53)	(54)	(56)
税后现金流	**321**	**325**	**328**	**331**	**334**	**338**	**341**	**344**

使用税后折现率对上表中估计的现金流量进行折现，得出的使用价值为 1,904 元。

常见错误二：使用按税率还原税后折现率得出的税前折现率对税前现金流进行折现。这个税前折现率为 8%/(1 − 0.35) = 12.3%。这样，得出的使用价值为 1,866 元。

这些应用，或者因为没有考虑各个期间现金流的变化，或者由于忽略了递延所得税，都不会得出正确的结果。正确的使用价值可以通过使用

correct value in use can be achieved by taking the value in use from common error 1 and adjusting for the discounted cash outflows related to deferred tax. This is a complex iterative calculation as the discounted cash outflows in question relate to the pre-tax value in use-hence, the result of the calculation feeds back into the calculation itself. The calculation is best solved with the aid of a computer, but the following summarises the final calculation for the example above once the iteration has been completed.

Currency(C)	**20X0**	**20X1**	**20X2**	**20X3**	**20X4**	**20X5**	**20X6**	**20X7**	**20X8**
Pre – tax VIU(α)	1,729	1,513	1,296	1,080	864	648	432	216	0
Tax base(β)	800								
$\alpha - \beta$	929	1,513	1,296	1,080	864	648	432	216	0
Change in $\alpha - \beta$		584	(216)	(216)	(216)	(216)	(216)	(216)	(216)
@ 35% (tax)		204	(76)	(76)	(76)	(76)	(76)	(76)	(76)
Discounted (8%)	(175)								
Post – tax VIU	1,904								
Pre – tax VIU	**1,729**								

The 'post-tax VIU' number is as calculated in 'common error 1' above. The iterative process will complete when a set of figures for the first line have been derived which, when discounted at 8%, produce the same number as in the bottom 'pre-tax VIU' line.

Having derived the correct pre-tax VIU, and having the correct pre-tax cash flows, it is possible to 'back-solve' to obtain pre-tax discount rate that discounts the latter to the former. It is logical that the pre-tax discount rate is higher as a higher return would be required from the asset in order to cover the future tax payments to be made.

The result of C1,729 is a lower VIU than that originally calculated under common error 1. This is because the larger tax cash out flows for the remainder of the asset's life were not taken into account in common error 1.

The outcome of this test is a deficit of C191 (based upon a carrying value of C1,920 and a VIU of C1,729). This implies that there may be an impairment to recognise. However, this is not necessarily the case. Part or all of this

“常见错误一”中的使用价值，调整与递延所得税有关的折现现金流出得出。因为有问题的折现现金流出与税前使用价值相关，所以这是一个复杂的迭代计算——因此，计算结果反馈到计算过程本身。最好是在计算机的帮助下进行计算，下表汇总了上面例子在迭代计算完成后的最终计算结果。

币种(元)	**20X0**	**20X1**	**20X2**	**20X3**	**20X4**	**20X5**	**20X6**	**20X7**	**20X8**
税前 VIU(α)	1,729	1,513	1,296	1,080	864	648	432	216	0
纳税基础(β)	800								
$\alpha-\beta$	929	1,513	1,296	1,080	864	648	432	216	0
$\alpha-\beta$的变化		584	(216)	(216)	(216)	(216)	(216)	(216)	(216)
35%(税率)		204	(76)	(76)	(76)	(76)	(76)	(76)	(76)
折现后(8%)	(175)								
税后 VIU	1,904								
税前 VIU	**1,729**								

“税后 VIU”的金额与按上文“常见错误一”的方法计算得出的金额相同。当得出第一行的全部数值后，然后按 8% 的折现率进行折现，得出的结果和最后一行“税前 VIU”的数字相同时，迭代计算过程结束。

得出正确的税前 VIU 并且有了正确的税前现金流后，才有可能使用“回解法”得出税前折现率，可用以折现税前现金流来得出税前 VIU 的折现率。资产需获得较高的回报以弥补未来税务支出，这就需要较高的税前折现率，这是符合逻辑的。

1,729 元这个结果比之前在“常见错误一”中计算的 VIU 要低。这是因为在“常见错误一”中未考虑资产剩余使用年限内产生的较大的所得税现金流出。

这个测试的结果为负值 191 元（基于 1,920 元的账面价值和 1,729 元的 VIU 得出）。这暗示了可能需要确认减值。但是也非必须确认。这个负数金额的部分或全部可能已经作为递延所得税负债被确认在了资产负债表

deficit may already be recognised in the balance sheet as a deferred tax liability. Management should also determine the fair value less costs to sell for the asset. In this situation, it would be a reasonable assumption that the tax base of the asset would re-set to cost if the asset were acquired by a market participant. Therefore, the impact of the tax cash flows in a FVLCS calculation is unlikely to be as significant and, as a result, an impairment may not be required.

18. 222. 6 Deriving a pre-tax discount rate is a complex exercise. There are some practical methods to use to identify potential impairment losses and estimate the pre-tax impact.

18. 222. 7 One method is to calculate the post-tax cash flow discounted at the post-tax discount rate, as per Common Error 1. This calculation should give a reasonable indication of whether there has been an impairment using readily available data. If no impairment is identified, a judgement can then be made with regard to the headroom above carrying value-if the headroom is considered sufficiently high, then it will be possible to infer that the likelihood of an impairment arising on a pre-tax calculation is remote. The pre-tax rate can be estimated for disclosure purposes.

18. 222. 8 If there is not significant headroom in the post-tax calculation then a pre-tax analysis will be required to identify the correct pre-tax value in use from which the pre-tax impairment loss and the related deferred tax effects can be derived (and the pre-tax discount rate for disclosure purposes).

18. 222. 9 An alternative method to estimate the correct value in use is Common Error 2-estimating the pre-tax discount rate by grossing up the post-tax discount rate by an appropriate tax rate (for example, the estimated future cash tax rate). Care should be taken in this exercise. For instance the estimate made should be adjusted to reflect the effect of special factors that might materially distort the relationship between the post-tax rate and the pre-tax rate — for example, where the timing of the tax cash flows is very favourable to the entity because of accelerated capital allowances. Applying this estimated rate to the pre-tax cash flows would result in an estimated value in use (and an estimated impairment loss) of the asset or CGU. As above, judgement will be needed to assess the reasonableness of the estimate.

中。管理层也应确定该项资产的公允价值减去处置费用的金额。这种情况下，假设如果市场参与者可以直接购买该资产，该资产的纳税基础将被重新调整为新的购买成本的假设是合理的。因此，FVLCS 计算中的所得税现金流量的影响不大可能重大，可能并不需要确认减值。

18.222.6 得出税前折现率是一个复杂的计算过程。可以采用一些实用方法，识别潜在的减值损失，并估计税前影响。

18.222.7 一种方法是按照“常见错误一”的方法，按税后折现率进行税后现金流折现的计算。根据已经获得的数据，采用这种计算方法应该可以表明是否发生了减值。如果没有识别出减值，就可以对高出账面价值的金额，又称净空（headroom）作出判断——如果认为净空够高，则可推断出基于税前计算结果发生减值的可能性不大。为了披露的目的，可以对税前折现率进行估算。

18.222.8 如果在税后计算的过程中没有出现大额净空，那么要求对税前现金流和折现率进行分析，以识别正确的税前使用价值从而得出税前减值损失和相关递延所得税的影响（以及为披露目的的税前折现率）。

18.222.9 估算正确使用价值的另一个方法是采用“常见错误二”中的方法——用适当税率（如预计未来现金税率）还原税后折现率，从而估算出税前折现率。采用这种方法进行计算的过程中，应当小心。例如，应该对估算值进行调整，反映可能重大地扭曲税后折现率和税前折现率关系的特殊因素所产生的影响——比如，因为加速资本税前抵扣，所得税现金流的时点对主体非常有利。把这个估算的折现率应用在税前现金流上，可能会得出资产或 CGU 的估算使用价值（和估算的减值损失）。如上所述，需要对估算的合理性进行判断。

18.223 If neither of the approximations is deemed acceptable then a pre-tax analysis will be required. The required pre-tax rate is the rate of return that will, after tax has been deducted, give the required post-tax rate of return. The following example illustrates how the pre-tax rate may be derived from the post-tax rate.

Example – Deriving a pre-tax rate from a post-tax rate – a simple example

The post-tax market rate of return required from an asset is 14%. Profits are taxed at 30%; there is a tax allowance of 100% of the cost of the asset. All cash flows arise at the end of year 1.

For an asset costing C100, the required post-tax cash flows during year 1 are C114. Pre-tax cash flows of C120 must be earned in order to give the required post-tax return of C114. Pre-tax cash flows of C120 result in a tax charge of C6 — comprising tax on profit before depreciation of C36 (30% of C120) less tax relief on the cost of the asset of C30 (30% of C100). Thus the required pre-tax rate is 20%.

The value in use of C100 of an asset with the above cash flows can be derived either by discounting the post-tax cash flows of C114 at the post-tax rate of 14% or by discounting the pre-tax cash flows of C120 at the derived pre-tax rate of 20%. The same answer is obtained from both methods, because the cost of the asset is fully deductible for tax purposes as a result of the 100% capital allowances and, therefore, does not give rise to any taxable temporary differences.

18.224 The example demonstrates that the pre-tax rate has to be derived from the post-tax rate and the post-tax cash flows. Therefore, the starting point is a post-tax analysis, despite the value in use calculation being labelled as a pre-tax exercise.

18.225 Grossing up from a post-tax rate of 14 per cent to a pre-tax rate of 20 per cent reflects the assumed rate of corporation tax only because of its unrealistic simplicity. The relationship between the post-tax rate and the derived pre-tax rate will deviate from the standard rate as soon as real factors are introduced such as uneven multi-period cash flows, temporary differences between pre-tax cash flows and the related tax cash flows.

18.223　如果认为这两个近似值都不合适，那么应该作税前分析。所要求的税前折现率是扣除所得税项后，生成所要求的税后报酬率的报酬率。下面的例子说明的是，如何用税后折现率计算得出税前折现率。

示例——从税后折现率得出税前折现率——一个简单的例子

资产的税后市场报酬率为 14%。利润按 30% 纳税，资产的成本可以 100% 在计算所得税时抵扣。所有现金流均产生于第一年年底。

对成本为 100 元的资产来说，第一年所要求的税后现金流为 114 元。为了产生 114 元要求的税后报酬，必须挣到 120 元的税前现金流。120 元的税前现金流产生的税费为 6 元——它是折旧前利润上的所得税 36 元（120 的 30%）减去资产成本的抵税额 30 元（100 的 30%）后的金额。这样，所要求的税前折现率为 20%。

根据上述现金流，资产的使用价值 100 元可以通过对税后现金流 114 元按税后折现率 14% 进行折现，或者通过对税前现金流 120 元按税前折现率 20% 进行折现得出。使用上述两种方法，可以得出同样的答案，因为免税额为 100%，纳税时资产成本可以全额扣除，所以，不会产生任何应税暂时性差异。

18.224　这个例子说明，必须根据税后折现率和税后现金流计算税前折现率。因此，尽管使用价值的计算表面上看是税前的计算，但起始点是对税后的分析。

18.225　把 14% 的税后折现率还原到 20% 的税前折现率，它反映了假设的公司税税率，原因仅仅在于该例子不切实际的简单。一旦引入了实际的因素诸如不均衡的多期现金流、税前现金流和相关所得税现金流之间的暂时差异，税后折现率和计算得出的税前折现率之间的关系将会偏离标准税率。

Treatment of tax losses in impairment tests

18. 225. 1 Entities may have tax losses that could reduce taxes to be paid in the future. To what extent should tax losses be taken into account in impairment tests? A CGU that consists of a business that has a taxable identity may have brought forward tax losses. These tax losses may result in a lower level of cash tax being payable over future periods. Alternatively, there may be no tax losses specifically attributable to the CGU or asset being tested, but tax losses are available from elsewhere within the entity that could be allocated to the CGU or asset being tested.

18. 225. 2 The recoverable amount of a CGU should not change because there are tax losses attaching to the assets of the CGU. Any difference in value between otherwise identical CGUs with or without tax losses, relates to the value of the tax losses and not to the value of the assets subject to impairment testing in accordance with IAS 36. Any such losses should, therefore, be excluded from the impairment test.

18. 225. 3 Value-in-use impairment tests are required by IAS 36 to be performed at a pre-tax level. [IAS 36 para 50]. However, in practice, the discount rates applied in a value in use impairment test are often initially established at a post-tax level and then adjusted to derive a pre-tax equivalent. The tax losses may have been included in the forecast tax cash flows used to derive the pre-tax discount rate. If this is the case, the pre-tax discount rate will reflect the benefit of these tax losses. The forecast tax cash flows are adjusted to remove this benefit and any deferred tax assets recognised in relation to the tax losses are excluded from the carrying amount of the CGU.

18. 225. 4 The principle outlined above applies even though fair value less cost to sell is a post-tax measure. The existence of tax losses does not change the recoverable amount of the assets in the CGU and tax payable balances should, therefore, not take into account any tax losses carried forward. Tax losses are sometimes sold in conjunction with the disposal of a business. However, these are typically treated as a separate transaction, as there is uncertainty as to whether the new owner will be able to realise the benefit of those losses.

减值测试中对税务亏损的处理

18. 225. 1　主体可能有能够减少未来纳税金额的税务亏损。在多大程度上可以把税务亏损考虑在减值损失测试中？一个由纳税主体业务组成的 CGU 可能存在前期税务亏损。这些税务亏损可能能够减少未来期间的应付税款。另外一种可能是，可能没有具体归属于被测试 CGU 或资产的税务亏损，但是，主体内其他地方产生的税务亏损可以分配给被测试的 CGU 或资产。

18. 225. 2　CGU 的可收回金额不会因为 CGU 中的资产附带有税务亏损而发生改变。除了附带或不附带税务亏损之外、其他方面完全相同的 CGU，它们的可收回金额之间的差异与税务亏损的价值有关，而与按照 IAS 36 进行减值测试的资产的价值无关。因此，任何这种税务亏损都不应包括在减值测试的范围内。

18. 225. 3　IAS 36 要求按照税前水平作使用价值的减值测试。[IAS 36 第 50 段]。但是，在实务中，应用于使用价值减值测试的折现率常常是以税后折现率为基础，然后对税后折现率进行调整得出。税务亏损可能已经包括在用来计算出税前折现率的预测所得税现金流中。如果是这种情况，税前折现率将反映税务亏损的利益。预测所得税项现金流应进行调整以剔除这些利益，同时任何与税务亏损相关的递延所得税资产也不应包括在 CGU 的账面价值中。

18. 225. 4　上述原则也适用于采用税后计量的公允价值减去处置费用。税务亏损的存在不改变 CGU 中资产的可收回金额，因此应交税金余额不应考虑任何结转后期的税务亏损。有时税务亏损会与业务一起被出售。但是，一般情况下，税务亏损的出售是作为单独交易进行处理的，因为新所有者是否能够实现这些亏损的利益并不确定。

Establishing the carrying amount of a CGU

18. 225. 4. 1 Entities should ensure that the assets being tested are consistent with the cash flows being tested. The following section describes in more detail some of the areas that should be considered.

Allocating assets and liabilities to CGUs

18. 225. 5 The recoverable amount of a CGU is the higher of value in use and fair value less costs to sell, as for an individual asset. The way in which the carrying amount of a CGU is determined should be consistent with the determination of its recoverable amount. [IAS 36 paras 74, 75]. The carrying amount of a CGU is established by allocating assets and liabilities to individual CGUs. The carrying amount of a CGU consists of:

- Assets that are directly and exclusively attributable to the CGU.
- An allocation of assets that are indirectly attributable on a reasonable and consistent basis to the CGU including:
  - corporate assets; and
  - capitalised goodwill.
- Recognised liabilities, but only to the extent that the recoverable amount of the CGU cannot be determined without consideration of those liabilities.

[IAS 36 paras 76, 77].

18. 225. 6 The assets (and liabilities where appropriate) attributed to CGUs should be consistent with the cash flows that are identified for calculating recoverable amount. Cash flows prepared for fair value less costs to sell are prepared on a different basis to those for value in use. As a result, the carrying value of the CGU in a value in use test differs from that on a fair value less costs to sell basis.

18. 225. 7 Value in use cash flows should strictly exclude working capital cash flows, whereas they will be included in fair value less costs to sell cash flows. For

确定现金产出单元的账面价值

18.225.4.1　主体应该确保被测试的资产和被测试的现金流一致。下面一节对应该考虑的内容作了更加详细的说明。

将资产与负债分配至现金产出单元

18.225.5　与单项资产相同，CGU 的可收回金额是使用价值和公允价值减去处置费用的孰高者。CGU 账面价值的确定方法应该和 CGU 可收回金额的确定方法一致。[IAS 36 第 74 段、第 75 段]。CGU 的账面价值是通过把资产和负债分配给各个 CGU 而确定的。CGU 的账面价值由下列内容组成：

- 直接归属于和专属于 CGU 的资产。
- 按合理及一致的基础分配的间接归属于 CGU 的资产，包括：
  - 总部资产；和
  - 资本化的商誉。
- 确认的负债，但仅限于如不考虑则不能确定 CGU 可收回金额的负债。

[IAS 36 第 76 段、第 77 段]。

18.225.6　可归属于 CGU 的资产（适当情况下，还有负债）应该与为计算可收回金额而识别的现金流一致。为公允价值减去处置费用所编制的现金流与编制使用价值现金流所根据的基础不同。因此，使用价值测试中 CGU 的账面价值与公允价值减去处置费用的账面价值不一样。

18.225.7　严格意义上讲，使用价值现金流应该把营运资金现金流排除在外，然而，它们包括在公允价值减去处置费用的现金流中。为了在实务中便于应

practical reasons, even when value in use is being estimated, working capital is sometimes included. When this is done the carrying amount of the CGU should also be adjusted for these items.

18.225.8 Liabilities that relate to financing the operations of CGUs (including interest-bearing debt, dividends and interest payable) are not allocated in determining the carrying amount. This is because the related cash outflows are also excluded from the impairment calculations and such items are taken into account in the rate used to discount the future operating cash flows when calculating a CGU's value in use. The carrying amount of a CGU should exclude liabilities that relate to financing the CGU's operations. No distinction is made between external and intercompany financing. The associated cash outflows, both principal and interest, are not considered in determining recoverable amount. Finance costs are indirectly considered in the measurement of the recoverable amount by using the present value method to discount future cash flows.

Example 1 – Fixed asset impairment review when interest is capitalised

Entity A has constructed a fixed asset. In constructing the asset, entity A capitalised interest relating to the borrowings that it used to finance the construction in accordance with IAS 23, 'Borrowing costs'. The borrowings are still outstanding.

The carrying amount of the fixed asset includes capitalised interest. This will be included when recoverable amount is compared to carrying amount. However, the future net cash flows used in the impairment test should exclude cash flows relating to the outstanding borrowings. This is because the borrowings are not deducted from the carrying value of the CGU being tested for impairment and the interest cost is effectively included in the calculation of the recoverable amount by discounting the future cash flows.

Example 2 – Inter-company funding

Group A is carrying out a first-year impairment review of the goodwill allocated to entity B, which was acquired last year. Entity B has net liabilities, which include inter-company funding from group A to allow the business to meet its short-term needs and to fund post-acquisition restructuring costs.

用，即便在对使用价值进行估值的过程中，有时也包括营运资金。此时，也应该就这些营运资金项目对 CGU 的账面价值进行调整。

18.225.8　为 CGU 的运营而融资产生的有关负债（包括附息债务、红利和应付利息），在确定账面价值时不作分配。这是因为相关的现金流出也未包括在减值计算内，这些项目在计算 CGU 的使用价值时，对未来运营现金流进行折现所使用的折现率中予以考虑。CGU 的账面价值不应该包括与 CGU 运营融资相关的负债。对外部融资和公司间的融资不作区分。确定可收回金额时，不考虑本金和利息的现金流出。财务成本是使用现值法对未来现金流进行折现来计量可收回金额的过程中的间接考虑因素。

示例 1——对利息进行资本化的同时，对固定资产作减值复核

主体 A 建造了一个固定资产。建造过程中，主体 A 按照《IAS 23——借款费用》，对建造融资的借款利息进行了资本化。借款尚未偿付。

固定资产的账面价值包含资本化的利息。把可收回金额和账面价值进行比较时，里面包含资本化的利息。但是，减值测试中使用的未来净现金流不应该包括尚未偿付的借款的现金流。这是因为，减值测试 CGU 的账面价值中没有扣除借款，且通过对未来现金流进行折现来确定可收回金额的计算过程中已经有效地包括了利息成本。

示例 2——公司间融资

集团 A 正在对分配给去年购买的主体 B 的商誉作第一年减值复核。主体 B 资不抵债，负债包括为满足短期业务需要及筹集购买后的重组成本而从集团 A 借入的公司间融资。

The carrying amount of entity B should exclude the inter-company funding, as the carrying value of a CGU should exclude the carrying amount of a recognised liability, unless the recoverable amount cannot be determined without it. The cash flows associated with the funding are excluded from the calculation of value in use.

18.225.9 Tax balances are not allocated for a value in use calculation, because the discounted cash flow forecasts are prepared on a pre-tax basis. In contrast in a fair value less costs to sell calculation current and deferred tax balances and their associated cash flows are taken into account.

18.225.10 The standard does not specify how leased assets should be treated. Under the standard's impairment review methodology, the approach would be as follows. For finance leases, the carrying value of the leased asset would be included in the carrying amount of the CGU; the lease liability and the lease payments would be excluded from the impairment calculations because they relate to financing. For operating leases, no assets would be recognised in the carrying amount of the CGU; the lease payments would be treated as operating cash outflows in the calculation of value in use.

Example – Leased assets within a CGU

Entity A is a shipping company. It runs a fleet of ten ships, all of which it leases from external ship-owning companies. Of the ten ships, eight are classified as finance leases and are held on balance sheet. The remaining two ships are held on operating leases with the lease payments recognised in the income statement over the life of the lease. All the ships have similar specifications and are used on the same routes. Entity A manages the fleet as a whole, deploying the ships as necessary to maximise the profitability of the fleet.

Entity A's management has determined that the fleet is a CGU. When doing impairment testing, the cash flows from all the ships are included in the calculation, including the cash inflows and lease payment outflows for the ships under operating leases. The value in use is then compared to the carrying value of the CGU, including the book value of the ships under finance leases.

主体 B 的账面价值应该把公司间的融资排除在外，因为 CGU 的账面价值不应该包括已经确认的负债的账面价值，除非没有它就不能确定可收回金额。使用价值的计算不包括与融资有关的现金流。

18.225.9 使用价值的计算中不对税项余额进行分配，因为折现现金流预测是以税前为基础进行编制的。相反，在计算公允价值减去处置费用的过程中，要考虑当期和递延所得税余额以及相关的现金流。

18.225.10 准则没有对如何处理租赁资产作出具体规定。根据准则的减值复核方法，租赁资产的处理方法如下。对于融资租赁，租赁资产的账面价值将包括在 CGU 的账面价值中；租赁负债和租赁偿付款不包括在减值计算中，因为它们与融资相关。对于经营租赁，无经营租赁资产确认在 CGU 的账面价值中；计算使用价值时，把租赁偿付款作为营运现金流出进行处理。

示例——CGU 内的租赁资产

主体 A 是一家航运公司，经营一支拥有十艘货轮的船队，所有船只均是从外部轮船公司租赁而来。这十艘货轮中，有八艘被分类至融资租赁并且计入资产负债表。另外两艘为经营租赁，支付的租赁费在租赁期间计入损益表。所有的船只拥有相似的特性并且航行在相同的航线上。主体 A 将该船队视为一个整体进行管理，根据需要进行轮船配置以达到利润最大化。

主体 A 的管理层决定将该船队作为一个 CGU。当进行减值测试时，所有轮船的现金流量均包含在计算中，包括现金流入以及为经营租赁的轮船支付租金的现金流出。然后将 CGU 的使用价值与账面价值相比较，该账面价值包含融资租赁船只的账面价值。

To the extent that the fleet is managed in this way, it is important to consider the finance and operating leases together. If the fleet as a whole is profitable and the carrying value is supported, it would not be appropriate, for example, to look at one operating lease in isolation and to book an onerous lease provision because that ship was trading on an unprofitable route. The unit of account is the fleet as a whole. Any loss in value would first be taken as an impairment charge to reduce the book value of the fleet. Only after the carrying value was reduced to nil would any provision be booked if the definition of a liability was met. See further paragraph 18. 247. 1.

18. 225. 11 There may be circumstances when it is not possible to determine recoverable amount without taking account of a recognised liability. For example if the disposal of a CGU would require the buyer to take over a liability, the fair value less costs to sell (or estimated cash flow from ultimate disposal when calculating value in use) is the price for the assets and the liability together, less costs of disposal. So that the comparison of recoverable amount and carrying amount are on a consistent basis, the liability should also be included in the carrying amount of the CGU. [IAS 36 para 78].

Example – Restoration obligation part of the CGU's carrying amount

The entity operates a mine and has made provision in accordance with IAS 37, 'Provisions, contingent liabilities and contingent assets', for the costs of restoration of the site when mining operations are completed. The provision represents the cost of restoring the damage done to the site when the mine was opened and the same amount has been capitalised as part of the cost of the mine and is being depreciated over the mine's life. The mine is a single CGU and any purchaser would be required to take over the obligation for restoration should the mine be sold. The entity is carrying out an impairment review of the CGU and in determining recoverable amount must take into account the cash outflows that will be required to settle this obligation. Therefore, in comparing the recoverable amount with the carrying amount of the CGU it must also take the recognised liability for restoration costs into account in determining the carrying amount of the CGU.

鉴于船队的管理方法，将融资租赁和经营租赁一起考虑是很重要的。如果船队作为一个整体是盈利的并且可以承受其账面价值，下列做法是不合适的：举例而言，单独考虑一个航行在不盈利的航线上的经营租赁货轮并为其计提金额重大的租赁亏损准备。计量单位是作为整体的船队。价值上的任何损失将首先做为减值费用减少船队的账面价值。只有账面价值减至为零以后，且符合负债定义的情况下才记录预计负债。进一步解释请参见第 18. 247. 1 段。

18. 225. 11　可能会出现这样的情况，即不考虑已经确认的负债，就不能确定可收回金额。例如，处置一个 CGU 时，可能要求买方接管负债，公允价值减去处置费用（或计算使用价值时，最终处置所产生的预计现金流）是资产与负债合计后的价格减去处置费用。因此，可收回金额与账面价值的比较在一致的基础上进行的话，CGU 的账面价值中也应该包括该负债。[IAS 36 第 78 段]。

示例——作为 CGU 账面价值一部分的恢复义务

主体经营着一个矿井，并且已经按照《IAS 37——准备、或有负债和或有资产》为矿井经营结束时现场的恢复费用提取了准备。准备代表着恢复在开矿井时对现场破坏所需要的费用，相同的金额已经资本化作为矿井成本的一部分，并且正在矿井的使用寿命内进行折旧。这个矿井是一个单独的 CGU，如果出售该矿井，则要求任何买家都要接管恢复的义务。主体正在对 CGU 进行减值复核，在确定可收回金额的过程中，必须考虑要求履行这一义务的现金流出。因此，把 CGU 的可收回金额与账面价值进行比较，确定 CGU 的账面价值时，也必须考虑已经确认的恢复费用负债。

Goodwill

18.225.12 Goodwill acquired in a business combination (purchased goodwill) represents future economic benefits arising from assets that are not capable of being individually identified and separately recognised. [IFRS 3 App A]. Such assets might, for example, be a skilled workforce or a non-contractual customer relationship. Goodwill does not generate cash flows independently from other assets or groups of assets and so the recoverable amount of goodwill as an individual asset cannot be determined. However, goodwill often contributes to the cash flows of individual or multiple CGUs. Therefore, goodwill acquired in a business combination must be allocated from the acquisition date to each of the acquirer's CGUs or groups of CGUs that are expected to benefit from the synergies of the business combination. [IAS 36 paras 80, 81].

18.225.13 The allocation of purchased goodwill is made independently of the allocation of the acquiree's other assets and liabilities. Acquired assets or liabilities do not need to be allocated to the CGU. [IAS 36 para 80]. The allocation of goodwill is made based on the synergies expected to be derived from the combination. The synergies are represented by those unrecognised assets of the acquired entity, such as market share, that are effectively transferred to the CGU, rather than by the recognised assets and liabilities that may or may not be transferred to it.

Example – Goodwill allocated to new and existing businesses

An entity acquires a group of companies one of whose subsidiaries, subsidiary A, is a competitor of one of the entity's existing operations. Subsidiary A will be closed and its customers will be served by the entity's existing operation. The goodwill relating to subsidiary A will be allocated to a CGU or group of CGUs of the entity's existing operation. The other assets and liabilities of subsidiary A may not be allocated to those CGUs.

18.225.14 CGUs to which goodwill is allocated from the date of acquisition should be chosen using the following criteria:

- the CGU should represent the lowest level within the entity at which management

商誉

18.225.12　业务合并中取得的商誉（或购买的商誉）代表着不能单独识别和确认的资产所产生的未来经济利益。[IFRS 3 附录 A]。例如，这些资产可能是熟练工人或非合同客户关系。商誉不独立于其他资产或资产组合产生现金流，所以商誉作为一项独立资产，不能确定其可收回金额。然而，商誉经常对单项或多个 CGU 的现金流有贡献，因此，必须自购买日起把业务合并中取得的商誉分配给预期从业务合并的协同效益中受益的购买方的 CGU 或 CGU 组。[IAS 36 第 80 段、第 81 段]。

18.225.13　所购买的商誉的分配独立于被购买方的其他资产和负债的分配而进行。无需把被购买的资产或负债分配给 CGU。[IAS 36 第 80 段]。商誉的分配以业务合并预期所产生的协同效益为基础。协同效益体现为被有效地转移给了 CGU 的被购买主体的未确认资产，比如市场占有率，而不是由可能转移给 CGU 也可能不会转移给 CGU 的、已经确认的资产和负债所体现。

示例——分配给新业务和现有业务的商誉

一个主体购买了一个集团公司，其中的一家子公司，即子公司 A，是该主体现有某一经营业务的竞争对手。子公司 A 将被关闭，由该主体的现有经营业务为子公司 A 的客户继续提供服务。与子公司 A 有关的商誉将被分配给该主体现有经营业务的一个或一组 CGU。子公司 A 的其他资产和负债可以不分配给这些 CGU。

18.225.14　自购买之日起，将被分配到商誉的 CGU，应该按下列条件进行选择：

■ 该 CGU 应该代表主体内、管理层在内部监督商誉的最低层级；且

monitors goodwill for internal purposes; and

- the CGU should not be larger than an operating segment (as defined by para 5 of IFRS 8, 'Operating segments') before aggregation.

[IAS 36 paras 80, 81.]

Example – Testing a segment for impairment

Entity A manufactures and sells envelopes and commenced operations in Melbourne in 19X6. In January 20X0, entity A purchased the assets and liabilities of entity B, a business located in Sydney, and recorded goodwill of C6m upon acquisition. One year later, in 20X1, entity A purchased the assets and liabilities of entity C, a business located in Perth, and recorded goodwill of C11m upon acquisition. Entity B and entity C also manufacture and sell envelopes.

The goodwill arose from the value attributed by entity A to the assembled workforce in each business and the benefit of combining the back office functions with those functions already carried out by entity A.

All pricing, purchasing, marketing, advertising and human resource decisions are made centrally except for hiring operational staff. Management has assigned responsibility for this function to entity B and entity C's local management.

The three business units entity A, entity B and entity C have different customer bases and are located in different states. Management has identified each business as a separate CGU for the purpose of testing assets other than goodwill for impairment. Entity A, entity B and entity C are one operating segment for the purpose of segment reporting.

The carrying amount of goodwill in entity A's financial statements is C14m. Management cannot allocate the goodwill to each of the three CGUs except on an arbitrary basis. Internal management reporting is organised to measure performance at the corporate level.

In this example, goodwill should be tested for impairment by aggregating the three CGUs: entity A, entity B and entity C. All three CGUs benefit

■ 该 CGU 不应该大于汇总前，（按《IFRS 8——经营分部》第 5 段所定义）的经营分部。

[IAS 36 第 80 段、第 81 段。]

示例——分部减值测试

主体 A 生产并销售信封，自 19X6 年起，开始在墨尔本进行经营。20X0 年 1 月，主体 A 购买了主体 B 的资产和负债，主体 B 是一家位于悉尼的企业，购买时，所记录的商誉为 6 百万元。一年后，20X1 年，主体 A 购买了主体 C 的资产和负债，主体 C 是一家位于珀思的企业，购买时所记录的商誉为 11 百万元。主体 B 和主体 C 也生产并销售信封。

商誉产生于主体 A 整合每个企业劳动力所产生的价值，以及合并内勤部门所产生的利益。

除了雇佣经营人员外，所有定价、采购、市场营销、广告、人力资源方面的决定都由管理层统一作出。管理层已经将雇佣经营人员的职能分派给了主体 B 和主体 C 的地方管理层。

主体 A、主体 B 和主体 C 三个业务单元分别拥有不同的客户群，且它们分别位于不同的州。为了对商誉以外的资产进行减值测试，管理层已经把每个业务单元确定为一个独立的 CGU。为了分部报告之目的，主体 A、主体 B、主体 C 组成一个经营分部。

主体 A 的财务报表中，商誉的账面价值为 14 百万元。管理层不能把该商誉分配至每一 CGU 中，除非基于任意基础。主体 A 组织编写的内部管理报告，是从公司层面来计量绩效。

本例中，应该把三个 CGU（主体 A、主体 B、主体 C）汇总起来作商誉减值测试。所有三个 CGU 都从上述每个业务合并的协同效益中

from the synergies ascribed to each business combination.
The combination of the three CGUs represent the lowest level at which management captures information for internal management reporting purposes about the benefits of the goodwill. The combined CGUs are not larger than an operating segment.

18. 225. 14. 1 The following table illustrates the impact of adopting IFRS 8 on goodwill impairment testing.

Table 18. 1A – Effect of adopting IFRS 8 on goodwill impairment testing

France Telecom S. A – Annual Report – 31 December 2009

1. 2 Basis of preparation of 2009 consolidated financial statements (extract)

IFRS 8 Operating Segments

IFRS 8 《Operating Segments》 supersedes IAS 14 《Segment Reporting》. Operating segments are components of the Group that engage in business activities and whose operating results based on the internal reporting are regularly reviewed by the chief operating decision maker (the Chief Executive Officer for the Group) in order to decide the allocation of resources and the assessment of the operating segments' performance. Segment information shall correspond to operating segments or relevant aggregation of operating segments.

In order to reflect organizational changes, whereby its integrated carrier strategy and synergies are rolled out in individual countries, the Group changed its segment reporting as of January 1, 2009, from an analysis by business activity (Personal Communication Services, Home Communication Services and Enterprise Communication Services) to an analysis mainly to a country-based reporting structure. 7 new operating segments are now reported: France, United Kingdom, Poland, Spain, Rest of the World, Enterprise and International Carrier and Shared Services (IC & SS). The reportable segment Rest of the World aggregates the business activities in the countries of AMEA (Africa, Middle East and Asia) and EME (Europe and Middle East).

IAS 36 amended by IFRS 8 Impairment Tests

IAS 36 has been modified by IFRS 8 with a compulsory application date similar to that of IFRS 8, namely January 1, 2009, first-application date retained by the Group. For impairment test purposes, IAS 36 required that goodwill should be allocated to groups of Cash-Generating Units (CGUs) that correspond to the level at which goodwill is internally monitored, which is not larger than a business segment (first level of segment reporting for

受益。

合并三个 CGU 体现了管理层为内部管理报告之目的而捕捉商誉所带来的利益的信息的最低层面，合并后的 CGU 不能大过一个经营分部。

18.225.14.1　下文表格说明了采用 IFRS 8 对商誉减值测试的影响。

表格 18.1A——采用 IFRS 8 对商誉减值测试的影响

法国电信 S. A——年度报告——2009 年 12 月 31 日

1.2　2009 年合并财务报表编制基础（节选）

IFRS 8　经营分部

《IFRS 8——经营分部》取代了《IAS 14——分部报告》。经营分部是参与商业活动的集团的组成部分，且其基于内部报告的经营成果定期由首席经营决策者（主体的首席行政长官）审查，以决定向其分配资源和评价其业绩。分部信息应与经营分部或相关经营分部汇总一致。

为反映组织结构变化，也由于综合运营策略和协同效益体现在单个国家，集团自 2009 年 1 月 1 日起变更其分部报告形式，由商业活动分析（个人通信服务，家庭通信服务以及企业通信服务）变更为国别报告结果的分析。现在报告七个新经营分部：法国、英国、波兰、西班牙、其他国家、企业和国际运营商和共享服务（IC&SS）。其他国家报告分部汇集了 AMEA（非洲、中东和亚洲）和 EME（欧洲和中东）国家的业务活动。

因 IFRS 8 修订后的 IAS 36 减值测试

IAS 36 因 IFRS 8 作过修订，并设置了与 IFRS 8 类似的强制生效日期，即 2009 年 1 月 1 日，但首次生效日期由集团决定。针对减值测试目的，IAS 36 原来要求商誉应在符合商誉内部监控层级的现金产出单元（CGU）组之间分配，现金产出单元组不能大于业务分部（集团分部报告的第一层级）或者地理分部（集团分部报告的第二层级）。因此，集团对波兰、约旦和塞内加尔的商誉监控时以国别为基础，并在这个基础上

Con.

the Group) or the geographic segment (second level of segment reporting for the Group). Therefore, the Group monitored goodwill for Poland, Jordan and Senegal by country and tested it at this level, aggregating Home and Personal businesses.

From now on, in the amended IAS 36, the largest level for impairment testing is the operating segment as defined by IFRS 8. In the absence of transitional provisions, the IFRIC received a request for guidance on the transition arrangements in IFRS 8 and its interaction with IAS 36. The IFRIC identified two alternative treatments: either prior period adjustment or current period adjustment, but the IFRIC decided not to add the issue to its agenda. The Group has applied the IAS 8 general principle of retrospective application. This leads to identify the operating segments in accordance with the principles of IFRS 8 in the internal reporting used until December 31, 2008. Since Group's internal and external reporting are aligned, operating segments as defined by IFRS 8 are the business segments over the 2005 – 2008 period.

As a consequence, goodwill relating to Home and Personal businesses for the three-abovementioned countries has been tested separately on a retrospective basis. This leads to additional impairment relating to Poland and Jordan Home businesses compared with the historical impairment accounted for, respectively amounting to 507 and 48 million euros as at January 1, 2007. This impairment is accounted for retrospectively as a change in accounting policy against equity as at January 1, 2007 (see below).

The accounting consequences of the change in accounting policy resulting from the amendment to IAS 36 by IFRS 8 are:

(**in millions of euros**)	January 1, 2007			December 31, 2007			December 31, 2008		
	Before the change in accounting policy	Impact of IAS 36 amended by IFRS 8	Restated	Published	Impact of IAS 36 amended by IFRS 8	Restated	Published	Impact of IAS 36 amended by IFRS 8	Restated
Goodwill	31,517	(555)	30,962	31,389	(582)	30,807	30,811	(510)	30,301
Retained Earnings	(886)	(518)	(1,404)	2,315	(518)	1,797	1,506	(518)	988
Components of other comprehensive income	2,272	(37)	2,235	1,964	(64)	1,900	309	8	317
Equity attributable to the parent	**26,992**	(555)	**26,437**	**30,053**	(582)	**29,471**	**27,600**	(**510**)	**27,090**
Non-controlling interests	4,844	–	4,844	4,470	–	4,470	3,598	–	3,598
TOTAL EQUITY	**31,836**	(555)	**31,281**	**34,523**	(582)	**33,941**	**31,198**	(**510**)	**30,688**

续表

进行测试,该层面包含了家庭以及个人业务。

从现在起,在修订后的 IAS 36 中,减值测试的最高层级为 IFRS 8 中定义的经营分部。在缺乏过渡性规定的情况下,IFRIC 收到请求,要求提供关于 IFRS 过渡性安排以及它与 IAS 36 相互关系的指南。IFRIC 找了两种解决方法:或者作为前期调整或者作为当期调整,但是 IFRIC 决定不把这个问题加入它的议程。集团采用了 IAS 8 追溯调整法的主要原则,这要求在截至 2008 年 12 月 31 日的内部报告中根据 IFRS 8 的原则确定经营分部。由于集团内部和外部报告是一致的,IFRS 8 定义的经营分部在 2005 年至 2008 年期间为业务分部。

因此,上述三个国家与家庭和个人业务相关的商誉已在追溯基础上单独进行了测试。该测试使得于 2007 年 1 月 1 日,与已经确认的历史减值金额相比较,与波兰、约旦家庭业务相关的额外减值金额分别为 5.07 亿和 4800 万欧元。这笔减值作为会计政策变更,追溯调整了 2007 年 1 月 1 日的权益。

根据 IFRS 8 而作出的对 IAS 36 的修订,它引起的会计政策变更的会计结果如下:

百万欧元	2007 年 1 月 1 日			2007 年 12 月 31 日			2008 年 12 月 31 日		
	会计政策变更之前	根据 IFRS 8 修订的 IAS 36 的影响	重述	已公布	根据 IFRS 8 修订的 IAS 36 的影响	重述	已公布	根据 IFRS 8 修订的 IAS 36 的影响	重述
商誉	31,517	(555)	30,962	31,389	(582)	30,807	30,811	(510)	30,301
留存收益	(886)	(518)	(1,404)	2,315	(518)	1,797	1,506	(518)	988
其他综合收益	2,272	(37)	2,235	1,964	(64)	1,900	309	8	317
归属于母公司权益	**26,992**	**(555)**	**26,437**	**30,053**	**(582)**	**29,471**	**27,600**	**(510)**	**27,090**
非控制性权益	4,844	-	4,844	4,470	-	4,470	3,598	-	3,598
权益合计	**31,836**	**(555)**	**31,281**	**34,523**	**(582)**	**33,941**	**31,198**	**(510)**	**30,688**

18. 225. 14. 2 IFRS 8 requires goodwill to be allocated to operating segments. In April 2009 the IASB issued 'Improvements to IFRS', which has amended IAS 36 and has clarified that the largest unit permitted for goodwill impairment is the lowest level of operating segment as defined in paragraph 5 of IFRS 8, before the aggregation permitted by paragraph 12 of IFRS 8. Because IFRS 8 is applied retrospectively as a change in accounting policy, impairments that result from the lower disaggregation of cash-generating units upon adopting IFRS 8 may be accounted for as a prior year adjustment and not reflected through current year profit or loss. Entities that currently use aggregated operating segments to determine their cash generating units will be forced to disaggregate when the amendment becomes effective. As this amendment is effective prospectively, any resulting impairment will be recognised in profit or loss in the year the amendment is adopted. Entities must adopt IFRS 8 in 2009 and the amendment to IAS 36 in 2010 (unless they elect to early adopt the amendment). On the assumption that entities would prefer to recognise any impairment arising from the amendment as a prior year adjustment, entities should ensure that their cash-generating units are aligned with their operating segments (prior to aggregation) on adoption of IFRS 8 and before adopting the amendment. An example where the adoption of IFRS 8 has led to goodwill being tested for impairment by reference to operating segments under IFRS 8 that are different from segments under IAS 14, with a resulting recognition of impairment, is given in Table 18. 1. A. The adjustment is treated as a prior year adjustment, because it results from the lower disaggregation of cash generating units upon adopting IFRS 8.

18. 225. 14. 3 The requirement that a CGU cannot be larger than an operating segment can have implications in vertically integrated businesses. IFRS 8 is clear that an internal operation can met the definition of an operating segment. Furthermore, IFRS 8 does not require that there is an active market for the output of an operation in order for that operation to be an operating segment. The potential impact of this is illustrated in the example below.

Example – Internal operating segment is a CGU

Entity E produces only one product. The final product is produced centrally in region A. 30% of the sales to third parties are within region A itself. However the market is region A does not meet the definition of an active

18.225.14.2　IFRS 8 要求将商誉分配至经营分部。2009 年 4 月，国际会计准则理事会发布了“对 IFRS 的修订”，其中修订了 IAS 36，明确了商誉减值所允许的最大单元为经营分部的最小层级，该经营分部是按 IFRS 8 的第 12 段允许的汇总之前、按 IFRS 8 第 5 段所定义的经营分部。因为 IFRS 8 作为会计政策变更进行追溯应用，采用 IFRS 8 时对现金产出单元进行的细化拆分而引起的减值可以作为以前年度调整入账，不体现在当年的损益当中。当修订生效时，现在使用汇总经营分部以决定现金产出单元的主体将被迫面临拆分。由于该修订是未来适用，任何可能产生的减值将在修订被采用当年的损益中确认。主体必须于 2009 年采用 IFRS 8，于 2010 年采用对 IAS 36 的修订（除非他们选择提前应用该修订）。假设主体希望将应用该修订产生的减值确认为以前年度调整，主体应确保他们在采用该修订之前、应用 IFRS 8 时的现金产出单元与他们的经营分部（汇总前）一致。表格 18.1A 结出了一个应用 IFRS 8 划分的经营分部执行商誉减值测试，因与根据 IAS 14 划分的分部的结果不一致导致减值的示例。此调整作为以前年度调整，因为其产生于采用 IFRS 8 拆分现金产出单元造成的减值。

18.225.14.3　现金产出单元不能大过经营分部的规定对垂直一体化业务产生影响。IFRS 8 清楚的说明内部经营可以符合经营分部的定义。而且，IFRS 8 不要求一项经营的产出必须有活跃市场才可将其确认为经营分部。下文的示例将说明这一点的潜在影响。

示例——内部经营分部作为一个 CGU

主体 E 只生产一种产品。最终产品集中在区域 A 生产。对第三方销售的 30% 发生在区域 A。但是，区域 A 的市场并不符合 IAS 36 第 6 段对活跃市场的定义，因为交易的项目不是同质的。剩余 70% 的销售发生在区域

market in paragraph 6 of IAS 36, because the items being traded are not homogeneous. The remaining 70% of sales occur in regions B, C, D and E. Regions B, C, D and E are distribution organisations with no production facilities, but they have office buildings, software and customer bases. All regions are independent in negotiating sales conditions with their local clients. In accordance with IFRS 8, the operating segments are the different regions (A, B, C, D and E). The cost of sales in the budgets of the sales regions are determined by transfer prices for these goods and not by the allocation of production costs from region A to these regions.

Impairment testing would be performed in line with the separate CGUs (regions A – E). Each sales region generates cash inflows that are largely independent of the cash flows from other assets or groups of assets. Region A sells its products to third parties also generating largely independent cash flows. This approach is in line with the requirements of IAS 36 that CGUs are not larger than operating segments.

18.225.15 The reason for choosing these criteria is that the goodwill may then be monitored and tested for impairment in a way that is consistent with management's internal management systems, thus avoiding additional development of systems specifically to deal with goodwill. [IAS 36 para 82]. The standard notes that allocating goodwill to CGUs for impairment purposes may not coincide with how it is allocated for the purpose of IAS 21, 'The effects of changes in foreign exchange rates'. It states that if goodwill is allocated at relatively low levels for the purpose of IAS 21 that does not mean that it has to be reviewed for impairment at those low levels, unless management monitors the goodwill at that level for internal management purposes. [IAS 36 para 83].

18.225.16 The allocation of goodwill should normally be completed before the end of the financial year in which the combination takes place. However, the standard also states that if the initial allocation of goodwill cannot be completed within the year of acquisition, that initial allocation is completed before the end of the first financial year beginning after the acquisition date. Goodwill is normally tested once the allocation is completed within the time limit. However, where there is a triggering event for an impairment test on a CGU where the goodwill allocation

B、C、D 和 E。区域 B、C、D 和 E 均为分销组织，没有生产设备，但是他们拥有办公大楼、软件和客户群。在与当地客户协商销售条件方面，所有区域均是独立的。根据 IFRS 8，经营分部是不同的区域（A、B、C、D 和 E）。销售区域预算中的销售成本是由商品的转移定价决定的，而不是由区域 A 的生产成本分配给其他区域确定的。

减值测试根据不同 CGU（区域 A—E）执行。每个销售区域产生的现金流入在很大程度上相对独立于其他资产或资产组。区域 A 销售产品给第三方也产生很大程度上独立的现金流量。这个方法与 IAS 36 的要求一致，即 CGU 不能大过经营分部。

18.225.15　选择这些条件的原因在于，可以采用和管理层内部管理体系一致的方法监管商誉，并对商誉作减值测试，从而避免专门为处理商誉而另外制订一套系统。[IAS 36 第 82 段]。准则注意到，为了减值之目的，对 CGU 所作的商誉分配可能和为《IAS 21——汇率变动的影响》中所规定的分配不一致。IAS 36 规定，如果为了 IAS 21 之目的，在相对较低的层级对商誉进行分配，并不意味着必须在该较低的层级上作减值测试，除非管理层为了内部管理之目的也在该层级对商誉进行监管。[IAS 36 第 83 段]。

18.225.16　在正常情况下，应该在合并发生的当年财务年度截止日之前把商誉分配完毕。但是，准则也规定，如果商誉的初始分配不能在购买当年完成的，初始分配应该在购买日后第一个财务年度截止日之前完成。一般情况下，一旦在规定的时间内完成商誉的分配，则需对商誉进行减值测试。但是，在商誉分配过程尚未结束时，与其相关的 CGU 发生了减值测试的事项，我们则认为，仅仅因为初始分配过程还没有结束，就不对商誉作减值测试，是不合适的。我们认为，应该对该商誉作减值测试。主体对商誉作减值测试的层级

process has not yet been completed, we believe that it would be inappropriate to leave goodwill untested solely because the initial allocation process has not been completed. We believe a test should be performed on this goodwill. The level at which an entity would test this goodwill would depend on facts and circumstances, including the level of information available at the year end. Any adjustment of the impairment charge arising from the finalisation of the purchase price allocation and allocation of goodwill would be accounted for retrospectively.

Example – Maximum period allowed to allocate goodwill

An acquisition takes place in January 20X8. Paragraph 96 of IAS 36 requires the goodwill arising on a business combination in the current year to be tested for impairment before the end of the current year, so the goodwill should be tested by the end of 20X8. However, the entity has not completed its purchase accounting by the end of this date. It cannot allocate goodwill until the amount is known. There have been no trigger events suggesting that the acquired goodwill might be impaired.

IFRS 3 allows an entity 12 months from the acquisition date to complete the purchase accounting. For this acquisition the entity must complete the purchase accounting by January 20X9. At this time the goodwill number is known so the goodwill must be allocated to CGUs or groups of CGUs by the end of period ending December 20X9. (Note that, this example assumes that the entity does not have interim reporting dates.)

18.225.17 The standard requires additional disclosures to be made where the allocation of goodwill to CGUs has not been completed by the end of the period in which the combination took place. These are described in paragraph 18.302.

18.225.18 Where a CGU to which goodwill has been allocated is disposed of, the goodwill is included in the assets and liabilities of the CGU used in calculating the profit or loss on disposal. A more difficult situation is where an operation within a group of CGUs to which goodwill has been allocated is disposed of. Goodwill attributable to the operation disposed of should be included in the assets disposed of and should be apportioned by measuring it on the basis of the relative values of the operation disposed of and the portion of the CGU retained. This method is to be

取决于当时的事实和情况，包括年末获得的信息的层级。因最终确定购买价格分配和商誉分配而对减值费用所作的调整应追溯作会计处理。

示例——允许分配减值的最长期间

2008 年 1 月，主体进行了一次购买。IAS 36 第 96 段规定，对当年中业务合并所产生的商誉，需要在当年年度结束前作减值测试，因此，应该在 2008 年年底前对商誉作减值测试。但是，主体在 2008 年年末日之前尚未完成对这次购买的会计处理。在商誉金额确定之前主体不能对商誉进行分配。同时，也没有出现可能引起所购买的商誉发生减值的事项。

IFRS 3 允许主体自购买日后 12 个月内完成对购买的会计处理。在这个购买例子中，主体必须于 2009 年 1 月前完成对购买的会计处理。到了这个时间点，商誉金额是已知的，所以必须在 2009 年年底前的期间内把商誉分配给 CGU 或 CGU 组。（注意，本例假定主体没有中期报告日。）

18.225.17 准则要求，业务合并发生的期间结束时，商誉分配给 CGU 的工作还没有完成的，需要给予额外披露。这些内容在第 18.302 段进行描述。

18.225.18 分配了商誉的 CGU 进行处置时，商誉包括在 CGU 的资产和负债中用于计算处置利润或亏损。一种较困难的情况是对分配了商誉的 CGU 组中一个运营单元进行的处置。可归属于被处置的运营单元的商誉，应该包括在处置资产中，并以被处置的运营单元的相对价值和所保留的 CGU 部分的相对价值为基础，进行分摊。除非主体能够证明其他方法能够更好地反映与被处置的运营单元有关的商誉，否则应该使用这种方法来分配商誉。[IAS 36 第 86 段]。

used, unless the entity can demonstrate that some other method better reflects the goodwill associated with the operation disposed of. [IAS 36 para 86].

18.225.19 The standard gives an example that clarifies the values to be used are the recoverable amounts of the operation disposed of and the operation retained at the date of disposal. The recoverable amount of the operation disposed of is relatively easy to obtain; it will be the fair value less costs to sell, which should normally be the proceeds less costs. For the operation retained, the latest estimate of recoverable amount of the whole CGU might be used as a basis. This would be the estimate at the last year end, because IAS 36 requires CGUs that contain goodwill to be tested for impairment annually. This latest estimate would have to be updated for any events or circumstances up to the date of the disposal of the operation that formed part of the CGU. Any consequential effects of the disposal on the remaining part of the CGU would have to be taken into account. If such a process is impracticable or unreliable, a new calculation of the recoverable amount of the retained part of the CGU may be necessary.

Example – Allocation of goodwill on part disposal of a CGU

A CGU was reviewed for impairment at 31 December 20X4 and recoverable amount was estimated at C3m. Recoverable amount was based on the fair value less costs to sell. Goodwill of C600,000 has previously been allocated to the CGU and is not impaired at 31 December 20X4. In 20X5 part of the CGU is disposed of for C2m net of disposal costs. The entity has to allocate the goodwill of C600,000 between the portion of the CGU that is retained and the portion disposed of.

Assuming no change in the recoverable amount of the CGU up to the date of disposal and no other special effects of the disposal, using a relative fair value approach the allocation of the goodwill to the operation disposed of would be two thirds of total goodwill. That is, the value of the business disposed of, C2m, divided by the recoverable amount of the whole CGU C3m. Therefore, C400,000 of goodwill would be apportioned to the business disposed of. Another method of allocation could be used for the goodwill if it could be demonstrated that this better reflected the goodwill disposed of and the goodwill retained.

18.225.19　准则中给出了一个示例，明确了价值是处置日被处置的运营单元和留存的运营单元的可收回金额。被处置的运营单元的可收回金额相对容易获得，它是公允价值减去处置费用，通常是处置收入减去费用。对留存的运营单元来说，可能要以最新的、对整个 CGU 可收回金额的估值为基础。这个金额可能是上年底的估算，因为 IAS 36 要求每年对含有商誉的 CGU 作减值测试。在组成 CGU 一部分的运营单元的处置日之前，如果出现任何事项或情况，则需要更新这个估值。应考虑处置对 CGU 留存部分所产生的影响。如果这个过程是不实际或不可靠的，可能有必要重新计算 CGU 留存部分的可收回金额。

示例——对 CGU 部分处置上商誉的分配

2004 年 12 月 31 日，主体对一个 CGU 作了减值复核，估计可收回金额为 3 百万。可收回金额是以公允价值减去处置费用为基础确定的。之前，曾经把 600,000 元的商誉分配给了该 CGU，截至 2004 年 12 月 31 日该商誉没有发生减值。2005 年，处置了部分 CGU，净处置收入为 2 百万。主体必须将 600,000 元的商誉在 CGU 的留存部分和处置部分之间进行分配。

假设截至处置日之前 CGU 的可收回金额没有发生变化，且该处置也没有产生其他特殊影响，采用相对公允价值方法，应分配给被处置的运营单元的商誉是总商誉的 2/3。该比例是被处置业务的价值 2 百万除以整个 CGU 可收回金额 3 百万。因此，有 400,000 元的商誉将被分配给被处置的业务。也可以采用其他分配方法，如果它们可以证明能够更好地反映处置的和留存的商誉的话。

18.225.20 If an entity carries out a restructuring that changes the composition of one or more CGUs to which goodwill has previously been allocated, it should reallocate that goodwill amongst the units affected. The way in which it reallocates the goodwill should be based on the same relative value approach as is described above for allocating goodwill on disposals of operations. This method should be adopted unless the entity can demonstrate that some other method better reflects the goodwill attributable to the reorganised CGUs. [IAS 36 para 87].

18.225.20.1 In some cases, the relative fair value approach may not be the most appropriate method for reallocating goodwill after an internal restructuring or for calculating goodwill disposed upon the disposal of part of a CGU. The relative fair value approach assumes that all CGUs or parts of CGUs contain a similar proportion of goodwill to one another. This may not be the case. Consider the example below:

Example – Alternative to relative fair value approach

Group S is a multinational group with a presence in various continents. In 20X6 group S acquired a South American subgroup. C1,000,000 of goodwill was generated upon acquisition and was allocated across three CGUs, (A, B and C) based upon geographical locations.

In 20X9, a restructuring exercise was carried out. The new CGUs in South America (X, Y and Z) are determined on a product basis. The group manufactures two products in South America and, in addition, has a consultancy business. Prior to the restructuring, the goodwill of C1,000,000 was assessed for impairment and was determined to be fully recoverable.

The fair value of identifiable net assets and the full fair value of each CGU is given in the table below.

	CGU X	CGU Y	CGU Z	Total
Fair value of identifiable net assets	C3,800,000	C6,000,000	C5,000,000	C14,800,000
Fair value in total	C4,000,000	C6,000,000	C10,000,000	C20,000,000

If the C1,000,000 of goodwill is re-allocated across CGUs X, Y and Z on a relative fair value basis, C200,000 would be allocated to CGU X, C300,000

18.225.20　如果主体进行重组，改变了之前分配了商誉的一个或多个 CGU 的构成成分，主体应该在受到影响的单元之间重新分配这些商誉。主体重新分配商誉的方法应该和上文运营单元处置中分配商誉所使用的相对价值法一样。应该采用这种方法，除非主体可以证明其他方法能够更好地反映可归属于被重组 CGU 的商誉。[IAS 36 第 87 段]。

18.225.20.1　在某些情况下，相对公允价值法可能不是内部重组后分配商誉或者计算 CGU 部分处置时被处置的商誉的最恰当的方法。相对公允价值法假设所有 CGU 或 CGU 的部分包含同等比例的商誉。事实可能并非如此。考虑下面的示例：

示例——相对公允价值法的替代法

S 集团是在各大洲存在经营的一个跨国集团。20X6 年，S 集团收购了一个南美洲的子集团。1,000,000 元的商誉是收购时产生的，该商誉根据地理位置分配在三个 CGU（A、B 和 C）之上。

20X9 年，开展了重组工作。南美洲的新的 CGU（X，Y 和 Z）基于产品基础而确定。该集团在南美生产两种产品，此外，还有一个咨询业务。重组之前，对 1,000,000 元的商誉进行了减值评估，被确定为可以完全收回。

可辨认净资产的公允价值和各 CGU 的全部公允价值如下表所示。

	CGU X	CGU Y	CGU Z	合计
可辨认净资产的公允价值	3,800,000	6,000,000	5,000,000	14,800,000
公允价值合计	4,000,000	6,000,000	10,000,000	20,000,000

如果 1,000,000 元的商誉重新在 CGUs X，Y 和 Z 之间按相对公允价值基础进行分配，200,000 元将被分配至 CGU X，300,000 元将被分配至 CGU Y， to CGU Y and C500,000 to CGU Z. This would result in the immediate impairment of goodwill allocated to CGU Y. This is because the relative fair value model does not take into account the difference between the businesses in question. CGUs X and Y, being manufacturing businesses, are highly asset intensive, whereas CGU Z, the consultancy business, has a smaller asset base. In this situation, an acceptable alternative to the relative fair value approach would be to 'perform a purchase price allocation' exercise for each CGU. The fair value of each CGU as a business would be compared to the fair value of the identifiable net assets to calculate a notional goodwill number. The recognised goodwill is then reallocated across the new CGUs based upon the relative values of this notional goodwill. In this case, there is notional goodwill of C200,000 in CGU X, Cnil in CGU Y and C5,000,000 in CGU Z. Thus C40,000 of goodwill would be allocated to CGU X (C200,000/C5,200,000 × C1,000,000), and C960,000 would be allocated to CGU Z. A similar situation to that above could occur on a partial disposal of a CGU if the part of the CGU disposed of was more or less asset intensive than that retained.

18.225.20.2 In addition, following a reorganisation a group may have to change its segment information and modify the level at which goodwill is tested. This is not considered to be a change in accounting policy, rather a change of circumstance and, therefore, IAS 8 does not apply and the impairment test would not need to be re-performed retrospectively.

Example – Allocation of goodwill after restructuring

An international chemicals business, entity D, acquired another chemicals business, entity E, with 80 factories operating in 10 countries. There is an external market for each factory's output, and each factory maintains its own accounting records and cash flow information. Entity E is managed by reference to geographical segments.

Management decided that the lowest level to which goodwill could be allocated on a reasonable and consistent basis was to each of the 10 countries. The compensation scheme of the territory management in each of the 10 countries includes certain financial ratios. These ratios take into

500,000 元将被分配至 CGU Z。这会使分配至 CGU Y 的商誉立即产生减值。这是因为相对公允价值模型未考虑业务之间的差异。CGUs X 和 Y 是资产密集型的制造业务，然而 CGU Z 是资产量较小的咨询业务。在这种情况下，一个可以接受的替代相对公允价值法的方法将是对各个 CGU “执行购买价格分配” 练习。作为一个业务的每个 CGU 的公允价值会与可辨认净资产公允价值进行比较以便计算名义商誉金额。已确认的商誉基于这个名义商誉的相对价值在新的 CGU 之间进行重新分配。本例中，归属于 CGU X 的名义商誉为 200, 000 元，归属于 CGU Y 的名义商誉为零，归属于 CGU Z 的名义商誉为 5,000,000 元。因此，40,000 元的商誉将会被分配至 CGU X（200,000/5,200,000 × 1,000,000），960,000 元将会被分配至 CGU Z。与上述相类似的情况可能发生在 CGU 的部分处置，如果处置的 CGU 部分与留存的部分相比，或多或少是资产密集型。

18. 225. 20. 2　此外，重组后集团可能不得不改变其分部信息并修改商誉测试的层级。这不被认为是会计政策的变更，而被认为是情况的改变，因此，IAS 8 不适用，不需要重新追溯进行减值测试。

示例——重组后商誉的分配

一家国际性化工企业——主体 D 购买了另一家化工企业主体 E，一个在 10 个国家运营着 80 家工厂的企业。每家工厂的产出都有外部市场，且每家工厂都有自己的会计记录和现金流信息。主体 E 是按地理分部进行管理的。

管理层决定，按合理一致的原则可以把商誉进行分配的最低层级是这 10 个国家中的每一个国家。这 10 个国家中，每个国家地域管理的补偿计划中包括一定的财务比率。这些比率在将购买中产生的商誉在 10 个国家运营中进行分配时予以考虑。购买主体 E 之前，主体 D 在这 10 个国家没有

account allocation of goodwill on the acquisition among operations in the 10 countries. Entity D did not operate in these 10 countries prior to entity E's acquisition.

Two years after the acquisition, entity D decides to restructure the acquired business in two countries and, as a result, decides to close five factories in those countries. Each factory is a separate cash-generating unit, so entity D should calculate the recoverable amount of the five factories it has decided to close for the purposes of impairment testing the factories. Goodwill cannot be allocated to the individual factories on a reasonable and consistent basis. The smallest cash-generating unit to which goodwill can be allocated on a reasonable and consistent basis is the countries in which the factories are located. Entity D calculates the recoverable amount of entity E's business in the two countries in which factories will be closed. The recoverable amount of those businesses is compared to the carrying amount of the business, including goodwill. Any impairment identified is applied first to reduce the goodwill's carrying amount and then to other non-monetary assets on a *pro rata* basis.

Four years after the acquisition, new products introduced by competitors supersede some of the products that entity E manufactures. Although all of the individual factories remain profitable, there is an indication that the goodwill on entity E's acquisition as a whole is impaired.

There are no indicators of impairment at individual factories, so it is not necessary to test for impairment at a factory level. There is an indication that goodwill is impaired, so goodwill should be tested for impairment at the level of the smallest cash generating unit to which goodwill can be allocated on a reasonable and consistent basis. The smallest cash generating unit to which goodwill can be allocated on a reasonable and consistent basis is entity E's business in each of the ten countries. Entity D calculates the recoverable amount of entity E's business in each country. The recoverable amount of those businesses is compared to the carrying amount of the business, including goodwill. Any impairment identified is applied first to reduce the carrying amount of the goodwill and then to other non-monetary assets on a *pro rata* basis.

运营。

购买两年后，主体 D 决定把在两个国家所取得的业务进行重组，重组的结果是决定关闭这两个国家的五家工厂。每个工厂都是一个独立的现金产出单元，因此，为了对这五家工厂作减值测试之目的，主体 D 应该计算决定被关闭的这五家工厂的可收回金额。商誉不能按合理一致的原则分配至每家工厂。按合理一致的原则可以对商誉进行分配的最小现金产出单元是这些工厂所在的国家。主体 D 计算将要被关闭的工厂所在国主体 E 业务的可收回金额。然后把这些业务的可收回金额与包括商誉在内的业务的账面价值进行比较。所识别出来的任何减值，首先用于冲减商誉的账面价值，然后按比例分配给其他非货币性资产。

购买四年后，竞争对手的新产品取代了主体 E 所生产的某些产品。尽管每家工厂仍然盈利，但是有迹象表明，主体 E 整体购买时所产生的商誉发生了减值。

因为没有迹象表明在每个工厂的层面发生了减值，所以没有必要在工厂的层面上作减值测试。由于有迹象表明商誉发生了减值，因此应该在以合理一致原则对商誉进行分配的最小现金产出单元的层级上，对商誉作减值测试。可以按照合理一致原则对商誉进行分配的最小现金产出单元是主体 E 在这 10 个国家中的每一个国家。主体 D 计算主体 E 在每个国家业务的可收回金额。然后把这些业务的可收回金额与包括商誉在内业务的账面价值进行比较。所识别出来的任何减值，首先用于冲减商誉的账面价值，然后按比例分配给其他非货币性资产。

18.225.20.3 In addition to reorganisations as a result of disposals or restructuring, entities may change the way they manage existing businesses, for example to save cost or to streamline processes. This may happen alongside a change in segments and/or CGUs, but it can also happen without any change to the composition of existing CGUs. IAS 36 does not envisage this situation and only discusses the reallocation of goodwill when there has been a change in the composition of CGUs. However, paragraph 80 of IAS 36 is clear that goodwill is allocated based upon the lowest level within the entity at which goodwill is monitored for internal management purposes. The question, therefore, arises as to whether goodwill can be reallocated following a change in management structure if there has been no change to the composition of CGUs.

Example – Allocation of goodwill after change in management structure

Entity A has previously allocated goodwill to CGU A, CGU B and CGU C. Following a change in management team, the managers of CGUs A, B and C have all been replaced by one manager who is in charge of the three businesses.

In this situation, it will be necessary to understand whether there has truly been a change in the way in which goodwill is monitored internally. If the internal reporting for each of CGUs A, B and C has been replaced with one report covering the combined businesses, we would consider it acceptable to reallocate the goodwill to the combination of the CGUs for the purposes of impairment testing. However, if the new manager is receiving disaggregated information for each CGU, this means that the goodwill is still being monitored in the same way as before (albeit by one person now as opposed to three people historically). That being the case, goodwill would continue to be reviewed for impairment on the basis of each separate CGU.

18.225.20.4 The reallocation of goodwill between CGUs should not be used as a method to mask impairments. As per paragraph 12(f) of IAS 36, where there has been significant change with an adverse effect on the entity, the restructuring of an operation is considered to be an impairment indicator. On this basis, an impairment review should be performed prior to any restructuring to ensure that the reallocation process does not mask any pre-existing impairments.

18.225.21 Purchased goodwill may relate to a single CGU or to a group of

18.225.20.3 除了由于出售或重新构建内部架构而导致的重组外，主体可能会因，例如，节省成本或简化流程，而改变他们管理现有业务的方式。这种情况可能同时会改变分部或CGU，但它也有可能发生时不改变现有CGU组成的情况下。IAS 36未考虑这种情况，只讨论了CGU组成部分出现变化时商誉的重新分配。然而，IAS 36第80段明确规定，商誉基于主体内为内部管理目的监管商誉的最低层级进行分配。因此，面临的问题是，当管理结构改变但CGU的组成并未出现变化时，商誉能否重新分配。

示例——管理结构改变后商誉的分配

主体A先前已分配商誉至CGU A、CGU B和CGU C。由于管理团队的变化，CGU A、B和C的所有经理被替换为一个经理，由这一个经理负责这三个业务部门。

在这种情况下，就必须了解内部监管商誉的方式是否真正发生了改变。如果各个CGU A、B和C的内部报告已经被一份涵盖合并后业务的报告所取代，我们认为，为减值测试目的，重新分配商誉至合并后的CGU，是可以接受。但是，如果新的经理收到的是各CGU独自的信息，这意味着商誉仍用以前相同的方式（尽管现在由一个人而非由历史上的三个人）来监管。在这种情况下，商誉将继续在每个独立CGU的基础上进行减值复核。

18.225.20.4 商誉在CGU之间的重新分配，不应被用来作为掩盖减值的方法。按照IAS 36第12(f)段的要求，当重大变化对主体带来不利影响时，业务重组被认为是一个减值迹象。在此基础上，任何重组之前应进行减值复核，以确保重新分配过程不会掩盖任何已经存在的减值。

18.225.21 所购买的商誉可能和一个CGU或一组CGU相关。为了内部管理

CGUs. Goodwill is allocated to CGUs at the lowest level at which management monitors goodwill for internal purposes. Because management may monitor goodwill on a broader basis than other assets this means that there may be some CGUs to which goodwill is attributable but has not been allocated because the CGU is one of a group of CGUs to which goodwill has been allocated.

18. 225. 22 When goodwill relates to a CGU, but has not been allocated to it for one of the reasons described in the preceding paragraph, the CGU does not have to be reviewed for impairment annually (although the goodwill will require an annual impairment test). However, it should be tested for impairment whenever there is an indication of impairment. The impairment test compares the unit's carrying amount (excluding any goodwill) with its recoverable amount and any impairment loss is recognised. [IAS 36 para 88].

18. 225. 23 Goodwill may be allocated to individual CGUs or to groups of CGUs. Any CGU or group of CGUs, to which goodwill has been allocated must be tested for impairment annually. They must also be tested when there is an indication of impairment. The impairment test compares the carrying amount of the CGU or group of CGUs, including the allocated goodwill, with the recoverable amount of the CGU or group of CGUs. If the recoverable amount is less than the carrying amount an impairment loss is recognised. [IAS 36 para 90].

18. 225. 24 The annual impairment test for CGUs containing goodwill may be carried out at any time in the financial year, but must be done at the same time each year. Different CGUs may be tested for impairment at different times in the year. However, if some or all of the goodwill allocated to a CGU was acquired in the current financial year the CGU must be tested for impairment before the end of that financial year. [IAS 36 para 96].

18. 225. 26 Individual assets comprising a CGU may be tested for impairment at different times from the CGU itself and CGUs making up a group of CGUs may be tested for impairment at different times from the group as a whole. However, if individual assets are tested at the same time as the CGU to which they belong, they must be tested first and the CGU is then tested afterwards. Similarly individual CGUs that are tested at the same time as a group to which they belong must be

之目的，商誉应分配至管理层为了内部管理之目的监管商誉时最低层级的CGU。因为管理层可以在比其他资产更加广泛的基础上监管商誉，这意味着，某些 CGU 可能有可归属的但是并未分配给的商誉，因为这些 CGU 是分配了商誉的 CGU 组的其中一个。

18.225.22　当商誉和某 CGU 相关，但是由于上段所述的原因并未被分配给该 CGU 时，则不必每年对该 CGU 作减值复核（尽管要求每年均需对商誉进行减值测试）。但是，任何时候出现了减值迹象，则该 CGU 都应该做减值测试。减值测试是将该现金产出单元的账面价值（不包括任何商誉）和其可收回金额进行比较，确认减值损失。[IAS 36 第 88 段]。

18.225.23　可以把商誉分配给单个 CGU 或 CGU 组。分配了商誉的 CGU 或 CGU 组必须每年作减值测试。如果有减值迹象，也必须对它们作减值测试。减值测试是将 CGU 或 CGU 组的账面价值，包括商誉，和其可收回金额进行比较。如果可收回金额小于账面价值，确认减值损失。[IAS 36 第 90 段]。

18.225.24　包含商誉的 CGU 的年度减值测试，可以在财务年度的任何时候进行，但是必须在每年的同一时间进行。对不同的 CGU 可以在一年当中的不同时间进行减值测试。但是，如果分配给一个 CGU 的部分或全部商誉是在当前财务年度取得的，在该财务年度结束前，必须对 CGU 作减值测试。[IAS 36 第 96 段]。

18.225.26　构成 CGU 组成部分的单项资产的减值测试时间可以不同于 CGU 本身的减值测试时间；组成 CGU 组的 CGU 的减值测试时间可以不同于整个 CGU 组的减值测试时间。但是，如果单项资产与其所属的 CGU 同时进行减值测试的，则必须首先对单项资产作减值测试，然后再对 CGU 作减值测试。类似地，单个 CGU 和其所属的 CGU 组同时进行减值测试的，则必须先对单个 CGU 作减值测试，然后再对 CGU 组作减值测试。[IAS 36 第 97 段、第 98

tested separately before the group is tested. [IAS 36 paras 97, 98].

18.225.27 The requirement to test individual assets and smaller CGUs in a group first is important. These tests exclude goodwill, which is not allocated to individual assets or to individual CGUs within a group of CGUs. It is the group of CGUs to which the goodwill is allocated. Therefore, these tests identify impairments other than impairments of goodwill. If an impairment loss arises from that preliminary test, it is recognised. The carrying amount of the CGU (or group of CGUs) is reduced accordingly. The second stage is the test of the CGU (containing the assets that have just been individually tested) or the group of CGUs (each of which has just been individually tested). This second stage is a comparison of the recoverable amount of the CGU (or group of CGUs) with the restated carrying amount of the CGU (or group of CGUs) including goodwill as reduced by the impairment loss already recognised. Any impairment loss that is recognised on the subsequent test of the CGU (or group of CGUs) will not duplicate the impairment loss recognised following the test of the individual assets of the CGU (or of the CGUs making up the group of CGUs) but will be additional to it.

18.225.28 This two stage test procedure is not perfect. If a group of CGUs includes some CGUs that are very profitable and some that are not it is quite possible that the recoverable amount of the profitable CGUs will mask any impairment loss that would have been disclosed had goodwill been allocated at a lower level to each of the CGUs in the group. However, it is a practical method of carrying out a review where it is difficult to allocate goodwill to individual CGUs. It matches the allocation and testing to the level at which management monitors goodwill. The two stage approach also ensures that other assets excluding goodwill are tested separately for impairment at the level of the individual asset or (for groups of CGUs) at the individual CGU level and goodwill allocated to the CGU or group of CGUs is tested at the CGU (or at the combined group of CGUs) level.

18.225.29 The example below illustrates the two stage approach. The first part of the example illustrates where goodwill can be allocated to the individual CGU. The second part of the example deals with the situation where an individual CGU to which goodwill is not allocated forms part of a group of CGUs to which goodwill has been allocated and where the individual CGU and the group of CGUs are tested

段］。

18.225.27　先对单项资产和一个 CGU 组内较小 CGU 作减值测试的要求非常重要。这些减值测试不包括商誉，商誉没有分配给单项资产或 CGU 组内单独的 CGU。商誉只被分配至了一组 CGU。因此，这些减值测试识别的是商誉减值以外的其他减值。如果初步测试表明发生了减值损失，则对该减值损失进行确认。相应减少该 CGU（或 CGU 组）的账面价值。第二步，对 CGU（包含第一步中已经单独作了减值测试的资产）或 CGU 组（包含已经在第一步中单独作了减值测试的 CGU）进行减值测试。这第二步是把 CGU（或 CGU 组）的可收回金额和重新确定的减去了已经确认的减值损失的 CGU（或 CGU 组）的账面价值（包括商誉）进行比较。对 CGU（或 CGU 组）进行的进一步减值测试所确认的减值损失，不会重复已在 CGU 单项资产（或 CGU 组中 CGU）做完减值测试后已经确认的减值损失，它们是额外的减值损失。

18.225.28　这个分两步进行的测试程序并不完美。如果一个 CGU 组既包括非常赚钱的 CGU，也包括不盈利的 CGU，则很有可能出现的情况是：盈利 CGU 的可收回金额将掩盖这个 CGU 组内如果把商誉分配至较低的每一个 CGU 层面可能披露出来的减值损失。但是，在难以把商誉分配给单项 CGU 时，这个方法则是减值复核的实用方法，它使分配和测试与管理层监督商誉的层级相匹配。这个两步法也能够保证，对除商誉之外的其他资产，在单项资产或单个 CGU（对 CGU 组而言）的层级分别作减值测试，分配给 CGU 或 CGU 组的商誉，则在 CGU 层级（或在合并后的 CGU 组）的层级作减值测试。

18.225.29　下面的示例对这个两步法进行了说明。示例的第一部分说明的是当商誉可以分配至单个 CGU 时的情况。示例的第二部分说明的是，作为分配了商誉的 CGU 组的组成部分但本身并未被分配商誉的单个 CGU，且其和 CGU 组同时作减值测试的情况。在这个示例中，假定使用价值大于公允价值减去处置费用，因此，使用价值作为可收回金额。

for impairment at the same time. In this example the value in use is assumed to be higher than fair value less costs to sell and, therefore, is taken as the recoverable amount.

Example – Two stage approach to impairment testing

The entity acquired a group of companies some years ago. At the current year end there is an indicator that one subsidiary, entity A may be impaired. Entity A is a cash-generating unit.

A – Recognition of impairment where goodwill has been allocated to the CGU

The carrying value of entity A and its recoverable amount are compared as follows to determine the impairment loss.

Cash generating unit	**A**
	Cm
Net assets	220
Goodwill	40
Total net assets	260
Value in use	200
Impairment	60

In this example, where purchased goodwill is allocated to the individual CGU there is an impairment loss of C60m in entity A, reducing the carrying value of its net assets and goodwill to C200m. The impairment loss is attributed C40m to goodwill and C20m to other assets on a *pro rata* basis (see from para 18.240).

The carrying values after recognising the impairment loss are as follows:

Carrying value after impairment	**A**
	Cm
Net assets	200
Goodwill	–
Total net assets	200

示例——减值测试两步法

几年前，主体购买了一组公司。本年度年末，有迹象表明其中的一个子公司——主体 A，可能发生了减值。主体 A 是一个现金产出单元。

A——分配了商誉的 CGU 的减值确认

为确定减值损失，对主体 A 的账面价值和可收回金额比较如下。

现金产出单元	**A**
	百万元
净资产	220
商誉	40
净资产合计	260
使用价值	200
减值	60

本例中，所购买的商誉分配给了单项 CGU，主体 A 有 60 百万元的减值损失，该减值损失把 CGU 净资产和商誉的账面价值减少到了 200 百万元。减值损失中，40 百万元归属于商誉，另外的 20 百万元按比例归属于其他资产（见第 18.240 段）。

确认减值损失后的账面价值如下：

减值损失后的账面价值	**A**
	百万元
净资产	200
商誉	–
净资产合计	200

B – Recognition of impairment where goodwill has not been allocated to the individual CGU

The entity first calculates impairment loss (if any) based on entity A's net assets excluding goodwill.

Cash generating unit	**A**
	Cm
Net assets	220
Value in use	200
Impairment	20

Entity A's net assets are reduced by the impairment loss to C200m (allocation of the impairment loss is on a *pro rata* basis).

In order to test goodwill the entity then tests the group of CGUs that includes entity A and to which goodwill has been allocated. The group of CGUs consists of the operations of entity A and entity B combined. (The impairment test of this group of CGUs must be done annually in any case and at other times where there is an indication of impairment, because it contains goodwill.) The calculation of the impairment loss is then as follows:

Cash generating unit	**A**	**B**	**Goodwill**	**Larger CGU**
	Cm	**Cm**	**Cm**	**Cm**
Net assets	200	110	80	390
Value in use	200	180		380
Impairment	–	–	10	10
Carrying values after impairment	**A**	**B**	**Goodwill**	**Larger CGU**
	Cm	**Cm**	**Cm**	**Cm**
Net assets	200	110	70	380

The total impairment charge is thus C30m, being C20m from the first stage and C10m from the second stage. This is the difference between the carrying amount of entity A's assets of C220m and their revised carrying amount of C200m plus the difference between the carrying amount of goodwill of C80m and its revised carrying amount of C70m .

B——商誉未被分配给单项 CGU 的减值确认

主体首先根据主体 A 的净资产（不包括商誉），计算减值损失（如有）。

现金产出单元	**A**
	百万元
净资产	220
使用价值	200
减值	20

因为减值，主体 A 的净资产减至 200 百万元（按比例对减值损失进行分配）。

为了测试商誉的减值损失，主体对包括主体 A 在内的 CGU 组和被分配在该 CGU 组的商誉进行减值测试。CGU 组由主体 A 和主体 B 合并后的业务构成。(因为包含商誉，任何情况下，对这个 CGU 组的减值测试必须每年进行，以及在出现减值迹象时进行)。减值损失的计算结果如下：

现金产出单元	**A**	**B**	**商誉**	**较大的 CGU**
	百万元	**百万元**	**百万元**	**百万元**
净资产	200	110	80	390
使用价值	200	180		380
减值	–	–	10	10
减值后的账面价值	**A**	**B**	**商誉**	**较大的 CGU**
	百万元	**百万元**	**百万元**	**百万元**
净资产	200	110	70	380

因此，减值费用总计为 30 百万元，第一步的减值费用为 20 百万元，第二步为 10 百万元。这是主体 A 资产的账面价值 220 百万元与它们修正后的账面价值 200 百万元之差，加上商誉的账面价值 80 百万元和它修正后的账面价值 70 百万元之差的合计。

18. 225. 31 Groups need to keep detailed records of the composition of the aggregate amount of purchased goodwill to avoid having to carry out impairment tests of all CGUs annually. The records should explain to which parts of the group the goodwill relates and to which CGUs and groups of CGUs it has been allocated. CGUs or groups of CGUs to which goodwill is allocated must be tested for impairment annually and whenever there are indications of impairment. Other CGUs to which goodwill has not been allocated only need to be tested when there are indications of impairment. Records of the allocation of goodwill to CGUs are also necessary to account for subsequent disposals (to determine how much goodwill should be written off when a business is sold or reorganised).

18. 225. 32 There is only limited guidance in the accounting standards on how to allocate purchased goodwill to different business units. Goodwill should be allocated on a reasonable basis. In theory, goodwill is allocated to the CGUs or groups of CGUs that are expected to benefit from the synergies of the combination. This can include CGUs or groups of CGUs of the existing business. In practice, goodwill is typically allocated to groups of CGUs rather than individual CGUs.

[The next paragraph is 18. 225. 34.]

18. 225. 34 Given the lack of guidance on acceptable methods of allocation, an appropriate basis needs to be selected by entity management. Discounted cash flow based methods are, in general, likely to be appropriate for most acquisitions, because asset-based methods do not generally reflect the relative profitability of different businesses. A cash flow approach is also consistent with the principles for subsequent impairment calculations.

[The next paragraph is 18. 225. 38.]

Identified intangibles and goodwill – The 'deferred tax problem'

18. 225. 38 Where intangible assets are acquired within a business combination, there is no exemption from the necessity of applying IAS 12. If the intangible in question is not tax deductible on either consumption or sale, a deferred tax liability based on the value of the intangible and the prevailing tax rate will be recognised. The

18.225.31 为了避免每年都不得不对所有 CGU 作减值测试，集团公司需要对所购买商誉汇总金额的构成元素作详细记录。这些记录应该能够解释，商誉与集团公司的哪些组成部分相关，以及把商誉分配给了哪些 CGU 或 CGU 组。对分配了商誉的 CGU 或 CGU 组每年必须作减值测试，且当有迹象表明发生了减值时，随时作减值测试。没有分配商誉的 CGU 则只需当出现减值迹象时，才作减值测试。为了对后续处置进行会计处理（确定在业务被出售或重组时应转销多少商誉），也有必要对把商誉分配给 CGU 的情况进行记录。

18.225.32 会计准则中对如何把购买的商誉分配给不同的业务单元仅提供了有限的指南。商誉应以合理的基础进行分配。从理论上来说，应把商誉分配给预期从业务合并的协同效益中受益的 CGU 或 CGU 组，可以包括购买方现有业务中的 CGU 或 CGU 组。实务中，通常把商誉分配给 CGU 组，而不是单项 CGU。

[下一段是第 18.225.34 段。]

18.225.34 考虑到对可接受的分配方法缺乏指引，主体的管理层需要选择一个恰当的基础。总的来说，现金流量折现法可能适用于大多数购买情况，因为以资产为基础的方法一般不能反映不同业务的相关盈利能力。现金流量法也跟后续减值计算的原则一致。

[下一段是第 18.225.38 段。]

可辨认的无形资产和商誉——“递延所得税问题”

18.225.38 在业务合并中取得的无形资产也要适用 IAS 12 的规定。如果无形资产无论使用还是出售均不能税前抵扣，那么则应基于无形资产的价值和现行税率确认一项递延所得税负债。按照 IAS 12 第 22（a）段中的规定，对应的借方科目则是增加商誉的金额。

corresponding debit entry, per paragraph 22(a) of IAS 12, will increase goodwill.

18.225.38.1 In certain jurisdictions, the amortisation of intangible assets is deductible for tax purposes. This generates additional benefits for the owner of the asset which impacts the fair value of the asset. This is the tax amortisation benefit (TAB). On a business combination any TAB that would be available if the asset were acquired separately should be reflected in the fair value of the asset. The TAB will increase the intangible value and reduce goodwill. However, the additional deferred tax on the intangible asset will increase goodwill.

18.225.39 Deferred tax liabilities on intangible assets in a business combination may be significant, as there may be no tax deduction for these assets. This leads to the recognition of a higher amount of goodwill. A value in use calculation, which is a pre-tax value, may lead to an impairment charge soon after an acquisition is made, due to the higher amount of goodwill that is recorded as a result of recognising a deferred tax liability.

18.225.40 In order to address this anomaly, a test should be performed using fair value less costs to sell at the date of acquisition and subsequently, if a value in use calculation triggers an impairment charge. The fair value less costs to sell is a post-tax measure of recoverable value. The carrying value of a CGU under the fair value less costs to sell method, should include the deferred tax liabilities The comparison of discounted post-tax cash flows and the carrying value of the CGU including deferred tax liabilities may eliminate or reduce the amount of the impairment charge.

18.225.41 While IAS 36 requires tax to be excluded from a value in use calculation, paragraph 76 of IAS 36 also states that the carrying amount of a CGU will not include the carrying amount of any recognised liability, unless the CGU's recoverable amount cannot be determined without consideration of this liability. When a CGU's recoverable amount is determined based on fair value less costs to sell, the carrying amount is determined on a post-tax basis, net of deferred tax liabilities.

18.225.41.1 IAS 36 defines the recoverable amount as the higher of value in use and fair value less costs to sell. Given the computational differences between the two measures in relation to tax balances and cash flows, it is possible that the impairment test using the higher measure shows an impairment but the test using

18.225.38.1　在某些税收管辖区，为了纳税之目的，可以扣除无形资产的摊销费用。这额外增加了资产所有者的利益，从而影响资产的公允价值。这就是税额摊销利益（TAB）。业务合并中，如果资产在单独购买时能获得 TAB，则该 TAB 应该在资产的公允价值中反映出来。TAB 将增加无形资产的价值，从而减少商誉的金额。但是，相应增加的递延所得税将增加商誉的金额。

18.225.39　在业务合并中，与无形资产相关的递延所得税负债金额可能很大，因为这些资产可能不能在计算所得税时扣减。这会导致确认较高金额的商誉。由于因确认了递延所得税负债，导致所记录的商誉金额较高，以税前价值为基础的使用价值的计算可能在购买后不久导致出现减值费用。

18.225.40　为了解决这种异常情况，如果使用价值的计算会导致减值，应该在购买日及后续期间按公允价值减去处置费用作减值测试。公允价值减去处置费用为可收回价值的税后计量。公允价值减去处置费用方法下 CGU 的账面价值应该包括递延所得税负债。税后现金流量折现与包含递延所得税负债的 CGU 账面价值的比较可以消除或减少减值费用的金额。

18.225.41　IAS 36 规定，使用价值的计算不包括所得税金额，IAS 36 第 76 段同时也规定，CGU 的账面价值不包括任何已确认负债的账面价值，除非不考虑这个负债就不能确定该 CGU 的可收回金额。当用公允价值减去处置费用确定 CGU 的可收回金额时，账面价值也应按税后金额，即扣除递延所得税负债后的金额确定。

18.225.41.1　IAS 36 将可收回金额定义为使用价值与公允价值减去处置费用两者中的孰高者。考虑到两种计量之间因所得税余额和所得税现金流量而产生的计算差异，很有可能减值测试时使用金额高的计量导致减值，而测试时金额低的计量显示较小的减值金额或者不需减值。在这种情况下，我们认为

the lower measure shows a smaller impairment or no impairment at all. In such a situation, we would consider it appropriate to recognise the smaller (or no) impairment. This is because we believe the requirement to consider the higher of the two measures is designed to ensure that the lowest impairment charge generated by the two measures is the amount actually recognised in profit or loss.

Example – Lower of value in use and fair value less costs to sell gives a lower impairment charge

Entity A has performed an impairment calculation on a CGU. The carrying value of the CGU excluding tax balances is C1,000. The CGU also has an associated C200 deferred tax liability.

The value in use, calculated on a pre-tax basis, is C900. The fair value less costs to sell, calculated on a post-tax basis, is C750.

When the value in use is compared to the carrying value excluding the tax balances, this shows a deficit of C100 (C900 – C1,000). When the fair value less costs to sell is compared to the carrying value including tax balances, this shows a deficit of C50 (C750 – C800).

IAS 36 defines recoverable value as the higher of value in use and fair value less costs to sell. This would imply that the value in use measure should be taken and, therefore, an impairment charge of C100 would be recognised.

However, in this situation, we would consider it appropriate to recognise the lower impairment charge of C50.

Non- controlling interests

18.225.42 Under IFRS 3, there is a policy choice in relation to recognising goodwill in a business combination where there is a non-controlling interest. Goodwill may be recognised only to the extent of the acquirer's interest in the net assets acquired ('the partial goodwill method') or goodwill may be recognised based on the fair value of the whole business acquired ('the full goodwill method'). Where goodwill relating to any non-controlling interest is not recognised (the partial goodwill method), This causes a complication when a CGU to which

确认较小金额的（或不确认）减值是恰当的。这是因为，我们认为要求考虑两种计量结果中的较高者，是为确保两种计量产生的最低的减值支出为实际确认在损益表中的金额。

示例——使用价值和公允价值减去处置费用较低者给出较低的减值支出

主体 A 对一个 CGU 执行减值计算。该 CGU 不含所得税余额的账面价值为 1,000 元。该 CGU 同时也有一个相关的价值为 200 元的递延所得税负债。

在税前基础上计算的使用价值为 900 元。在税后基础上计算的公允价值减去处置费用为 750 元。

当使用价值与不含所得税余额的账面价值相比较时，结果为减值 100 元（900 - 1,000）。当公允价值减去处置费用与包含所得税余额的账面价值相比较时，结果为减值 50 元（750 - 800）。

IAS 36 将可收回价值定义为使用价值和公允价值减去处置费用两者中的孰高者。这意味着应考虑使用价值计量，因此将确认 100 元的减值支出。

但是，在这种情况下，我们认为确认较小的减值支出 50 元是适当的。

非控制性权益

18.225.42　根据 IFRS 3，对于存在非控制性权益的业务合并，确认商誉时涉及一个政策选择的问题。商誉可以只确认购买的净资产中购买方的权益范围内的部分（“部分商誉法”），也可以在整个被购买业务的公允价值基础上进行确认（“完全商誉法”）。在未确认与非控制性权益有关的商誉（部分商誉法）的情况下，对分配了商誉的 CGU 作减值测试时，就出现了困难。难点在于 CGU 资产和负债（商誉除外）的账面金额包括这些资产和负债上少数股东的份额以及可以归属于母公司权益的商誉，它不包括少数股东权益的商誉。但

goodwill has been allocated is reviewed for impairment. The complication is that the carrying amount of the assets and liabilities (other than goodwill) of the CGU includes the minority share of those assets and liabilities together with the goodwill attributable to the parent's interest. It does not include the minority interest in goodwill. However the recoverable amount of the CGU takes no account of the fact that goodwill on the minority share has been omitted from the carrying amount. In order to compare 'like with like' the calculation needs to be adjusted.

18.225.43 In carrying out an impairment test of a CGU with a non-controlling interest that has been accounted for using the partial goodwill method, this 'mismatch' has to be addressed. This is done as follows:

- First the carrying amount of the CGU is notionally adjusted to include goodwill attributable to the non-controlling interest. This is done by grossing up the carrying amount of goodwill allocated to the CGU to include the goodwill attributable to the non-controlling interest.
- The notional carrying amount of the CGU is then compared with the recoverable amount of the CGU.
- If the recoverable amount is lower than the notional carrying amount an impairment loss is recognised.
- This impairment loss will include a loss attributable to the non-controlling interest's notional share of goodwill. That element of the loss needs to be identified and excluded from the amount of the loss that is recognised. This is done in proportion to the amount of the loss that is attributable to the notional goodwill as a whole.
- The impairment loss (as adjusted for the non-controlling interest share) is first applied to write down the goodwill that has been recognised. This is the goodwill attributable to the parent's interest that is actually recognised in the financial statements, not the 'notional' goodwill that includes the non-controlling interest's share. Any excess of impairment losses over the carrying amount of goodwill is then applied *pro rata* against the remaining non-monetary assets on the basis of their carrying amounts.

[IAS 36 paras 92 to 94].

是，CGU 的可收回金额并未考虑账面价值中少数股东股份上的商誉未被包含在内的事实。为了能够将“同类与同类”进行比较，需要对计算进行调整。

18.225.43 对包含采用部分商誉法进行会计处理的非控制性权益的 CGU 作减值测试时，必须解决这种“不匹配性”。通过下列方法可以解决该不匹配性：

- 首先，对 CGU 的账面价值作名义上的调整，使它包含可归属于非控制性权益的商誉。具体是通过还原分配给 CGU 的商誉的账面价值，使其包含可归属于非控制性权益的商誉来实现。

- 然后，把 CGU 的名义账面价值与 CGU 的可收回金额进行比较。

- 如果可收回金额小于名义账面价值，确认减值损失。

- 这个减值损失包含可归属于非控制性权益名义商誉份额上的损失。需要对该部分损失进行识别，它不包含在确认的损失金额内。该部分损失的金额是按将损失总金额归属于整体名义商誉后计算非控制性权益商誉所占的比例来确定的。

- （扣减了非控制性权益名义商誉份额上应承担的减值损失后的）减值损失首先冲减确认的商誉。该商誉是实际上在财务报表中进行了确认的可归属于母公司权益的商誉，而不包含非控制性权益份额的“名义”商誉。超出商誉账面价值的减值损失部分，以剩余非货币资产的账面价值为基础，按比例分配。

［IAS 36 第92—94 段］。

18. 225. 43. 1 If the entity chooses to fair value the non-controlling interest (that is, to use full goodwill method) then this will mean that the goodwill on the consolidated balance sheet will represent goodwill on 100 per cent of the business. Therefore, for testing purposes no notional adjustment will be needed to gross up the goodwill as it is already shown at 100 per cent.

18. 225. 44 IAS 36 contains an example of how the above works in practice. The following example is based on the one in the standard.

Example 1 – Calculation of impairment when there is a non-controlling interest in the CGU

Entity X acquires an 80% interest in entity A for C2. 4m on 1 January 20X6. The identifiable net assets and contingent liabilities (after fair valuing) of entity A are C1. 8m on that date. Entity X applies the partial goodwill method, recognising goodwill only to the extent of its own 80% interest in entity A. Entity X, therefore, recognises in its financial statements:

- The fair value of net assets and contingent liabilities C1. 80m.
- Goodwill of C0. 96m (calculated as C2. 40m – (C1. 80 × 80%)).
- Non-controlling interest of C0. 36m (C1. 80m × 20%).

Entity A is a CGU. Goodwill has been allocated to entity A, therefore, it must be tested annually for impairment and more frequently whenever there is an indication of impairment. It must also be tested before the end of the accounting period in which the acquisition took place.

At the end of 20X6 entity X assesses the CGU's (entity A) recoverable amount as C1m. Entity X uses straight-line depreciation and a 10 year useful life for entity A's depreciable assets and anticipates no residual value. (It is assumed for simplicity that the depreciable assets are C1. 8m.) In accordance with IFRS 3 goodwill is not amortised.

Part of the recoverable amount of C1m is attributable to the Non-controlling interest's share of goodwill that has not been recognised. In accordance with IAS 36, the carrying amount of entity A should first be notionally increased for the purpose of the impairment test by the goodwill attributable to the non-

18.225.43.1　如果主体选择了将非控制性权益按公允价值计量（即使用完全商誉法），这将意味着合并资产负债表中的商誉为业务100%的商誉。因此，就测试目的而言，无需对商誉进行任何名义调整，因为它已经是100%的商誉了。

18.225.44　IAS 36给出了一个示例，内容是如何在会计实务中进行上面所提到的工作。下面的例子就是根据准则中的示例给出的。

示例1——CGU中包含非控制性权益时的减值计算

20X6年1月1日，主体X以2.4百万的价格购买了主体A 80%的权益。该日，主体A的可辨认净资产和或有负债为1.8百万（评估后）。主体X使用部分商誉法，仅对其在主体A中的80%的权益确认了商誉。因此，主体X在其财务报表中确认了下列内容：

- 净资产和或有负债的公允价值为1.80百万。
- 0.96百万的商誉［计算如下：2.40百万－（1.80百万×80%）］。
- 0.36百万的非控制性权益（1.80百万×20%）。

主体A是一个CGU。已经把商誉分配给了主体A，因此，主体A必须每年对商誉作减值测试，如果出现减值迹象，作减值测试的次数还要更加频繁。主体A也必须在购买发生的会计期间结束前作减值测试。

20X6年年底，主体X把CGU（主体A）的可收回金额评估为1百万。主体X用直线折旧法和10年的使用寿命，对主体A的可折旧资产进行折旧，预计无残余价值。（为了简化起见，假定可折旧资产为1.8百万）。根据IFRS 3，对商誉不作摊销。

1百万可收回金额的一部分归属于尚未确认的非控制性权益商誉份额。根据IAS 36，为了减值测试之目的，首先应该名义上将可归属于非控制性权益的商誉增加到主体A的账面价值中。然后把名义上增加后的账面价值与1百万的可收回金额进行比较。结果见下表。

controlling interest. That notionally increased carrying amount is then compared with the recoverable amount of C1m. This is shown in the following table.

	Carrying value of CGU	
	Cm	**Cm**
Goodwill (attributable to parent's interest)		0.96
Unrecognised non-controlling interest in goodwill *		0.24
Gross carrying amount of identifiable net assets	1.80	
Accumulated depreciation	0.18	
Carrying amount of identifiable net assets		1.62
Notionally adjusted carrying amount		2.82
Recoverable amount		1.00
Impairment loss (notional)		1.82

* The goodwill attributable to entity X's interest of 80% was C0.96m at the acquisition date. Therefore, the goodwill attributable to the non-controlling interest's 20% interest is one quarter of that or C0.24m.

The impairment loss then needs to be allocated. This is first attributed to goodwill (of which only 0.96m is in entity A's balance sheet (as the 0.24 is attributable to the non-controlling interests) and then allocated to the net assets.

	Carrying value of CGU		Allocation of impairment	After impairment
	Cm	**Cm**	**Cm**	
Goodwill (attributable to parent's interest)		0.96	(0.96)	
Gross carrying amount of identifiable net assets	1.80			
Accumulated depreciation	0.18			
Carrying amount of identifiable net assets		1.62	(0.62)	1.00
Carrying amount[1]		2.58		1.00
Recoverable amount		1.00		
Impairment loss (total booked)		(1.58)	(1.58)	

	CGU 的账面价值	
	百万元	**百万元**
（可归属于母公司的权益的）商誉		0.96
未确认的非控制性权益的商誉*		0.24
可辨认净资产的总账面价值	1.80	
累计折旧	0.18	
可辨认净资产的账面价值		1.62
名义调整后的账面价值		2.82
可收回金额		1.00
（名义上的）减值损失		1.82

* 购买日，可归属于主体 X 的 80% 权益上的商誉为 0.96 百万。因此，可归属于非控制性权益的 20% 权益上的商誉是 0.96 百万的四分之一，或 0.24 百万。

接下来，需要分配减值损失。首先把减值损失分配给商誉（其中，在主体 A 资产负债表上反映的仅仅为 0.96 百万，因为 0.24 百万归属于非控制性权益），然后再分配给净资产。

	CGU 的账面价值		减值分配	减值后
	百万元	**百万元**	**百万元**	
（可归属于母公司权益的）商誉		0.96	(0.96)	
可辨认净资产的总账面价值	1.80			
累计折旧	0.18			
可辨认净资产的账面价值		1.62	(0.62)	1.00
账面价值[1]		2.58		1.00
可收回金额		1.00		
（确认的总）减值损失		(1.58)	(1.58)	

The balance of the impairment loss of C0. 62m is recognised in full, because it relates to net assets (including both parent and non-controlling interest's share) that are also recognised in full in the financial statements. This remaining impairment loss is allocated *pro rata* to the identifiable assets (excluding goodwill) on the basis of their carrying amounts. The total impairment loss recognised in entity X's consolidated financial statements is therefore C0. 96m + C0. 62m or C1. 58m.

[1] Excludes notional amount of non-controlling interest's goodwill.

Corporate assets

18. 225. 45 Corporate assets (such as head office buildings for an entity or a division of the entity, computer centres or research facilities) should be identified and the appropriate proportion allocated to individual CGUs or groups of CGUs that are being reviewed for impairment. Corporate assets are defined as "*…assets other than goodwill that contribute to the future cash flows of both the cash-generating unit under review and other cash-generating units*". [IAS 36 paras 6, 102]. The structure of an entity determines whether an asset meets this definition for a particular CGU. The key characteristics of corporate assets are that they do not generate cash inflows independently of other assets or groups of assets and their carrying amount cannot be fully attributed to the CGU that is being reviewed for impairment. [IAS 36 para 100].

18. 225. 46 A corporate asset is usually tested for impairment only if there is an indicator that it is impaired (unless it is an indefinite-lived asset such as a brand that must be tested annually-see para 18. 123. 1). If there is an impairment indicator then the corporate asset must be tested as part of a CGU as it does not generate independent cash flows and so its standalone value in use cannot be estimated. A fair value may be able to be established for corporate assets. The corporate asset cannot be written down below its recoverable amount, which is the higher of fair value less costs to sell and value in use. However, if the fair value less costs to sell is higher than the carrying amount, the corporate asset is not impaired and a test at the CGU level, will not be necessary. [IAS 36 para 22(a)].

对0.62百万的减值损失余额全部作了确认，因为它与财务报表中全额确认的净资产（包括母公司股权份额和非控制性权益股权份额）有关。这个剩余减值损失基于可辨认资产（不包括商誉）的账面价值按比例进行分配。因此，主体X合并财务报表中的减值损失总额为0.96百万+0.62百万或1.58百万。

[1] 不包括非控制性权益商誉的名义金额。

总部资产

18.225.45　应该对总部资产（如主体或主体的部门的总部办公大楼、电脑中心或研究设施）进行识别，并把适当的部分分配给需要作减值测试的单个CGU或CGU组。总部资产的定义是："……*除商誉以外的，不仅为复核中的现金产出单元的未来现金流作出贡献，同时也为其他现金产出单元的未来现金流作出贡献的资产*。"[IAS 36第6段、第102段]。主体的组织架构决定一项资产对某一CGU而言是否符合总部资产的定义。总部资产的主要特征是，它们不独立于其他资产或资产组产生现金流入，而且不能把它们的账面价值全部归属到减值复核中的CGU。[IAS 36第100段]。

18.225.46　通常，只有在有迹象表明发生了减值的情况下（除非是像品牌这种使用寿命不确定的、必须每年作减值测试的资产——见第18.123.1段），才对总部资产作减值测试。由于总部资产不产生独立的现金流，所以它独立的使用价值无法估算，如果出现了减值迹象，必须把它作为CGU的一部分进行测试。有可能找到总部资产的公允价值。总部资产不能减记到低于其可收回金额，可收回金额为公允价值减去处置费用和使用价值两者之间的较高者。但是，如果公允价值减去处置费用高于账面价值，总部资产没有发生减值，则没必要在CGU层面上作减值测试。[IAS 36第22（a）段]。

18.225.47 An entity should ensure that the carrying values of all CGUs in a group should add up to the carrying value of the group's assets in aggregate. No assets should escape the impairment review. By including allocations of corporate assets within the CGU's carrying amount, the impairment review checks whether or not the CGU's net cash flows (exclusive of any cash outflows relating to the CGU's use of those corporate assets) will recover the carrying amounts of the CGU's own assets and the allocated portion of corporate assets. Any internal charges that are payable relating to the use of the corporate assets would need to be excluded from the CGU's cash flows; otherwise the consumption of corporate assets resources would be double-counted, because the carrying amount would be increased and the value in use decreased by the same item.

18.225.48 The standard prescribes an approach to allocation of corporate assets that is similar to that for goodwill and includes the same two stage approach where corporate assets cannot be allocated on a reasonable and consistent basis to a CGU. It requires that:

- If the carrying amount of the corporate asset *can* be allocated to the CGU on a reasonable and consistent basis the entity should compare the recoverable amount of the CGU with the carrying amount of the CGU including the allocated portion of corporate assets. Any impairment loss arising is then recognised.

- If corporate assets *cannot* be allocated on a reasonable and consistent basis to the CGU, the entity should apply a two stage test, that is it:

  (a) first compares the recoverable amount of the CGU with the carrying value of its net assets (excluding any allocation of corporate assets) and recognises any impairment loss resulting from this comparison; and

  (b) then identifies the next smallest group of CGUs that contains the CGU under review and to which corporate assets can be allocated on a reasonable and consistent basis, compares the recoverable amount of that larger group of CGUs with the carrying amount of their net assets (including the allocation of corporate assets) and recognises any further impairment loss resulting from that comparison.

[IAS 36 para 102].

18.225.47　主体应该确保，集团内所有 CGU 的账面价值加总，应该等于该集团资产合计账面价值。没有任何资产可以免除减值复核。把总部资产的分配包括在 CGU 账面价值内，减值复核可以检查 CGU 净现金流（不包括与 CGU 使用总部资产有关的任何现金流出）能否回收 CGU 自有资产的账面价值和总部资产分配给它的部分。与使用总部资产有关的任何内部支出不应包括在 CGU 的现金流中，否则，对总部资产资源的消耗将构成重复计算，因为该同一总部资产项目一边增加账面价值，一边减少使用价值。

18.225.48　当不能按合理一致的基础把总部资产分配给 CGU 时，准则规定了一种总部资产分配的方法，该方法和商誉的分配方法相似，包括了相同的两个步骤。它要求：

- 如果总部资产的账面价值可以按合理一致的基础分配给 CGU，主体应该把 CGU 的可收回金额与 CGU 的账面价值（包括对总部资产的分配部分）进行比较。如果发生了减值损失，则进行确认。

- 如果不能按合理一致的基础把总部资产分配给 CGU，那么主体应该采用两步测试法，即：

  （a）首先把 CGU 的可收回金额与其净资产的账面价值（不包括总部资产的分配部分）进行比较，确认减值损失；

  （b）接下来，识别含有减值复核下 CGU 的下一个最小 CGU 组，并且可以按合理一致的基础把总部资产分配给这个 CGU 组，把较大 CGU 组的可收回金额与它们的净资产（包括总部资产的分配部分）进行比较，对比较所得出的任何减值损失作进一步的确认。

［IAS 36 第 102 段］。

18. 225. 49 The method of allocation of corporate assets to CGUs is illustrated in an appendix to the standard. It uses the respective net asset carrying amounts of the CGUs' net assets weighted according to the expected useful lives of the CGUs. This is an appropriate basis where the relative carrying amounts of the net assets are a reasonable indication of the proportion of the corporate assets that are devoted to each CGU. It is not the only basis, however, and other bases may be appropriate depending on the entity's structure. Additionally, different bases of allocation may be appropriate for different types of corporate asset. For example the corporate assets in a central personnel department might be allocated on the basis of headcount in individual CGUs rather than by reference to their net assets. This guidance may also be applicable to brands. The following example is based on the one contained in the appendix to the standard.

Example – Testing corporate assets for impairment

The corporate assets (headquarters) have a carrying value of C300, comprising the headquarters building at C200 and a computer centre at C100. The computer centre cannot be reasonably allocated, but an allocation is made of the remaining C200 between the three cash generating units, based on the carrying amounts of the three units weighted by reference to the CGU's remaining useful lives as follows:

Cash generating unit	A	B	C	Total
	C	C	C	C
Carrying amount	200	200	300	700
Useful life	10 years	20 years	20 years	
Weighting based on useful life	1	2	2	
Carrying amount after weighting	200	400	600	1,200
Pro-rata allocation of the headquarter building	16.7%	33.3%	50%	100%
	(200/1,200)	(400/1,200)	(600/1,200)	
Allocation of carrying amount of building	33	67	100	200
Carrying amount after allocation	233	267	400	900

The computer centre is not allocated.

18.225.49　准则附录中讲述了把总部资产分配给 CGU 的方法。这种方法根据 CGU 的预期使用寿命，对 CGU 净资产的账面金额分别作加权处理。当净资产的相关账面价值是将总部资产分配给每个 CGU 的合理指标时，这是一个合理基础。但是，它不是唯一的基础，根据主体的组织架构，采用其他基础可能也是合适的。此外，针对不同类型的总部资产，可能需要不同的分配基础。例如，可以根据单个 CGU 的员工人数（而不是参考净资产）分配中心人事部的总部资产。这个指南可能也适用于品牌。下面的示例以准则附录中的例子为依据举出：

示例——对总部资产作减值测试

总部资产（总部）的账面价值为 300 元，其中总部建筑物为 200 元，电脑中心为 100 元。不能对电脑中心作合理分配，但是可以把剩余的总部建筑物 200 元在三个现金产出单元之间进行分配，分配依据是参考这三个 CGU 的剩余使用寿命，对它们的账面价值作加权处理，结果如下：

现金产出单元	A	B	C	总计
	元	元	元	元
账面价值	200	200	300	700
使用寿命	10 年	20 年	20 年	
使用寿命的权重	1	2	2	
加权后的账面价值	200	400	600	1,200
按比例对总部办公楼进行分配	16.7%	33.3%	50%	100%
	(200/1,200)	(400/1,200)	(600/1,200)	
办公楼账面价值的分配	33	67	100	200
分配后的账面价值	233	267	400	900

对电脑中心不作分配。

18. 225. 50 The example in IAS 36 continues by showing how the recoverable amount is determined for each CGU and illustrates the two stage tests that must both be carried out in this case, because the computer centre cannot be allocated to individual CGUs. The two stages are: (a) the normal impairment test of the individual CGUs including the allocated corporate assets followed by (b) the impairment test of the three CGUs together, including the remaining corporate asset that can be allocated only to the three CGUs together. The following is an abbreviated example based on the one in the standard and on the facts given in the above example.

Example – The two stage test

The entity first determines the recoverable amount and carrying amount of each CGU excluding the computer centre and carries out the impairment test for each CGU (assuming that there are indications of impairment for each CGU). The recoverable amounts are determined as 250, 230 and 350 respectively for A, B and C.

Normal impairment (first stage) test				
Cash generating unit	**A**	**B**	**C**	**Total**
Directly attributable net assets	200	200	300	700
Headquarter building	33	67	100	200
Total net assets	233	267	400	900
Value in use (recoverable amount)	250	230	350	830
Impairment loss	–	37	50	87
Net assets after impairment	233	230	350	813

The impairment loss is then allocated between the assets of the CGUs and the headquarter building on a *pro rata* basis as follows:

Cash generating unit	**B**		**C**	
To headquarter building	9	(37 × 67/267)	12	(50 × 100/400)
To assets in CGU	28	(37 × 200/267)	38	(50 × 300/400)
	37		50	

Second stage test Cash generating unit	**A**	**B**	**C**	**Headquarter building**	**Computer centre**	**Total**
	C	C	C	C	C	C

18.225.50　接下来，IAS 36 给出的示例继续讲述，如何确定每个 CGU 的可收回金额，并说明在这种情况下，因为不能把电脑中心分配给单个 CGU，必须采用两步法进行测试。这两个步骤是：（a）对包含已分配总部资产的单项 CGU 作正常减值测试；然后（b）将三个 CGU 加总，包括可以但只能分配给这三个 CGU 集合的剩余总部资产，一起作减值测试。下面是根据准则中的示例所做的一个简单例子，背景资料如上例所述。

示例——两步法测试

主体首先确定不包括电脑中心在内的每个 CGU 的可收回金额和账面价值，对每个 CGU 作减值测试（假定每个 CGU 都出现了减值迹象）。A、B 和 C 的可收回金额分别确定为 250、230 和 350。

第一步：正常减值测试				
现金产出单元	**A**	**B**	**C**	**总计**
直接可归属的净资产	200	200	300	700
总部办公楼	33	67	100	200
净资产合计	233	267	400	900
使用价值（可收回金额）	250	230	350	830
减值损失	–	37	50	87
减值后的净资产	233	230	350	813

接下来，把减值损失按比例在 CGU 资产和总部办公楼之间进行分配，结果如下：

现金产出单元	**B**		**C**	
分配给总部办公楼的	9	（37×67/267）	12	（50×100/400）
分配给 CGU 资产的	28	（37×200/267）	38	（50×300/400）
	37		50	

第二步：测试现金产出单元	**A**	**B**	**C**	**总部办公楼**	**电脑中心**	**总计**
	元	元	元	元	元	元

Con.

Directly attributable net assets	200	200	300	200	100	1,000
Impairment loss arising from normal impairment test	–	(28)	(38)	(21)	–	(87)
Carrying amount after normal impairment test	200	172	262	179	100	913
						830
Impairment loss from second stage test						83

The impairment loss of C83 arising on the second stage test is allocated *pro rata* to the assets of the total unit (that is, the CGUs, the headquarter building and the computer centre). [IAS 36 para 102, 104].

[The next paragraph is 18. 235.]

Recognition of impairment losses

18. 235 If the recoverable amount of an asset or CGU is less than its carrying amount an entity should reduce the carrying amount to the recoverable amount. The reduction is an impairment loss. [IAS 36 para 59].

18. 236 For assets carried on the depreciated historical cost basis the impairment loss should be recognised in profit or loss immediately. [IAS 36 para 60]. The loss is charged in arriving at profit or loss before tax. For assets that are carried at revalued amounts an impairment loss is treated as a revaluation decrease. The loss is first set against any revaluation surplus relating to the asset in other comprehensive income to the extent of the surplus and the balance of the loss is then treated as an expense in profit or loss. [IAS 36 para 61].

Example – Capitalisation of borrowing costs and impairment

Entity A's management is constructing a machine. The construction cost is financed by bank borrowings. The machine's carrying amount before borrowing costs is C300,000 and the recoverable amount is C280,000. The entity has incurred borrowing costs of C10,000 during the construction.

Management should continue to capitalise the interest cost. After the

续表

直接可归属的净资产	200	200	300	200	100	1,000
正常减值测试产生的减值损失	–	(28)	(38)	(21)	–	(87)
正常减值测试后的账面价值	200	172	262	179	100	913 830
第二步测试产生的减值损失						83

把第二步测试中发生的减值损失 83 元按比例分配给整个单元（既三个 CGU、总部办公楼和电脑中心）的资产。[IAS 36 第 102 段、第 104 段]。

［下一段为第 18.235 段。］

减值损失的确认

18.235 如果一项资产或 CGU 的可收回金额低于其账面价值，主体应该把账面价值减记至可收回金额。减少的部分即为减值损失。[IAS 36 第 59 段]。

18.236 对于按折旧后历史成本记账的资产，应该将减值损失立即确认在损益表中。[IAS 36 第 60 段]。减值损失在计算税前损益时扣除。对于按重估金额进行记账的资产，减值损失作为重估值的减少进行处理。减值损失首先冲减其他综合收益中与该资产相关的重估盈余，不足部分作为支出计入损益表中。[IAS 36 第 61 段]。

示例——借款费用的资本化和减值

主体 A 的管理层正在建造一台机器，建造费用通过银行借款筹集。不考虑借款费用，机器的账面价值是 300,000 元，可收回金额是 280,000 元。建造期间，主体发生了 10,000 元的借款费用。

管理层应该继续把利息费用资本化。对利息费用进行资本化以后，资产

capitalisation of the interest cost, the asset's carrying amount that is, C310,000 The recoverable amount of C280,000 is compared with the full carrying amount of C310,000, generating an impairment charge of C30,000.

An entity should continue to capitalise borrowing costs even if the asset's carrying amount exceeds its recoverable amount. The carrying amount should be written down, however, to recognise impairment losses.

18.237 Where the amount of an impairment loss exceeds the carrying amount of the asset to which it relates an entity should write the asset down to zero. The balance of the impairment loss should be recognised as a provision only if it meets the criteria for recognition in another international accounting standard. [IAS 36 paras 62, 108]. The standard most likely to apply is IAS 37, 'Provisions, contingent liabilities and contingent assets'. An example might be where an asset is destroyed before the end of its expected useful life and the entity has a legal obligation to restore the site from which it operated. In addition to writing off the asset's carrying amount, the entity would have to make provision (or increase any existing provision) for the site's restoration.

18.238 When an asset has been impaired, the remaining carrying value less residual value (if any) should be amortised over the remaining useful economic life. [IAS 36 para 63]. The principle in accounting for fixed assets is that asset lives and residual values should be reviewed at least annually to ensure they are realistic and be revised if this is not the case in the light of experience or changed circumstances [IAS 16 para 51]. An impairment would warrant particular attention, because it may indicate that previously estimated asset lives are unrealistically long and need to be shortened.

18.239 When an impairment loss is recognised any related deferred tax assets or liabilities are determined in accordance with IAS 12, 'Income taxes', by comparing the carrying amount of the asset to its tax base. [IAS 36 para 64]. IAS 12 is dealt with in chapter 13.

Allocation of impairment losses to assets of cash-generating units

18.240 Where the recoverable amounts of assets can be estimated individually,

的账面价值为310,000元。可收回金额280,000元与账面原值310,000元相比，产生减值支出30,000元。

即便资产的账面价值超过其可收回金额，主体也应该继续把借款费用资本化。但是，应该对账面价值作减记处理，确认减值损失。

18.237 当减值损失的金额超过有关资产的账面金额时，主体应该把资产减记为零。减值损失的余额只有在符合另一个国际会计准则确认条件的情况下，才可以确认为一项准备。[IAS 36 第62段、第108段]。最可能适用的准则是《IAS 37——准备、或有负债和或有资产》。可能的一个示例是，一项资产在预期使用寿命到期前被拆除，主体有法律上的义务，把其运营的现场恢复到原貌。主体除了注销资产的账面价值，还要为现场的复原提取准备（或增加其现有准备）。

18.238 资产已经发生减值的，应该在剩余可使用经济寿命期间对剩余账面金额减去残余价值（如有）进行摊销。[IAS 36 第63段]。对固定资产的会计处理原则是，至少应该每年复核一次资产的使用寿命和残余价值，确保两者都是现实的，如果根据经验或变化了的情况发现它们不现实，则应进行修正。[IAS 16 第51段]。对减值应该特别注意，因为它可能表明以前所估计的资产使用寿命长得不现实，应该予以缩短。

18.239 确认了减值损失后，把资产的账面价值和它的计税基础进行比较，按《IAS 12——所得税》确认相关的递延所得税资产或负债。[IAS 36 第64段]。第十三章讲述IAS 12。

向现金产出单元的资产分配减值损失

18.240 资产的可收回金额可以单独估计的，减值损失的确认相对简单。如

the recognition of impairment losses is straightforward. Where the recoverable amounts of assets including goodwill cannot be estimated individually, they need to be estimated in aggregate for the CGUs to which they belong. [IAS 36 para 66]. The question then arises as to which assets in the CGU should be written down where the carrying value of a CGU's net assets in aggregate exceeds its recoverable amount.

18.241 IAS 36 requires that an impairment loss attributable to a CGU should be allocated to write down the assets in the following order:

- Purchased goodwill.
- The other assets in the CGU on a *pro rata* basis based on the carrying amount of each asset in the CGU.

Example – Allocation of impairment to goodwill then a brand

Entity A is testing its CGU, which contains goodwill and 2 brands, X and Y. The CGU needs to be impaired since the recoverable amount is lower than the carrying amount. Entity A believes this is mainly due to the poor performance of the brand Y and wants to allocate the impairment charge to this brand.

If a CGU is considered to be impaired, the goodwill allocated to that CGU is written off first. Entity A must first impair the goodwill before any charge is allocated to the brand Y. If the brand was a separate CGU it should have been tested separately.

18.242 However, within this allocation framework each asset should be reduced only to the highest of:

- Its fair value less costs to sell (if this can be determined).
- Its value in use (if this can be determined).
- Zero.

[IAS 36 para 105].

[The next paragraph is 18.244.]

18.244 Where the recoverable amount of an individual asset is not known (because value in use cannot be determined) no impairment loss is recognised for

果资产（包括商誉）的可收回金额不能单独估计，则需要与其所属的CGU一起进行估计。[IAS 36 第 66 段]。这时，出现的问题是，当 CGU 净资产的账面价值总额超过了其可收回金额时，应该对 CGU 中的哪些资产作减值处理。

18.241　IAS 36 要求，按下列顺序，把归属于 CGU 的减值损失进行分配，对资产进行减记处理：

- 所购买的商誉。
- 基于 CGU 中每个资产的账面价值，按比例分配给 CGU 中的其他资产。

示例——把减值分配给商誉，然后分配给品牌

主体 A 正在对它的 CGU 作减值测试，这个 CGU 中含有商誉和两个品牌：X 和 Y。由于 CGU 的可收回金额小于账面价值，需要对它进行减值处理。主体 A 认为，这主要是由于品牌 Y 绩效不佳引起来的，想把减值费用分配给这个品牌。

如果认为一个 CGU 发生了减损，则首先对分配给它的商誉进行减记处理。主体 A 必须首先对商誉作减值处理，然后再向品牌 Y 分配减值费用。如果这个品牌是一个独立的 CGU，应该对它单独作减值测试。

18.242　但是，在这个分配框架内，只能把每个资产减少到下述三项中的最高值：

- 它的公允价值减去处置费用（如果可以确定）。
- 它的使用价值（如果可以确定）。
- 零。

[IAS 36 第 105 段]。

[下一段是第 18.244 段。]

18.244　单项资产的可收回金额未知的（因为不能确定其使用价值），如果该资产所属的 CGU 没有发生减值，则不对该资产确认减值损失，即便资产的

the asset if the CGU to which it belongs is not impaired. This applies even if the fair value less costs to sell of the asset is less than its carrying amount. The standard includes an example of a machine that is part of a production line. The machine has been damaged but still operates and there is no intention of scrapping or selling it. The machine's recoverable amount cannot be determined, because it does not generate cash flows independently of the production line. The machine could only be sold for scrap value, which is below its carrying amount. There is no intention to sell or scrap the machine. If the CGU's recoverable amount (the production line) to which the machine belongs is above the carrying amount of the CGU, no impairment should be recognised in respect of the damaged machine. However, the depreciation rates or the useful life of the machine may need to be reviewed. [IAS 36 para 107(b)].

18.245 The common factor above is that the asset's value in use cannot be determined, but its fair value less costs to sell is known. In the former case, the standard overcomes this by substituting for value in use the value attributed to the asset after allocation of part of the CGU's impairment loss. In the latter case, the standard ignores the value in use of the individual asset and uses the absence of any impairment in the CGU to which the asset belongs to assume in effect that the value in use of the individual asset is equal to or greater than its carrying amount. Because the recoverable amount is the higher of fair value less costs to sell and value in use, the fact that the fair value less costs to sell is lower than the carrying amount of the asset is then not significant. [IAS 36 para 107].

18.246 In some cases, it is not easy to determine the fair value less costs to sell for an individual asset when allocating an impairment loss. For assets such as used machinery, equipment or specialised buildings, it may not be possible to estimate fair value less costs to sell using an income approach due to a lack of comparable data or cash flows directly attributable to the single asset. In order to allocate the impairment loss as appropriate, entities may consider using a depreciated replacement cost approach to determine a proxy for fair value less costs to sell. Although the use of depreciated replacement cost is prohibited when determining the ceiling for recoverable amount (see para 18.124.11.1), we would consider it acceptable to use this measure when allocating an impairment loss if this is the only possible way to calculate a proxy for fair value less costs to sell. This method

公允价值减去处置费用低于账面价值。准则列举了一个机器的例子，这台机器是生产线的一部分。机器已经损坏，但是仍能运行，并且管理层也无意把它做报废或销售处理。机器的可收回金额不能确定，因为它不能独立于生产线而产生现金流。该机器只能按报废时的价值出售，报废时的价值低于账面价值。管理层无意把机器售出或报废。如果机器所属 CGU（生产线）的可收回金额大于 CGU 的账面金额，则不应该针对这台损坏的机器确认减值。但是，可能需要复核这台机器的折旧率或使用寿命。[IAS 36 第 107（b）段]。

18.245　上例中的共同点是不能确定资产的使用价值，但是它的公允价值减去处置费用是已知的。对于前一个例子，准则用将 CGU 减值损失分配后所确定的可归属于资产的价值作为使用价值。对于后一个例子，准则不考虑单项资产的使用价值，而是用资产所属 CGU 没有发生减值，来假定实际上单项资产的使用价值等于或大于其账面价值。因为可收回金额是公允价值减去处置费用和使用价值的孰高者，公允价值减去处置费用低于资产账面价值的事实就不那么重要了。[IAS 36 第 107 段]。

18.246　在某些情况下，分配减值损失时，很难确定一个单项资产的公允价值减去处置费用的金额。比如使用过的机器、设备或者特殊的建筑物等资产，由于缺少可比数据或者直接归属于单项资产的现金流量信息，要估计他们的公允价值减去处置费用可能是不可行的。为了恰当地分配减值损失，主体可以考虑采用折旧后重置成本法确定一个金额来代替公允价值减去处置费用。尽管在确定可收回金额上限时禁止采用折旧后重置成本法（参见第 18.124.11.1 段），但在分配减值损失时，如果这是计算公允价值减去处置费用的替代值的唯一可能方法，我们认为是可接受的。如果能够以单项资产为基础采用收益法，则这一方法不应被使用。实务中，这个问题可能产生在企业合并后，因为《国际财务报告准则第 3 号——企业合并》（IFRS 3）允许采用折旧后重置成本法对一项资产的公允价值进行初始确认。

should not be used if an income approach could be performed on a single asset basis. In practice, this issue may arise after a business combinations if the fair value of an asset at initial recognition was measured using a depreciated replacement cost approach as is allowed under IFRS 3, 'Business combinations'.

18.247 The following example illustrates how an impairment loss is allocated under IAS 36.

Example – Allocation of impairment losses to CGUs

There is an indication that a group of CGUs may be impaired. Management has carried out an impairment test and estimated that the group of CGU's recoverable amount is C700. Below are further details of the group of CGUs.

Assets	Carrying amount	Fair value less costs to sell	Value in use
	C	C	C
Goodwill	300	–	–
— CGU A	500	550	500
— CGU B	90	50	50
— CGU C	250	50	150
Total for group of CGUs	1,140	650	700
Total recoverable amount for CGU	700		
Impairment to allocate	440		

An impairment of C440 has been identified and needs to be allocated. The impairment loss arising will be allocated first to goodwill and then to each of the CGUs. The carrying amount of each CGU is reduced to the higher of fair value less costs to sell, value in use and zero in accordance with IAS 36.

18.247 下面的例子说明了如何根据 IAS 36 的规定分配减值损失。

示例——将减值损失分配给多个 CGU

有迹象表明，一个 CGU 组可能发生了减值。管理层已经作了减值测试，估计这个 CGU 组的可收回金额为 700 元。下表给出了这个 CGU 组的详细情况。

资产	账面价值	公允价值减去处置费用	使用价值
	元	元	元
商誉	300	–	–
— CGU A	500	550	500
— CGU B	90	50	50
— CGU C	250	50	150
CGU 组总计	1,140	650	700
CGU 可收回金额总计	700		
需要分配的减值	440		

确认出来 440 元的减值，需要对它进行分配。产生的减值损失首先分配给商誉，然后分配给每个 CGU。根据 IAS 36，每个 CGU 的账面价值减至公允价值减去处置费用、使用价值以及零这三者中的较高者。

Assets	Carrying amount	Fair value less costs to sell	Value in use	Allocation of impairment (i)	Revised carrying amount based on allocation
Goodwill	300	–	–	–300	–
— CGU A	500	550	500	(ii)	500
— CGU B	90	50	50	–40	50
— CGU C	250	50	150	–100	150
	1,140			–440	700

(i) An impairment loss is allocated first to goodwill allocated to the CGU's and then to the cash generating units on a pro rata basis based on the carrying amount of each CGU.

(ii) No impairment allocated because fair value less costs to sell or value in use is greater than original carrying value.

As no impairment loss is allocated to CGU A, the balance of the impairment after the goodwill writedown is 140, which should be allocated pro rata to the carrying amount of CGU B (C90) and CGU C (C250). This would lead to C103 being allocated to CGU C. However this would bring the carrying amount below the recoverable amount of C150. Therefore the amount of impairment loss allocated to CGU C is capped at C100. The remaining C3 must be allocated to CGU B. This means the total allocated to CGU B is C40 (being (140 × (90 ÷ (250 + 90))) + 3).

18.247.1 In the example above the impairment charge is fully allocated. However, each asset will be reduced to the higher of its fair value less costs to sell, its value in use or zero. In some circumstances this may mean that the impairment charge is not fully allocated. if the assets do not have sufficient value to absorb the charge in its entirety. In these circumstances no liability for the unallocated impairment charge will be recognised unless the liability meets the definition of a liability under another standard. [IAS 36 para 108].

资产	账面价值	公允价值减去处置费　用	使用价值	减值的分配(i)	以分配结果为依据,修正后的账面价值
Goodwill	300	-	-	-300	-
— CGU A	500	550	500	(ii)	500
— CGU B	90	50	50	-40	50
— CGU C	250	50	150	-100	150
	1,140			-440	700

(1) 首先将减值损失分配给分至这些 CGU 的商誉，然后按照每个 CGU 的账面价值按比例分配给这些现金产出单元（CGU）。

(2) 因其公允价值减去处置费用或者使用价值大于原账面价值，不分配减值。

对商誉进行减记后，剩余的减值为 140，因为没有将减值损失分配给 CGU A，这 140 将按照 CGU B 和 CGU C 的账面价值（90 元、250 元）的比例进行分配。这样做的结果会将 103 元分配给 CGU C。但是，这会使其账面价值低于可收回金额（150 元）。因此，分配给 CGU C 的减值损失的上限为 100 元，剩余的 3 元必须分配给 CGU B。这就是说，分配给 CGU B 的总额为 40 元{140 × [90 ÷ (250 + 90)] + 3}。

18.247.1　上例中减值被全部分配完了。但是，要把每项资产减至公允价值减去处置费用、使用价值或零三者中的较高者。这可能意味着在有些情况下，如果资产价值不够完全吸收产生的费用，则减值不能被全部分配。在这种情况下，未分配完的减值不确认为负债，除非该负债符合其他国际会计准则中对负债的定义。[IAS 36 第 108 段]。

Assets or CGUs held for disposal

18.248 If a decision is made to sell an asset, a practical issue is when the expected sale proceeds should be used in the value in use calculation in place of the cash flows from continued use. This may affect the timing and measurement of any impairment losses.

18.249 IAS 36 paragraph 21 states: "If there is no reason to believe that an asset's value in use materially exceeds its fair value less costs to sell, the asset's fair value less costs to sell may be used as its recoverable amount. This will often be the case for an asset that is held for disposal. This is because the value in use of an asset held for disposal will consist mainly of the net disposal proceeds, as the future cash flows from continuing use of the asset until its disposal are likely to be negligible". This suggests that the measurement of recoverable amount would normally anticipate the disposal when it is formally brought into management's cash flow projections. Value in use (which includes the estimated cash flows from the asset's ultimate disposal) would then be similar to fair value less costs to sell; hence, the future cash flows of the CGU to which the asset may have formerly belonged are no longer taken into account.

18.250 Similarly, when a decision is made to sell or terminate a business, the amounts expected to be recoverable from the sale or closure of the business would provide the basis for measuring the recoverable amount of its assets and goodwill. In the case of a business for sale, if the carrying values of the net assets and capitalised goodwill exceed in aggregate their recoverable amount (which would be based on the expected sale proceeds), the assets are impaired.

18.251 Once an asset or CGU qualifies as a non current asset (or disposal group) held-for-sale in accordance with IFRS 5, 'Non-current assets held-for-sale and discontinued operations', it is in fact excluded from the scope of IAS 36. An asset or CGU qualifies as held-for-sale under IFRS 5 if its carrying amount will be recovered principally through a sale transaction, rather than through continued use. [IFRS 5 para 6]. This applies only to assets or CGUs that are to be sold and not to assets or CGUs that are to be abandoned or liquidated. This is because in the latter situation the carrying amount will be recovered through continued use by the entity

持有待处置资产或现金产出单元

18.248　如果作出一项出售资产的决定，接下来的一个实际问题是，在使用价值的计算中，应该何时用预期的处置收入代替持续使用的现金流。这可能影响减值损失的计量及时点。

18.249　IAS 36 第 21 段规定："如果没有理由相信资产的使用价值远远超过其公允价值减去处置费用，则资产的公允价值减去处置费用可视为其可收回金额。对于持有待处置的资产而言，往往属于这种情况。这是因为，资产的持续使用直至处置为止所产生的未来现金流量可能很少，持有待处置资产的使用价值主要是处置净收入"这表明，当一项处置被正式纳入管理层的现金流预测时，它也就包含在可收回金额的计量中了。从而使用价值（包括预计的资产最终处置的现金流）将和公允价值减去处置费用相似；因此，不再考虑资产以前所属 CGU 的未来现金流。

18.250　类似地，作出一项出售或终止某业务的决定时，计量其资产和商誉可收回金额的基础应该是预计出售或关闭这项业务将收回的金额。在出售业务的情况下，如果其净资产及资本化的商誉的账面价值合计超过了它们的可收回金额（以预期的出售所得为基础），资产就发生了减值。

18.251　一旦一项资产或 CGU 符合 IFRS 5——持有待售的非流动资产和终止经营中持有待售的非流动资产（或处置组）的条件，它实际上就不包括在 IAS 36 的范围内了。如果一项资产或 CGU 的账面价值将主要通过出售而不是持续使用得以收回，它就符合 IFRS 5 所规定的持有待售。[IFRS 5 第 6 段]。这个规定仅适用于即将出售的资产或 CGU，而不适用于将被弃置或清算的资产或 CGU。这是因为在后一种情况中，账面价值将通过主体持续使用直至弃置日或关闭日而得以收回的。

up to the date of abandonment or closure.

18. 252 To qualify as held-for-sale under IFRS 5 an asset or CGU (group of assets) must meet strict conditions. These are:

- The asset or CGU is available for immediate sale in its present condition, subject only to terms that are usual and customary for sales of such assets or CGUs and the sale must be highly probable.
- For a sale to be highly probable, management must be committed to a plan to sell the asset or CGU and an active programme to locate a buyer and complete the plan must have been initiated. The asset or CGU must be actively marketed at a price that is reasonable in relation to its current fair value. The completion of the sale must be expected within one year from the date of classification as held-for-sale, except in certain limited circumstances and it must be unlikely that significant changes will be made to the plan or that it will be withdrawn.

[IFRS 5 paras 7, 8].

18. 253 If these conditions are satisfied, the asset or CGU is measured at the lower of carrying amount and fair value less costs to sell at the date of classification as held-for-sale. IFRS 5 also states that an asset or CGU should be "measured in accordance with applicable IFRSs" immediately before the initial classification as held-for-sale.

18. 254 An impairment test is required under IAS 36 for non-current assets and disposal groups before classification as 'held-for-sale', as a plan to dispose of an asset or CGU is an internal indicator of impairment. The value in use and fair value less costs to sell of an asset or CGU that is expected to be sold converge to the same number, as the value will be realised from sale and the cash flows up to the point of sale will be much less significant. The convergence of value in use and fair value less costs to sell of an asset or CGU is progressive. The values gradually move closer until IFRS 5's criteria are met. The measurement principles of IFRS 5 are discussed in more detail in chapter 26.

18. 255 The interaction between IAS 36 measurement requirements and IFRS 5 presentation requirements is illustrated in the following example.

18.252　要符合 IFRS 5 所规定的持有待售的标准，一项资产或 CGU（资产组）必须符合严格的条件，这些条件是：

- 资产或 CGU 在其当前状况下，仅根据出售此类资产或 CGU 的通常和惯用条款，即可以立即出售，而且出售必须极可能发生。

- 所谓极可能出售，管理层必须有承诺出售资产或 CGU 的计划，并且已积极地展开寻找买方和完成该计划的活动。必须以跟该资产或 CGU 当前公允价值相比合理的价格积极寻求在市场上销售。自划归为持有待售之日起，该项出售必须预计在一年内完成（某些特殊情况除外），同时，不大可能对出售计划作出重大修改或予以撤销。

[IFRS 5 第 7 段、第 8 段]。

18.253　如果满足了这些条件，资产或 CGU 自划归为持有待售之日起，按照其账面价值和公允价值减去处置费用孰低计量。IFRS 5 也规定，资产或 CGU 在初始划归到持有待售之前，应“按照适用的国际财务报告准则的规定进行计量”。

18.254　一项处置资产或 CGU 的计划是减值的内部迹象，因此 IAS 36 要求在非流动资产或处置组被划归为“持有待售”之前，要先作减值测试。预期将被出售的资产或 CGU，其使用价值和公允价值减去处置费用会趋于同一个数额，因为其价值将通过出售得以实现，而出售之前的现金流则将不那么重要。资产或 CGU 的使用价值和公允价值减去处置费用将逐渐趋同。这两个数值逐渐越来越接近，直至符合 IFRS 5 的标准。IFRS 5 的计量原则在第 26 章进行更为详细的讨论。

18.255　IAS 36 的计量要求与 IFRS 5 的列报要求的相互作用将通过下面的示例予以说明。

Example – Impairment where an operation is held-for-sale

An entity reports quarterly. In the third quarter an impairment is identified in the assets of an operation that the entity is considering selling.

The impairment has to be charged in arriving at profit before tax in the third quarter under IAS 36 (because the operation does not classify as held-for-sale and, therefore, will not qualify as a discontinued operation under IFRS 5). However, if the operation is being actively marketed by the end of the fourth quarter (that is, by the end of the full year) and the operation qualifies as a discontinued operation under IFRS 5, could the impairment charge be shown in the full year's financial statements below the tax line as part of the results of the discontinued operation?

The above requirements of IFRS 5 need to be considered in responding to the question and can be applied as follows.

1 The operation does not qualify as 'held-for-sale' or as a discontinued operation in the third quarter. However, there is an impairment indicator (proposed sale in the near future) and the operation must, therefore, be reviewed for impairment. The recoverable amount is the higher of value in use and fair value less costs to sell and this is compared with the carrying amount and an impairment loss is recognised if necessary. It is possible that the recoverable amount may be fair value less costs to sell as the disposal is contemplated but this is not a foregone conclusion (the value in use may be higher). The impairment loss if any is recognised in arriving at profit before tax under one of the format headings set out in IAS 1.

2 At the end of the year the operation is being actively marketed. Assuming it meets all necessary conditions the operation is classified in the closing balance sheet as a disposal group held-for-sale. The disposal group is measured at the lower of carrying amount and fair value less costs to sell. A further impairment loss may or may not arise at this stage.

3 The impairment losses incurred in the third and fourth quarters are presented in the income statement for the full year as part of the results of discontinued operations.

[IFRS 5 para 33].

示例——持有待售的运营中的减值

主体每季度出一次报告。第三季度，发现其正考虑要出售的一项运营中，有项资产发生了减值。

根据 IAS 36，减值费用必须计入第三季度的税前利润（因为该运营未被划归为持有待售，从而不符合 IFRS 5 中终止经营的标准）。然而，如果在第四季度末（即全年的年末），主体为该运营积极地寻找着市场，该运营符合 IFRS 5 中终止经营的标准，那么，在整年度的财务报表中，减值费用能否列报在税项栏的下面，体现为终止经营结果的一部分呢?

回答这个问题时需要考虑 IFRS 5 的上述要求，可以这样考虑：

1. 在第三季度，该运营不符合“持有待售”或终止经营的条件。但是存在减值迹象（提议在不久的将来出售），因此必须对该运营是否减值进行复核。可收回金额是使用价值与公允价值减去处置费用两者中的较高者，可收回金额与账面价值进行比较以确认减值损失（如果必要）。因为正计划处置，可收回金额有可能就是公允价值减去处置费用，但这也并非是必然结果（使用价值有可能更高）。如果出现任何减值损失，按 IAS 1 中的一个格式标题，将确认在税前利润中。

2. 年底，主体在市场上积极地推销着该项运营。假设该运营符合所有必要的条件，在年末的资产负债表中，该运营被分类为持有待售的处置组。按账面价值和公允价值减去处置费用两者孰低对处置组进行计量。在这一步，可能出现更多的减值损失，也可能不会出现。

3. 第三季度和第四季度发生的减值损失在全年的利润表中体现为终止经营结果的一部分。

[IFRS 5 第 33 段]。

18.256 Provisions under IAS 37 do not include amounts written off assets. The expression that is sometimes used 'provision for loss on disposal of fixed assets' is not a provision in the sense of IAS 37 and any such loss should not be shown as a provision or liability. Paragraph 79 of IAS 37 refers to the need for asset values to be reviewed for impairment before any provisions are recognised.

Asset subject to sale and finance leaseback

18.256.1 Where there is an impairment test on assets that have been subject to a sale and finance leaseback where a gain arose on the transaction, there is a policy choice available to the entity. One treatment would be to allow a reduction in the deferred gain by the value of the impairment loss. Alternatively the entity may choose to net the deferred gain against the asset's carrying value. This net amount reflects the CGU's carrying amount, which may be less than the recoverable amount and, therefore, may result in no impairment charge. It is, however, considered inappropriate to recognise an impairment loss where the entity has recognised a deferred gain on the sale and leaseback. This can be illustrated with the following example:

Example – Asset subject to sale and finance leaseback is impaired

Entity A acquired a vessel in 20X0 for C100m; on31 December 20X6 the vessel was the subject of a sale and finance leaseback transaction. Entity A received C200m for the asset when the carrying amount was C80m. The values, therefore, at 31 December 20X6 on entity A's balance sheet are:

	Cm
Vessel	200
Deferred gain	120(200 – 80)
Finance lease liability	200

At 31 December 20X8, before the impairment test the carrying amount of the above are:

18.256　IAS 37 中所称的准备不包括减记的资产金额。有时会出现“固定资产处置损失准备”这样的表述，这不是 IAS 37 意义上的准备，任何此类损失不应该体现为一项准备或负债。IAS 37 第 79 段提到，在确认任何准备之前，需要先复核资产的价值，看其是否发生了减值。

售后融资租回的资产

18.256.1　在对售后融资租回（且该交易产生收益）的资产进行减值测试时，主体可以选择其会计政策。一种处理方法是允许将减值损失的金额从递延收益中扣除。主体可以选择的另一种处理方法是将递延收益抵减资产的账面价值。抵减后的净值反映了 CGU 的账面价值，而这个账面价值可能小于其可收回金额，从而可能不会产生减值费用。然而，在主体已经就售后租回确认了一项递延收益的情况下，再确认减值损失是不恰当的。这点可以通过下面的示例来进行说明。

示例——售后融资租回的资产发生了减值

20X0 年，主体 A 以 100 百万元购买了一艘轮船，20X6 年 12 月 31 日，将这艘船进行了售后融资租回。主体 A 收到 200 百万元，而资产的账面价值为 80 百万元。因此，20X6 年 12 月 31 日，主体 A 资产负债表上的价值如下：

	百万元
轮船	200
递延收益	120（200 - 80）
融资租赁负债	200

20X8 年 12 月 31 日，减值测试前，上述各项的账面价值如下：

	Cm
Vessel	183
Deferred gain	100
Finance lease liability	160

The higher of value in use and fair value less cost to sell of the vessel at 31 December 20X8 is C150m. There are two options available to entity A:

Treatment 1:

Entity A should reduce the value of the vessel by C33m to C150m and should offset this with a reduction in the deferred gain of C33m. This gives a net impact of nil in the income statement. The asset write-down should still be described as an impairment.

Treatment 2:

Alternatively no impairment charge should be recognised because the deferred gain could be netted off against the carrying amount of the asset. The net amount reflects the carrying amount of the CGU C83m (C183m - C100m), which is less than its recoverable amount of C150m.

[The next paragraph is 18. 263.]

Subsidiaries that are part of larger CGUs

18. 263 IAS 36 is principally targeted at identifying and recognising impairment losses from a group perspective. Thus the whole group as a reporting entity is divided into separate CGUs for the purpose of impairment reviews, such that the CGUs in aggregate cover the whole group and are non-overlapping.

18. 264 Individual subsidiaries may also be separate reporting entities, but the allocation of a group's activities between separate companies within a group does not necessarily coincide with the way the group's CGUs are defined.

18. 265 Issues arise where a subsidiary's activities form part of a larger CGU in

	百万元
轮船	183
递延收益	100
融资租赁负债	160

20X8 年 12 月 31 日，使用价值和公允价值减去处置费用两者中的较高者为 150 百万元。主体 A 有两种选择：

处理方法 1：

主体 A 应该把轮船的价值减少 33 百万元，减至 150 百万元，并将递延收益减少 33 百万元，以与之相抵销。这样，在利润表中的净影响为零。不过，此项资产减记仍然应该描述为一项减值。

处理方法 2：

另一种方法下，由于可以用递延收益去抵减资产的账面价值，从而没有需要确认的减值费用。抵减后的净值反映了 CGU 的账面价值为 83 百万元（183 - 100），低于 150 百万元的可收回金额。

[下一段是第 18.263 段。]

子公司是一个较大的现金产出单元的一部分

18.263　IAS 36 主要针对的是，从集团的角度识别并确认减值损失。这样，整个集团作为一个报告主体，为了减值复核之目的分成了一个个单独的 CGU，这样，汇总的 CGU 涵盖了整个集团，而且也不出现重叠。

18.264　单个子公司也可以是单独的报告主体，但是，集团的活动在集团内不同公司之间的分配不必和集团 CGU 的定义方式一样。

18.265　当一家子公司的活动构成集团中一个较大 CGU 的一部分时，会出现

the group. In particular, the cash flows of an individual subsidiary may appear not to support the carrying values of its fixed assets, yet from a group perspective there is no impairment because the subsidiary is part of a profitable CGU.

18.266 Such situations may be numerous where wholly-owned subsidiaries are concerned and can be illustrated by reference to the examples in the standard that discuss how CGUs are identified. For example, a low-return supporting route operated by a transport group may reside in a separate subsidiary entity, yet be part of a CGU that includes a profitable trunk route that is fed by the supporting route. Another example is where a factory owned by a subsidiary entity is operating with surplus capacity, but the CGU comprises this and a number of other sites (owned by other subsidiary entities) at which the product can be made — overall there is no impairment at the CGU level because demand is such that there is not enough surplus capacity to close any one site.

18.267 Transfer pricing also creates difficulties. A subsidiary may be only breaking even because it sells its output to a fellow subsidiary at cost, yet they are part of the same CGU from a group perspective. Where subsidiaries are separate CGUs, one subsidiary may be unprofitable, because it sells output to a fellow subsidiary at below-market prices. Conversely, the transferee subsidiary might be profitable, because it buys goods and services from its fellow subsidiary at below-market prices. The standard indicates (from a group's perspective) that the cash inflows of the transferor CGU and the cash outflows of the transferee CGU that are used in the value in use calculations should be adjusted to reflect market prices rather than internal transfer prices. [IAS 36 para 70].

18.268 If the subsidiary earns an economic return on its assets after adjusting for market prices, it may be possible to argue that no impairment is required. This would be on the basis that the subsidiary could obtain a market rate of return on its investment and therefore the recoverable amount (being the higher of value in use and fair value less costs to sell) is higher than the actual cash flows being generated. In such a situation, disclosure would be required to explain the basis upon which the recoverable amount was determined. See further from paragraph 18.286. Where a subsidiary is not earning an economic return on its assets even after adjusting to market prices in terms of its separate cash flows, the subsidiary should be booking an impairment on those assets in its entity financial statements.

问题。尤其是单个子公司的现金流看上去可能无法支持其固定资产的账面价值，而从集团的角度来看，因为该子公司是一个盈利的 CGU 的一部分，所以没有发生减值。

18.266 如果想到全资子公司，会发现可能有许多这样的情况，可以参考准则中有关如何识别 CGU 的示例来说明。例如，某运输集团中，一家单独的子公司可能在运营一条低回报的辅助路线，但是它是一个盈利干线的 CGU 的一部分，该盈利干线由辅助路线供应。另一个示例是，一个子公司拥有的一家工厂产能过剩，但是这家工厂和几个位于其他地点的工厂（为其他子公司所拥有）共同组成一个 CGU，这样才能生产出产品——从总体上说，因为需求如此旺盛，没有足够的过剩生产能力来关闭任何一个工厂，所以在 CGU 层面没有发生减值。

18.267 转移价格也会制造难题。一家子公司因为以成本价把产品销售给同一个集团下的另一家子公司，从而只能做到收支平衡；但是从集团的角度看，它们是同一个 CGU 的组成部分。当子公司是独立 CGU 的情况下，一家子公司因为其以低于市场的价格把产品销售给同一集团下的另一家子公司，从而可能没有盈利。相反地，转入方的子公司由于以低于市场的价格从同集团的子公司中购买了产品与服务，从而可能盈利。该准则指出（从集团的角度），在使用价值的计算中，应当对所使用的转出方 CGU 的现金流入和转入方 CGU 的现金流出进行调整，以反映市场价格而不是内部转移价格。[IAS 36 第 70 段]。

18.268 调整至市场价格后，如果子公司从其资产中获得经济回报，则可能可以据此争论无需减值。其依据的基础是子公司的投资能够获得市场回报率，因此可收回金额（使用价值与公允价值减去处置费用中孰高者）高于实际产生的现金流量。这种情况下，需要进行披露来解释确定可收回金额的基础。参见自第 18.286 段起的进一步讨论。如果在将其单独的现金流按照市场价格调整之后，子公司仍然不能从其资产中获得经济回报的，子公司应该在其主体财务报表上对这些资产确认减值。

Reversals of impairment losses

General rules

18.269 IAS 36 requires that an entity should assess at each reporting date whether there is any indication that an impairment loss recognised in a previous period for an asset other than goodwill either no longer exists or has decreased. If there is any such indication the entity should estimate the recoverable amount. This applies both to individual assets other than goodwill and to CGUs. [IAS 36 paras 109, 110].

18.270 Indicators that impairment losses may have reversed are mainly the opposite of those that gave rise to the impairment loss in the first place (see para 18.55). [IAS 36 para 112]. However, the indicators of reversal listed in the standard do not include the reverse of one of the external and one of the internal impairment indicators. These are that first the carrying amount of the entity's net assets are in excess of its market capitalisation; and secondly, that there is evidence of obsolescence or physical damage of an asset. However, it may be that each of these is effectively covered by the other indicators, for example the obsolescence indicator would be covered by the indicator of an asset's market value having increased significantly in the period. Similarly, it would be expected that an entity's market capitalisation would increase if "*significant changes with a favourable effect on the entity have taken place during the period*". Companies should, therefore, consider whether there have been favourable events or changes in circumstances since the impairment loss was recognised that would indicate that the impairment loss no longer exists or may have decreased. If there are indicators, the recoverable amount of the relevant assets or CGUs should be estimated again. Such changes include situations where the recoverable amount increases as a result of further capital investment to improve an asset's performance or a restructuring, the benefits of which had been excluded from the original measurement of value in use. [IAS 36 para 111]. (See paras 18.197 and 18.205.)

18.271 For tangible and intangible fixed assets (other than goodwill) and for

减值损失的转回

总则

18.269　IAS 36 要求，主体应该在每个报告日评估是否有迹象表明以前期间确认的除商誉以外的资产减值损失不再存在或已减少。如果存在这种迹象，主体应该估计可收回金额。这对 CGU 和除商誉外的单项资产都适用。［IAS 36 第 109 段、第 110 段］。

18.270　减值损失可能已转回的迹象和一开始导致产生减值损失的迹象大部分是相反的（参见第 18.55 段）。［IAS 36 第 112 段］。但是，IAS 36 中所列出的转回迹象中，不包括一项外部减值迹象和一项内部减值迹象的转回。其中第一项是主体净资产的账面金额超过了市场资本化金额；第二项是有证据表明资产已经陈旧过时或者实体损坏。不过，这两项中的每一项都有可能实际上已被包含在其他迹象中，例如，陈旧过时的迹象可能包含在资产的市价在当期大幅上涨的迹象中。类似地，如果“*当期发生了对主体有利的重大变化*”，则预期的主体的市场资本化金额将提高。因此公司在确认了减值损失之后，应该考虑周围环境是否发生了有利的事项或变化，表明减值损失不再存在或者可能已减少。如果有这些迹象，应该重新评估有关资产或 CGU 的可收回金额。这样的变化包括为了提高资产绩效而进一步增加资本投资或进行重组，使得可收回金额增加，而起初对使用价值的计量中未包括这些提高资产绩效或重组所产生的利益。［IAS 36 第 111 段］。（见第 18.197 段和第 18.205 段。）

18.271　对于有形资产、无形资产（除商誉外）、对子公司、联营企业、合

investments in subsidiaries, associates and joint ventures, the reversal of an impairment loss should be recognised if, and only if, there has been a change in the estimates used to determine the asset's recoverable amount since the last impairment test was carried out. A reversal of an impairment loss recognises an increase in the estimated service potential of an asset, either from use or sale since the last impairment test. Entities are required to identify the change in the estimates that cause the increase in estimated service potential. Changes may result from:

- A change in the basis for recoverable amount that is whether it is based on fair value less costs to sell or value in use.
- If recoverable amount was based on value in use: a change in the amount or timing of estimated future cash flows or in the discount rate.
- If recoverable amount was based on fair value less costs to sell: a change in the estimate of the fair value less costs to sell.

[IAS 36 paras 114, 115].

Impairment losses relating to goodwill may not be reversed (see para 18.281 below).

Example – Reversal of impairment of fixed assets

Entity O is a South American entity, producing orange juice, most of which is sold to overseas customers. Three years ago, entity O recognised an impairment loss on fixed assets based on value in use. Entity O's functional currency is the local currency. At that time, management estimated that prices of its products would fall over the following four years.

During the current year, the orange crop in the northern hemisphere was mostly destroyed by a very severe winter. Orange juice prices rose significantly as a result. The entity is also entering into long-term agreements with overseas customers, under which higher volumes will be exported during the subsequent years.

The combinations of prices and volumes used as references for the cash flow estimates in the value in use calculation have changed. This is an indicator that the previously recognised impairment may have reversed. [IAS 36 para 111(b)].

营企业的投资，当且仅当用于确定资产可收回金额的估计在上次进行减值测试后发生了变化的情况下，才应转回减值损失。减值损失的转回，体现了一项资产的预计服务潜能（通过使用或者销售）自上次减值测试之后的增加。主体需要认定在其估算中、引起预计服务潜能增加的变化。产生这些变化的原因可能有：

- 可收回金额的基础发生变化，即是以公允价值减去处置费用为基础、还是以使用价值为基础。
- 如果可收回金额的确定是以使用价值为基础的：预计未来现金流的金额或时间或折现率发生了变化。
- 如果可收回金额的确定是以公允价值减去处置费用为基础的：公允价值减去处置费用的估计发生了变化。

［IAS 36 第 114 段、第 115 段］。

与商誉有关的减值损失不能转回（参见下面的第 18. 281 段）。

示例——固定资产减值的转回

主体 O 是一家南美主体，生产橙汁，其中大部分橙汁销售给海外客户。三年前，主体 O 以使用价值为基础，确认了固定资产减值损失。主体 O 的功能货币是当地货币。当时，管理层预计其产品价格在接下来的四年中将下降。

今年，北半球由于严冬，橙子的大部分收成被毁。结果，橙汁的价格大幅上扬。主体也和海外客户签订了长期协议，根据这个协议，今后几年橙汁的出口量将增加。

在使用价值的计算中，现金流预测要同时参考价格与销售量，现在他们已经发生了变化。这就是一个以前所确认的减值损失可能已经转回的迹象。［IAS 36 第 111（b）段］。

Management should update its estimates and determine the assets' revised recoverable amounts. [IAS 36 para 114, 115]. Reversals of previously recognised impairment losses are limited to the carrying amount which would have been determined at the current date, had the impairment not been recognised. [IAS 36 para 117].

18.272 The standard explains that increases in value in use should not be recognised as reversals of impairment losses if they arise simply from the passage of time, resulting from the unwinding of the discount rate that was applied to arrive at the present value of expected future cash flows. This is so even if the effect of the discount unwinding is to increase the recoverable amount of the asset above its carrying amount. The reason why the unwinding of the discount does not give rise to the reversal of an impairment loss is that, while the value in use admittedly increases, the underlying reasons for the original impairment have not been removed -the service potential of the asset has not increased. [IAS 36 para 116]. The effect is illustrated in the following example:

Example – Subsequent depreciation is not an indication that an impairment has reversed

An asset cost C100 on 1 January 20X0. Its expected useful life is 5 years; depreciation is on a straight-line basis. An impairment review is carried out as at 31 December 20X0 when the carrying value is C80. The projected cash flows are as follows:

	20X1	20X2	20X3	20X4
Cash flows (nominal total C82; present value C 64)	13	22	23	24

Using a discount rate of 10%, the present value of the cash flows (value in use) at 31 December 20X0 is C64. Thus an impairment loss of C16 is recognised.

The impaired carrying value of C64 is then depreciated on a straight-line basis over the remaining 4 years of its expected useful life. Assuming the cash flows materialise as projected in the impairment calculation, the carrying value

管理层应该更新其估计，确定修订后的资产可回收金额［IAS 36 第 114 段、第 115 段］。对以前所确认减值损失的转回，不应超过该资产如果没有确认减值、在当前应有的账面价值。［IAS 36 第 117 段］。

18.272　准则解释说，如果使用价值的增加仅仅是随着时间的推移，在计算预计未来现金流量现值时所采用的折现率的展开而导致的，则这样的增加不确认减值损失转回。即使折现的展开导致资产的可收回金额增加至超出其账面价值，也是如此。减值损失不因为折现的展开而转回的原因在于，尽管使用价值的确增加了，但是当初产生减值的原因并没有消除——资产的服务潜能并没有增加。［IAS 36 第 116 段］。
下面的示例说明了其影响：

示例——后续折旧不是减值损失已经转回的迹象

20X0 年 1 月 1 日,一项资产的成本为 100 元。预期使用寿命是 5 年,以直线法计提折旧。20X0 年 12 月 31 日,对资产进行减值复核,其账面金额为 80 元。预计的现金流量如下：

	20X1	20X2	20X3	20X4
现金流（名义合计金额为 82 元;现值为 64 元）	13	22	23	24

采用 10% 的折现率，20X0 年 12 月 31 日，现金流的现值（使用价值）为 64 元。因此，确认了 16 元的减值损失。

计提减值之后的账面价值 64 元，按照直线法，在该资产预计剩余使用寿命 4 年中计提折旧。假设现金流与减值计算中所预计的一样，每年年底，账面价值和使用价值（剩余现金流按 10% 的折现率折现后的现值）

and value in use (present value of remaining cash flows discounted at 10%) at each year end are as follows:

	20X0	20X1	20X2	20X3	20X4
Carrying value	64	48	32	16	–
Value in use	64	57	41	22	–

It can be seen that the value in use at 31 December 20X1, 20X2 and 20X3 exceeds the carrying amount. The reason is the unwinding of the discount (as the future cash flows get nearer, their present value increases). But there is no reversal of the original impairment loss.

18.273 Where a reversal of an impairment loss is recognised because economic conditions have changed, IAS 36 does not suggest that any increase in value in use that is due to 'the passage of time' should be estimated as a separate component and excluded from the reversal. In most practical situations this would be quite unrealistic.

18.274 The amount of any reversal that can be recognised is restricted to increasing the carrying value of the relevant assets to the carrying value that would have been recognised had the original impairment not occurred (that is, after taking account of normal depreciation that would have been charged had no impairment occurred). [IAS 36 para 117]. In respect of depreciable assets, any reversals of impairment losses will not be as large as the original impairment loss. Any increase above the carrying amount (net of depreciation) that would have applied had no impairment charge been recognised originally is treated as a revaluation (see para 18.278). [IAS 36 para 118].

18.275 If there is an indication that a previously recognised impairment loss may have decreased or ceased to exist, this may also indicate that the useful life, depreciation method or the residual value of the asset may need to be reviewed and adjusted in accordance with the relevant international standard (IAS 16 or IAS 38). This may be necessary even if no impairment loss is reversed for the asset. [IAS 36 para 113].

18.276 To illustrate accounting for reversals see example above in paragraph 18.197.

如下：

	20X0	20X1	20X2	20X3	20X4
账面价值	64	48	32	16	–
使用价值	64	57	41	22	–

可以看到，20X1 年 12 月 31 日、20X2 年 12 月 31 日、20X3 年 12 月 31 日，使用价值都超过了账面价值。原因在于折现的展开（随着未来现金流越来越接近，它们的现值增加）。但是，原始减值损失并没有转回。

18.273 由于经济条件发生了变化而转回减值损失时，IAS 36 并未指出在使用价值的增加中，应当将由于“时间的推移”而导致的增加部分作为一项单独因素进行估计，从转回金额中扣除。在大部分实务中，这将非常不现实。

18.274 减值损失可以转回的金额，不得超过将相关资产的账面价值增加至和当初如果没有发生减值而应该确认的账面价值一样的金额（也就是说，考虑了如果没有发生减值、需要计提的正常折旧之后）。[IAS 36 第 117 段]。对于可折旧资产，减值损失的转回金额不能和原减值损失的金额一样多。超过如果当初不确认减值而应有的账面价值（扣除折旧）的部分，作为重估处理（参见第 18.278 段）。[IAS 36 第 118 段]。

18.275 如果有迹象表明，以前所确认的减值损失可能已减少或不再存在的，这可能也表明资产的使用寿命、折旧方法或残值需要按照相关国际准则（IAS 16或 IAS 38）进行复核和调整。即使资产的减值损失没有转回，可能也有必要这么做。[IAS 36 第 113 段]。

18.276 转回的会计处理，参见上文第 18.197 段中的示例。

18.277 Accounting for the reversal of an impairment loss should be consistent with the treatment adopted when the impairment was recognised. Where the asset is held at historical cost, the reversal should be recognised in the current year's income statement, since the original loss would have been charged in profit or loss. [IAS 36 para 119].

18.278 For a revalued asset, the reversal of an impairment loss should be recognised in profit or loss to the extent that the original impairment loss (adjusted for subsequent depreciation) was recognised in profit or loss. Any remaining balance of the reversal of an impairment loss should be recognised in other comprehensive income, since part of the original impairment loss would have been charged there. [IAS 36 para 120]. The standard does not specifically say that the reversal credited to profit or loss should not exceed the original impairment loss charged there *as adjusted by depreciation.* However, the increased carrying amount of the asset cannot exceed the carrying amount as it would have been without the original impairment as adjusted for the depreciation that would have applied. [IAS 36 para 117]. It makes sense for this limitation to be applied to the amount of the reversal credited to profit or loss rather than to the amount credited to other comprehensive income, because the depreciation would have been charged to profit or loss.

18.279 The reversal calculations for revalued assets can be rather complex, as illustrated in the following example.

Example – Recognition and reversal of impairment loss on revalued asset

At 31 December 20X1 an asset was purchased for C100,000. Its expected useful economic life is 20 years. Three years later it was revalued to C136,000.

At 31 December 20X6 the asset was reviewed for impairment and written down to its recoverable amount of C65,000.

The following table shows the movements in the asset's book value on a depreciated historical cost basis and as actually recognised in the financial statements.

18.277　减值损失转回的会计处理方法应该和当初确认减值损失的方法一致。若资产是以历史成本计量的，由于原来的减值损失应该是计入损益的，所以减值损失的转回也应该确认在当年的利润表中。[IAS 36 第 119 段]。

18.278　对于经过重估的资产，在损益表中转回的减值损失，应该以当初在损益表中确认的减值损失（经过后续折旧的调整）为限。剩余的减值损失转回，应该计入其他综合收益，因为原先一部分减值损失应该是记在其他综合收益中的。[IAS 36 第 120 段]。该准则并没有明确规定贷记损益表的转回金额不得超过原记在损益表中的减值损失（折旧调整后）。但是资产账面价值的增加额不得超过如果原来没有减值、经过折旧调整后的账面价值。[IAS 36 第 117 段]。将这个限制适用于贷记损益表的转回金额，而不是贷记其他综合收益的转回金额是合理的，因为折旧费用是计入损益表的。

18.279　重估资产的转回计算可能会比较复杂，通过下面的例子予以说明。

示例——重估资产减值损失的确认和转回

20X1 年 12 月 31 日，一项资产以 100,000 元的价格购得。资产的预期经济使用寿命为 20 年。三年后经重估为 136,000 元。

20X6 年 12 月 31 日，对资产作了减值复核后，将其减记至可收回金额 65,000 元。

下表给出了该资产的账面价值按照折旧后的历史成本，和实际确认在财务报表中的变动情况。

	Depreciated historical cost	Revalued carrying value
	C000	C000
31 December 20X1 – cost	100	100
Depreciation (3 years)	(15)	(15)
Revaluation	–	51
31 December 20X4	85	136
Depreciation (2 years)	(10)	(16)
31 December 20X6	75	120
Impairment loss	(10)	(55)
31 December 20X6 after impairment loss	65	65

The impairment loss of C55,000 at 31 December 20X6 is charged to other comprehensive income until the carrying amount reaches depreciated historical cost and thereafter in profit or loss, as follows:

Other comprehensive income	45
Income statement	10
Impairment loss	55

The standard states that the impairment loss is charged to other comprehensive income to the extent of the revaluation surplus held in other comprehensive income that relates to the asset. In the above example there was a credit balance of C51,000 in 20X4. It has been assumed that, as permitted by paragraph 41 of IAS 16, a transfer has been made each year of the depreciation relating to the revalued amount from the revaluation surplus to retained earnings. This amount would be C6,000 and would reduce the available surplus in other comprehensive income from C51,000 to C45,000.

At 31 December 20X8 economic conditions have improved and the asset's recoverable amount is estimated to be C90,000.

	折旧后的历史成本 千元	重估后的账面价值 千元
20X1 年 12 月 31 日 – 成本	100	100
折旧(3 年)	(15)	(15)
重估	–	51
20X4 年 12 月 31 日	85	136
折旧(2 年)	(10)	(16)
20X6 年 12 月 31 日	75	120
减值损失	(10)	(55)
20X6 年 12 月 31 日计提减值损失后的金额	65	65

20X6 年 12 月 31 日，55,000 元的减值损失计入其他综合收益，直至账面价值调整至折旧后的历史成本，因此，损益表中的情况如下：

其他综合收益	45
利润表	10
减值损失	55

准则规定，计入其他综合收益的减值损失，以计入其他综合收益的该资产的重估盈余为限。上例中，20X4 年有贷方余额 51,000 元。假设按国际会计准则第 16 号第 41 段所允许的那样，每年已经从重估盈余中将与重估金额有关的折旧转到了留存收益。金额为 6,000 元，则从其他综合收益的可用盈余中减去这个数额，即从 51,000 元降到了 45,000 元。

20X8 年 12 月 31 日，经济情况有了好转，预计资产的可收回金额为 90,000 元。

If no impairment loss had been recognised, the carrying value at 31 December 20X8 would have been C104,000 (C120,000 at 31 December 20X6 less 2 years of further depreciation of C16,000), which is greater than the recoverable amount of C90,000. Therefore, the whole of the increase in the carrying value can be treated as a reversal of the previous impairment loss. If the carrying value had been increased to more than C104,000, the excess would be treated as a revaluation, not a reversal of the impairment. [IAS 36 para 118].

The impairment loss should be reversed, as indicated in the following table.

	Depreciated historical cost		**Carrying value**
	Before impairment	**After impairment**	
	C'000	**C'000**	**C'000**
31 December 20X6	75	65	65
Depreciation (2 years)	(10)	(9)	(9)
31 December 20X8	65	56	56
Reversal of impairment loss	–	9	34
31 December 20X8 after reversal	65	65	90

The reversal of the impairment loss of C34,000 is recognised as follows:

Income statement	9
Other comprehensive income	25
	34

The profit or loss figure of C9, 000 represents the amount of the original impairment loss that was charged in the income statement of C10, 000 less an adjustment for the additional depreciation that would have been charged had the asset been carried at depreciated historical cost of C1,000. This is calculated as the difference between the depreciation that would have been charged for the two years of C10, 000 had the asset been stated at depreciated historical cost and the depreciation actually charged of C9,000. The balance of the reversal of C25,000 is credited to other comprehensive income.

如果之前没有确认减值损失，20X8 年 12 月 31 日的账面价值应该为 104,000 元（20X6 年 12 月 31 日的 120,000 元减去 2 年的进一步折旧值 16,000 元），这个金额大于 90,000 元的可收回金额。因此，之前减值损失的转回，可以全部用于增加账面价值。如果账面价值增加到超过 104,000 元，则超出部分作为重估处理，不作为减值的转回。[IAS 36 第 118 段]。

减值损失应该被转回，如下表所示。

	折旧后的历史成本		账面价值
	减值前	减值后	
	千元	千元	千元
20X6 年 12 月 31 日	75	65	65
折旧（2 年）	（10）	（9）	（9）
20X8 年 12 月 31 日	65	56	56
减值损失的转回	–	9	34
20X8 年 12 月 31 日转回后的金额	65	65	90
对 34,000 元的减值损失转回确认如下：			
利润表			9
其他综合收益			25
			34

计入损益的 9,000 元的数字，代表了当初计入利润表中的减值损失金额 10,000 元，减去 1,000 元的折旧调整（如果资产按折旧后的历史成本记账的话）。这计算的是，如果该资产按折旧后的历史成本计量而应计提的两年的折旧 10,000 元与实际计提的折旧 9,000 元之间的差额。剩余的 25,000 元的转回贷计其他综合收益。

18.280 After a reversal of an impairment loss has been recognised the future depreciation charge for the asset should be adjusted to allocate the revised carrying amount less residual value over its remaining useful life on a systematic basis. [IAS 36 para 121].

Special rules for goodwill

18.281 The special rules for goodwill are simply that impairments of goodwill may not be reversed. The standard states that after goodwill has been impaired any subsequent increase in the recoverable amount of goodwill is likely to be internally generated goodwill rather than a reversal of an impairment of purchased goodwill. IAS 38, 'Intangible assets', prohibits the recognition of internally generated goodwill. This means that increases in the recoverable amount of goodwill following an impairment are treated as if they were internally generated goodwill and are not recognised. [IAS 36 paras 124, 125].

18.281.1 In certain circumstances where an entity is planning a restructuring, this can mean recognising a charge twice, once for the impairment charge and secondly for the restructuring expenses. Even in this circumstance it would not be appropriate to reverse the impairment on goodwill as the impairment relates effectively to an overpayment for the entity in its current condition. The restructuring costs do not arise as a result of the business combination, but rather arise from management's intention to increase the entity's future value.

18.282 It should be noted that if the net assets of a business included impaired carrying values for both purchased goodwill and other fixed assets, the situation may occur where some impairment loss reversals are permitted (for the other fixed assets) and those for goodwill are not. This situation may occur with business restructurings. Goodwill and other fixed assets of businesses in need of reorganisation may have to be written down; if their values are restored as a result of reorganisation, only the impairment losses relating to the fixed assets other than goodwill may be written back. An example of this is given in paragraph 18.197 above.

18.280　确认了减值损失的转回后，应该调整资产未来的折旧费用，对修订后的账面价值减去残值后的金额在其剩余使用寿命中进行系统分配。[IAS 36 第 121 段]。

商誉的特殊规则

18.281　商誉的特殊规则很简单，商誉的减值不能转回。准则指出，商誉发生减值之后，商誉可收回金额的任何增加都很可能是自创商誉，而不是购入商誉的减值的转回。IAS 38——无形资产禁止确认自创商誉。这意味着，发生减值损失后，商誉可收回金额的增加被作为自创商誉进行处理，不予确认。[IAS 36 第 124 段、第 125 段]。

18.281.1　在主体正计划一项重组的情况下，这可能意味着一项费用要确认两次，一次是确认减值的费用，第二次是确认重组的费用。即便在这种情况下，转回商誉的减值也是不恰当的，因为该减值实际上是与主体在当前状况下的一项超额支付有关的。重组费用不是业务合并所导致的，而是管理层意图增加主体未来价值所导致的。

18.282　应该注意到，如果一项业务的净资产中，既包括外购商誉计提减值后的账面价值，也包括其他固定资产计提减值后的账面价值，则会出现这样的情况：一部分减值损失允许转回（与其他固定资产有关的），而与商誉有关的那部分不允许转回。这种情况可能发生在业务重组时。需要进行重组的业务的商誉和其他固定资产可能必须要被减记；如果重组的结果使得它们的价值得以恢复，只有与固定资产（而非商誉）有关的减值损失可以被转回。上文第 18.197 段给出了这样的示例。

Impairment losses recognised in interim periods

18. 282. 1 IAS 34 requires an entity to apply the same accounting policies in its interim financial statements as at the end of its financial year. An entity may be required to recognise an impairment in an interim period; but by the end of the financial year the impairment may have reversed either in full or partially. IFRIC 10 ' Interim reporting and impairment ', addressed this issue and states that an impairment loss recognised in an interim period on goodwill should not be reversed.

Allocation of reversal of impairment losses to assets of a CGU

18. 283 The allocation of the reversal of impairment losses for a CGU is accounted for in a similar way to the allocation of the original loss (see para 18. 241), except that reversal of impairment losses on goodwill may not be recognised. Thus the rules are that the reversal is allocated to assets other than goodwill on a pro-rata basis based on the carrying amount of each asset in the CGU. [IAS 36 para 122].

18. 284 In allocating the reversal of an impairment loss the standard does not permit an asset's carrying amount to be increased above the lower of:

- its recoverable amount (if determinable) ; and
- the carrying amount that would have been determined had no impairment loss been recognised previously adjusted for subsequent depreciation or amortisation.

Any surplus reversal arising from the application of this limitation to a particular asset should be allocated to the CGU's remaining assets (except goodwill) on a pro-rata basis. [IAS 36 para 123].

18. 285 The following example illustrates the allocation of the reversal of an impairment loss for a CGU. The original impairment was C495 based on an

在中期确认的减值损失

18.282.1　IAS 34 规定，主体在中期财务报表所采用的会计政策要和财务年度年末时的一样。主体可能在中期按要求要确认一项减值，但是到了财务年度结束的时候，该减值可能已经全部或部分转回。《国际财务报告解释公告第10号——中期财务报告和减值》（IFRIC 10）解决了这个问题，指出，在中期确认的商誉减值损失不应该被转回。

将减值损失的转回在现金产出单元的资产中分配

18.283　除了商誉的减值损失不能转回之外，对 CGU 减值损失转回的分配方式与原发生损失的分配方式相似（参见第 18.241 段）。因此，分配的规则是，根据 CGU 中除商誉以外的资产的账面价值，将转回按比例分配给各项资产。［IAS 36 第 122 段］。

18.284　对减值损失的转回进行分配时，准则不允许将资产的账面价值增至高于以下两者的较低者：

- 资产的可收回金额（如果可以确定）；
- 假如以前年度没有确认减值损失，资产应有的账面价值（经过后续的折旧或摊销调整之后）。

某一项资产由于采用这一限制而产生的剩余的转回金额，应该按比例分配给该 CGU 的剩余资产（商誉除外）。［IAS 36 第 123 段］。

18.285　下面的例子对 CGU 减值损失转回的分配进行了说明。CGU 的原账面价值为 1,395 元，减去 900 元的可收回金额，从而原先的减值为 495 元。减

original carrying amount of the CGU of C1,395 less recoverable amount of C900. Of the impairment loss C295 was allocated to write off goodwill. Several years later the recoverable amount of the CGU is estimated at C1,000. The carrying amounts of the net assets of the CGU at that time is C800. There is thus a reversal of the impairment loss of C200.

Details of the original impairment allocation and the present carrying amounts and the amounts that the assets would have been carried at had the original impairment not occurred are as follows:

Asset	**Original carrying amount** **C**	**Impairment** **C**	**Original carrying amount after impairment** **C**	**Present carrying amount (after depreciation)** **C**	**Carrying amount without impairment (after depreciation)** **C**
Goodwill	295	(295)	Nil	Nil	295
Property A	505	(5)	500	480	480
Machine A	90	(10)	80	60	70
Machine B	125	(46)	79	65	100
Machine C	130	(48)	82	65	110
Intangible A	250	(91)	159	130	230
Total	1,395	(495)	900	800	1,285

Note: The figures in the last two columns are not precise and assume in some cases changes in depreciation rates/useful lives following recognition of the original impairment.

The details of the revised estimates of recoverable amount and allocation of the reversal of the impairment loss are as follows. The recoverable amount has been shown as one figure, but represents the higher of fair value less costs to sell and value in use.

值损失中 295 元被分配去冲减了商誉。几年后，该 CGU 的预计可收回金额为 1,000 元。此时，该 CGU 净资产的账面价值为 800 元。因此转回减值损失 200 元。

原减值的分配、当前的账面价值、若未发生减值当前该资产应有的账面价值的详细情况如下：

	原始账面价值	减值	原始账面价值扣除减值	当前账面价值（折旧后）	没有减值的账面价值（折旧后）
资产	元	元	元	元	元
商誉	295	(295)	无	无	295
不动产 A	505	(5)	500	480	480
机器 A	90	(10)	80	60	70
机器 B	125	(46)	79	65	100
机器 C	130	(48)	82	65	110
无形资产 A	250	(91)	159	130	230
总计	1,395	(495)	900	800	1,285

注：最后两栏中的数字并不准确，假设在某些情况下，原确认减值之后，折旧率/使用寿命发生了变化。

修改后的预计可收回金额和减值损失转回分配的详细情况如下。虽然可收回金额已经作为一个数字显示出来，但是它代表的是公允价值减去处置费用和使用价值两者中的较高者。

Asset	Carrying amount	Recoverable amount	Reversal 1st allocation	Revised carrying amount	Reversal 2nd allocation	Revised carrying amount
	C	C	C	C	C	C
Goodwill	Nil	30	Nil(1)	Nil	Nil	Nil
Property A	480	510	Nil(2)	480	Nil	480
Machine A	60	70	10(3)	70	Nil	70
Machine B	65	80	15(3)	80	Nil	80
Machine C	65	90	25(3)	90	Nil	90
Intangible A	130	220	81(4)	211	9(4)	220
Total	800	1,000	131	931	9	940
Revised carrying amount						940
Unallocated reversal						60(5)
Recoverable amount						1,000

Notes:

1. No allocation of the reversal is made to goodwill as reversals of impairments of goodwill are not permitted by IAS 36.

2. No allocation is made to property A because its carrying amount equals its depreciated historical cost excluding the original impairment.

3. The amount of the reversal allocated to each machine is limited to the lower of its recoverable amount and its carrying amount calculated as if the original impairment had not taken place, but after depreciation on that amount. In each case the recoverable amount is equal to or below that latter figure so the reversal is limited to the difference between present carrying value and recoverable amount.

4. The full pro-rata allocation of the reversal is allocated to the intangible. As the revised carrying amount (C211) is still less than the recoverable amount (C220) and what the carrying amount would have been without the original impairment (C230) there is a second allocation of 9 to increase the carrying amount to the lower of these two figures (C220). The first allocation of 81 is

资产	账面价值 元	可收回金额 元	对转回的第一次分配 元	修改后的账面价值 元	对转回的第二次分配 元	修改后的账面价值 元
商誉	无	30	无(1)	无	无	无
不动产 A	480	510	无(2)	480	无	480
机器 A	60	70	10(3)	70	无	70
机器 B	65	80	15(3)	80	无	80
机器 C	65	90	25(3)	90	无	90
无形资产 A	130	220	81(4)	211	9(4)	220
总计	800	1,000	131	931	9	940
修改后的账面价值						940
未分配的转回						60(5)
可收回金额						1,000

注：

1. 转回的分配不涉及商誉，因为 IAS 36 不允许转回商誉的减值。

2. 转回没有被分配给不动产 A，是因为其账面价值等于折旧后历史成本（不考虑原来的减值）。

3. 分配给每一机器的转回金额，限于其可收回金额以及若原来没发生减值而应有的账面价值（但在该金额上扣除了折旧）两者中的较低者。每一个项目，其可收回金额都等于或低于若原来没发生减值而应有的账面价值（但在该金额上扣除了折旧），所以转回的金额限于可收回金额与当前的账面价值之间的差额。

4. 无形资产完整的分配到了全部按比例分配的转回。调整后的账面价值（211 元）仍低于可收回金额（220 元）和若原来没有发生减值而原有的账面金额（230 元），再分配 9 以将其账面价值增加到可收回金额与若原来没有发生减值而原有的账面金额两者中的较低者（220 元）。第一次分配的 81 元，是减值转回的 200 元，按照无形资产账面价值与符合减值转回价值增加条件

calculated as the proportion of the 200 impairment reversal that relates to the carrying amount of the intangible when compared with the total assets which qualify for an increase in value from an impairment reversal, being Machines A-C and the intangible (C130 × C200/C320).

5. After increasing all the assets except goodwill to the lower of their recoverable amount and the carrying amount at which the assets would have been stated had the original impairment not occurred, there remains C60 that cannot be further allocated due to the limits set out in paragraph 18.284. This amount represents reversals that cannot be allocated to:

Machine A	27	(60 × 200/320) - 10
Machine B	26	(65 × 200/320) - 15
Machine C	16	(65 × 200/320) - 25
Sub-total	69	
Less: reallocated to intangible	(9)	
	60	

The allocations were based on the asset's carrying amount times the amount of the reversal (C200) divided by the carrying amount of the assets over which the reversal could be allocated (C320, being the sum of the carrying amounts of machines A, B and C and intangible A).

Separate financial statements

18.285.1 Investments in separate financial statements that are within IAS 36's scope-subsidiaries, associates and joint ventures that are carried at cost-generate cash flows as discrete assets and should normally be considered individually. To be consistent with the way such entities are accounted for, their value in use would normally be based on the estimated future net cash flows of the underlying entities that are attributable to the group's interest. Any impairments in the underlying assets should already be picked up in the financial statements of the subsidiaries associates or joint ventures. However, further adjustments may be required in the

的资产总和（即机器 A－机器 C 及无形资产）相比较的比例计算的(130 元×200 元/320 元)。

5. 将除商誉以外的其他所有资产增加到他们的可收回金额和若原来没有发生减值而应有的账面价值两者中的较低者之后，还有 60 元由于第 18.284 段的限制而不能进一步分配。这个金额体现的是不能分配给下列资产的转回：

机器 A	27	(60×200/320)－10
机器 B	26	(65×200/320)－15
机器 C	16	(65×200/320)－25
小计	69	
减:重新分配给无形资产的金额	(9)	
	60	

分配是以资产的账面价值，乘以转回金额（200 元）除以能够分配转回的资产的账面价值（320 元，即机器 A、B、C 和无形资产 A 账面价值总和)。

单独财务报表

18.285.1　在 IAS 36 范围之内的单独财务报表中的投资——即按成本计量的子公司、联营、合营企业——作为单独资产产生现金流，一般情况下应单独考虑。使用价值通常基于其对应主体预计未来净现金流中可归属于集团的部分，以与对这些主体进行会计处理的方法保持一致。在子公司、联营、合营企业的财务报表中应该已经就相应的资产减值计提了准备。但是，在投资者的账上，需要对投资者在相应主体中的权益投资和其他对该主体的贷款进行额外的减值测试，从而可能带来进一步的调整。

investor's books arising from the additional impairment testing required on the investor's equity interest in the underlying entity and other loans to the entity.

Issues for parent companies and subsidiaries

Parent's investment in subsidiaries

18.285.2 Where capitalised goodwill on consolidation is written down as a result of impairment, the carrying value of the parent entity's investment in the relevant subsidiary in the parent's separate financial statements should also be reviewed for impairment. This is because an impairment of goodwill on consolidation may mean that the carrying amount of the investment, determined at the date of acquisition and based on the same figures as those from which goodwill was derived, may also be impaired.

18.285.3 The recoverable amount (if determined by value in use) of an investment in a subsidiary would normally be based on the present value of the subsidiary's estimated future cash flows. This is justified based on the simplifying assumption that, as the parent controls the subsidiary, it will be able to extract the subsidiaries cash flows in the form of dividends.

Example – Impairment of investment in subsidiary

Entity A has an investment of C350 in its subsidiary entity B. Entity B has net assets of only C200 and, therefore, management believe that it needs to book an impairment of C150. This is not necessarily correct. Management needs to review the future discounted cash flow of entity B. In this instance the value in use and fair value less costs to sell of entity B are both C300. Management, therefore, should only book an impairment of C50. It is important to look at the underlying cash flows that support the investment when considering the investment for impairment.

18.285.3.1 When performing an impairment review of a subsidiary undertaking, it is necessary to consider non interest bearing inter-company balances, such as trading receivables and payables, between the parent and subsidiary. Any cash outflows payable to the parent for settlement of inter-

关于母公司和子公司的问题

母公司对子公司的投资

18.285.2　在合并财务报表中资本化下来的商誉因为减值而被减计的情况下，在母公司的单独财务报表中，母公司这一主体对相关子公司的投资的账面价值也应该进行减值复核。这是因为，合并财务报表中商誉的减值，可能意味着与商誉的形成是基于同样一些数据的、在购买日确定的投资的账面价值可能也发生了减值。

18.285.3　对子公司投资的可收回金额（如果是按使用价值来确定的），一般会以子公司的预计未来现金流现值为基础。其理由是基于一项简化的假设，即，母公司控制子公司，从而就有能力以股利的形式提取子公司的现金流。

示例——对子公司投资的减值

主体 A 对子公司主体 B 有投资 350 元。主体 B 的净资产仅为 200 元，因此，管理层认为需要确认 150 元的减值。这么做不一定正确。管理层需要复核主体 B 的未来折现现金流。在本例中，主体 B 的使用价值及公允价值减去处置费用的金额均为 300 元。所以管理层应该只确认 50 元的减值。在考虑投资的减值时，看一看支持该项投资的基础现金流，是非常重要的。

18.285.3.1　在对子公司进行减值测试时，有必要考虑不计息的内部往来余额，例如母公司和子公司之间的应收账款和应付账款。在确定减值计算中的子公司现金流时，任何应付母公司的用于支付公司间往来余额的现金流出都应包含在内。这是因为，从一个主体的角度来看，预期将有一笔现金流从该

company trading balances are included in determining the subsidiary's cash flows for use in the impairment calculation. This is because, from an entity perspective, it is expected that there will be a cash outflow from the subsidiary. Similarly, any cash inflows from the parent to the subsidiary are also taken into account. Any inter-company receivable in the parent's financial statements is separately evaluated based on the guidance in IAS 39, 'Financial instruments-Recognition and measurement'.

18.285.4 The goodwill and other net assets in the consolidated financial statements that are attributable to an impaired subsidiary will usually differ from the subsidiary's carrying value in the parent's balance sheet as time goes by after the acquisition. The likelihood that the parent's investment has also been impaired will depend partly on its accounting policy, which may be:

- cost less provision for impairment; or
- fair value (in accordance with IAS 39).

18.285.5 Often, an acquisition is undertaken by one company within a group, but the goodwill acquired is attributable to various CGUs and subsidiaries across the group. This could lead to a situation where the cost of investment in the subsidiary's entity financial statements is not fully recoverable (because the synergistic benefits associated with the acquisition do not all flow to the subsidiary) even if the goodwill is not impaired at a group level. This could lead to an impairment charge in the subsidiary's entity financial statements, unless it could be supported that the investment was part of a larger CGU or that part of the investment balance could be notionally allocated to another subsidiary as a capital contribution and the value was, therefore, recoverable via that other subsidiary.

Disclosure

18.286 IAS 1, 'Presentation of financial statements', requires disclosure of specific accounting policies used. It also requires disclosure of the judgements that management has used in applying the most significant accounting policies that affect the financial statements and the key assumptions and estimates used. [IAS 1

子公司流出。类似的，任何从母公司流入子公司的现金流也应考虑在内。母公司财务报表中的任何内部应收款将按照 IAS 39——金融工具：确认和计量的指引单独进行评估。

18.285.4　并购后，随着时间的推移，合并财务报表中与一家已经发生减值的子公司相关的商誉和其他净资产通常会与母公司资产负债表中该子公司的账面价值不同。母公司的投资也发生减值的可能性将部分取决于其会计政策。母公司的会计政策可能是：

- 成本减去减值准备；或
- 公允价值（按 IAS 39 确定）。

18.285.5　经常出现这样的情况，收购是由集团中的一家公司进行的，但是收购产生的商誉归属于集团内不同的 CGU 和子公司。这可能会引起一个问题：即使商誉在集团层面没有减值，在子公司的主体财务报表中投资成本无法完全收回（因为与收购相关的协同效应不是完全流向该子公司）。这可能导致在子公司的主体财务报表中确认减值费用，除非能证明该投资属于某一个较大的 CGU 的一部分、或者该投资余额的一部分可以被假设分配给另一家子公司作为资本投入，因此，其价值可以通过另一家子公司收回。

披露

18.286　《IAS 1——财务报表的列报》要求披露所使用的具体会计政策。还要求披露管理层在应用影响财务报表的最重要的会计政策时所用到的判断、使用的关键假设和估计。[IAS 1 第 103 段、第 113 段、第 116 段]。表 18.2 中给出了一个减值会计政策的实例以及重大估计和判断的详细信息。

paras 103, 113, 116]. An example of an accounting policy for impairment and details of significant estimates and judgements is given in Table 18. 2.

Table 18. 2 – Accounting policy for impairment

Vodafone Group plc – Annual Report for the year ended 31 March 2011

2. Significant accounting policies (extract)

Impairment of assets

Goodwill

Goodwill is not subject to amortisation but is tested for impairment annually or whenever there is an indication that the asset may be impaired.

For the purpose of impairment testing, assets are grouped at the lowest levels for which there are separately identifiable cash flows, known as cash-generating units. If the recoverable amount of the cash-generating unit is less than the carrying amount of the unit, the impairment loss is allocated first to reduce the carrying amount of any goodwill allocated to the unit and then to the other assets of the unit pro-rata on the basis of the carrying amount of each asset in the unit. Impairment losses recognised for goodwill are not reversed in a subsequent period.

Recoverable amount is the higher of fair value less costs to sell and value in use. In assessing value in use, the estimated future cash flows are discounted to their present value using a pre-tax discount rate that reflects current market assessments of the time value of money and the risks specific to the asset for which the estimates of future cash flows have not been adjusted.

The Group prepares and approves formal five year management plans for its operations, which are used in the value in use calculations. In certain developing markets the fifth year of the management plan is not indicative of the long term future performance as operations may not have reached maturity. For these operations, the Group extends the plan data for an additional five year period.

Property, plant and equipment and finite lived intangible assets

At each reporting period date, the Group reviews the carrying amounts of its property, plant and equipment and finite lived intangible assets to determine whether there is any indication that those assets have suffered an impairment loss. If any such indication exists, the recoverable amount of the asset is estimated in order to determine the extent, if any, of the impairment loss. Where it is not possible to estimate the recoverable amount of an individual asset, the Group estimates the recoverable amount of the cash-generating unit to which the asset belongs.

表 18.2——减值的会计政策

沃达丰集团公司——截止 2011 年 3 月 31 日止年度的年度报告

2. 重要会计政策（摘录）

资产减值

商誉

商誉不摊销，每年或者在有迹象表明其可能发生了减值时进行减值测试。

为了减值测试之目的，资产按照可以单独辨认现金流的最低水平进行分组，即所谓的现金产出单元。如果现金产出单元的可收回金额低于该单元的账面价值，减值损失首先分配去减少分配至该现金产出单元的商誉的账面价值，然后根据现金产出单元中其他每项资产的账面价值按比例进行分配。对商誉所确认的减值损失，在以后的期间不能转回。

可收回金额为公允价值减去处置费用和使用价值两者之间的较高者。对使用价值进行评估时，预计未来现金流按税前折现率折现为现值，税前折现率反映了当前市场对于货币时间价值及资产特定风险的评估，在预计未来现金流时并未就这些资产特定风险进行调整。

本集团编制并批准正式的五年管理层计划，其被用于使用价值的计算中。在某些发展中市场，由于其经营可能尚未达到成熟阶段，第五年的管理层计划不能反映长期的未来业绩。针对这些业务，本集团会多做五年的计划数据。

不动产、厂房、设备和有确定使用寿命的无形资产

在每个报告日，本集团对不动产、厂房、设备和有确定使用寿命的无形资产的账面价值进行复核，以确定是否有迹象表明这些资产已经出现了减值损失。若存在这种迹象，则对资产的可收回金额进行估计，来确定减值损失的范围（如有）。单项资产的可收回金额无法估计的，本集团对该资产所属的现金产出单元的可收回金额进行估计。

Con.

If the recoverable amount of an asset or cash-generating unit is estimated to be less than its carrying amount, the carrying amount of the asset or cash-generating unit is reduced to its recoverable amount. An impairment loss is recognised immediately in the income statement.

Where an impairment loss subsequently reverses the carrying amount of the asset or cash-generating unit is increased to the revised estimate of its recoverable amount, not to exceed the carrying amount that would have been determined had no impairment loss been recognised for the asset or cash-generating unit in prior years. A reversal of an impairment loss is recognised immediately in the income statement.

Critical accounting estimates (extract)

Impairment reviews

IFRS requires management to undertake an annual test for impairment of indefinite lived assets and, for finite lived assets, to test for impairment if events or changes in circumstances indicate that the carrying amount of an asset may not be recoverable.

Impairment testing is an area involving management judgement, requiring assessment as to whether the carrying value of assets can be supported by the net present value of future cash flows derived from such assets using cash flow projections which have been discounted at an appropriate rate. In calculating the net present value of the future cash flows, certain assumptions are required to be made in respect of highly uncertain matters including management's expectations of:

- growth in EBITDA, calculated as adjusted operating profit before depreciation and amortisation;
- timing and quantum of future capital expenditure;
- long term growth rates; and
- the selection of discount rates to reflect the risks involved.

The Group prepares and approves formal five year management plans for its operations, which are used in the value in use calculations. In certain developing markets the fifth year of the management plan is not indicative of the long-term future performance as operations may not have reached maturity. For these operations, the Group extends the plan data for an additional five year period.

For businesses where the five year management plans are used for the Group's value in use calculations, a long-term growth rate into perpetuity has been determined as the lower of:

续表

如果预计一项资产或现金产出单元的可收回金额低于其账面价值，则将该资产或现金产出单元的账面价值减至可收回金额。减值损失立即确认计入利润表。 减值损失后来发生转回的，将资产或现金产出单元的账面价值增加至修正后的预计可收回金额，但是不超过若以前年度没有对该资产或现金产出单元计提减值损失而应有的账面价值。减值损失的转回立即确认计入利润表。 **关键的会计估计（摘录）** **减值复核** 国际财务报告准则要求管理层对寿命不确定的资产每年进行减值测试；对于有确定寿命的资产，如果有事件或环境变化显示资产账面价值可能不能收回的，也要进行减值测试。 减值测试是一个涉及管理层判断的领域，要求评估资产未来现金流量的净现值，即采用恰当的折现率进行折现后的预计现金流量，能否支持资产的账面价值。计算未来现金流量的净现值时，需要就一些高度不确定的事项（包括管理层预期）作出假设，包括： • EBITDA（按照扣除折旧与摊销之前的营业利润来计算）的增长； • 未来资本性支出的金额和时点； • 长期增长率；以及 • 选择反映相关风险的折现率。 本集团编制并批准正式的五年管理层计划，其被用于使用价值的计算中。在某些发展中市场，由于其经营可能尚未达到成熟阶段，第五年的管理层计划不能反映长期的未来业绩。针对这些业务，本集团会多做五年的计划数据。 对于本集团采用五年管理层计划来计算使用价值的业务，以下述两者中的较低者来确定未来长期增长率：

Con.

- the nominal GDP rates for the country of operation; and
- the long-term compound annual growth rate in EBITDA in years six to ten estimated by management.

Changing the assumptions selected by management, in particular the discount rate and growth rate assumptions used in the cash flow projections, could significantly affect the Group's impairment evaluation and hence results.

The Group's review includes the key assumptions related to sensitivity in the cash flow projections. Further details are provided in note 10 to the consolidated financial statements.

18.286.1 The disclosure requirements for impairment are extensive. Regulators across the world raise comments on the inadequacy of entities' impairment disclosures. The disclosure requirements under value in use and fair value less costs to sell are basically similar, but some differences exist. [IAS 36 para 134]. The reason why the list of disclosures under value in use is longer than under fair value less costs to sell is the nature of the two models: while the value in use is always a discounted cash flow model, fair value less costs to sell can also be determined based on signed purchase contracts or market data. However, if fair value less costs to sell is being determined based on discounted cash flows, as is often the case in practice, the disclosures for both will be essentially the same.

18.287 The financial statements should disclose *for each class of assets*:

- The amount of impairment losses recognised in profit or loss for the period and the line item or items in the income statement in which the losses are included.
- The amount of reversals of impairment losses recognised in profit or loss for the period and the line item or items in which the reversals are included.
- The amount of impairment losses on revalued assets recognised directly in other comprehensive income in the period.
- The amount of reversals of impairment losses on revalued assets recognised directly in other comprehensive income in the period.

[IAS 36 para 126].

续表

• 经营所处国家的名义 GDP；以及 • 管理层计划中第 6 年至第 10 年的 EBITDA 的长期复合年增长率。 管理层所选择的假设发生改变，特别是在现金流预测中使用的折现率和增长率假设，将会对本集团的减值评估产生重大影响并进而影响减值结果。 本集团的复核包括现金流预测中关键假设的敏感度。合并财务报表的附注 10 给出了更多信息。

18.286.1　对减值的披露要求是广泛的。全世界的监管机构对各主体减值披露的不充分性都提出了意见。对使用价值和公允价值减去处置费用的披露要求基本相似，但仍有一些区别。[IAS 36 第 134 段]。使用价值的披露清单比公允价值减去处置费用的长，原因在于这两种模式的本质：使用价值总是折现后的现金流模式，而公允价值减去处置费用还可以根据已签署的购买合同或市场数据来确定。然而，如果公允价值减去处置费用是按照折现后的现金流来确定的（实务中经常这么做），则对两者的披露要求基本上是一样的。

18.287　*对每类资产*，财务报表中应该披露下列事项：

- 当期在损益中确认的减值损失的金额，以及在利润表中该损失所计入的报表项目。
- 当期在损益中确认的减值损失转回的金额，以及该项转回所计入的报表项目。
- 当期直接在其他综合收益中确认的重估资产的减值损失金额。
- 当期直接在其他综合收益中确认的重估资产减值损失的转回金额。

[IAS 36 第 126 段]。

18.288 For the purpose of this disclosure, a class of assets is a group of assets of a similar nature and use in the entity's business. [IAS 36 para 127]. Examples of classes of tangible fixed assets are:

- Land.
- Land and buildings.
- Machinery.
- Ships.
- Aircraft.
- Motor vehicles.
- Furniture and fixtures.
- Office equipment.

Examples of classes of intangible asset are:

- Goodwill.
- Brand names/trade marks.
- Mastheads and publishing titles.
- Computer software.
- Licences and franchises, copyrights, patents and other intellectual property rights, service and operating rights.
- Recipes, formulae, models designs and prototypes.
- Development costs.
- Customer relationships.
- Customer lists.

18.289 Table 18.3 discloses the total impairment charge to profit or loss. The note contains other information (not reproduced here but see table 18.1) that distinguishes the impairments by class of asset.

18.288　为了本披露之目的，一类资产是指在主体的业务中具有相似性质和用途的一组资产。[IAS 36 第 127 段]。有形的固定资产类别的例子有：

- 土地。
- 土地和建筑物。
- 机器。
- 轮船。
- 飞机。
- 机动车辆。
- 家具及固定装置。
- 办公设备。

无形资产类别的示例有：

- 商誉。
- 品牌/商标。
- 报头和出版标题。
- 电脑软件。
- 许可与特许权、版权、专利和其他知识产权、服务权及经营权。
- 配方、公式、模型设计和原型。
- 开发费用。
- 客户关系。
- 客户清单。

18.289　表 18.3 披露了计入损益的总的减值费用。该附注包含按资产类别区分的减值的其他信息（这里不再重复赘述请参见表 18.1）。

Table 18. 3 – Disclosure of total impairment charge to the income statement

Vodafone Group plc – Annual report for the year ended 31 March 2010

10 Impairment (extract)

Impairment losses (extract)

The net impairment losses recognised in the consolidated income statement, as a separate line item within operating profit, in respect of goodwill and licences and spectrum fees are as follows:

		2010	**2009**	**2008**
Cash generating unit:	Reportable segment:	**£m**	**£m**	**£m**
India	India	2,300	–	–
Spain	Spain	–	3,400	–
Turkey	Other Africa and Central Europe	(200)	2,250	–
Ghana	Other Africa and Central Europe	–	250	–
		2,100	**5,900**	

18. 290 The standard permits the information in paragraph 18. 287 to be given with other information disclosed for the class of asset, for example in the reconciliation of the carrying amount of property, plant and equipment at the beginning and end of the year, that is required by IAS 16. [IAS 36 para 128]. In fact IAS 16 and IAS 38 both require the amount of impairment losses recognised in the period to be disclosed in the reconciliation, including separate disclosure of both losses recognised in other comprehensive income and losses recognised in profit or loss. They also require separate disclosure of reversals of impairments recognised in other comprehensive income and in profit or loss. This disclosure is required for each class of asset. [IAS 16 para 73, IAS 38 para 118].

18. 291 Where an entity reports segmental information in accordance with IFRS 8, 'Operating segments', it should disclose, for each reportable segment based on its primary reporting format:

- The amount of impairment losses recognised in profit or loss and (separately) directly in other comprehensive income for the period.

表 18.3——计入利润表的总减值费用的披露

沃达丰集团公司——截至 2010 年 3 月 31 日止年度的年度报告

10. 减值（摘录）

减值损失（摘录）

作为经营利润的一个单列项目，在合并利润表中所确认的与商誉、许可证和频谱占用费有关的净减值损失如下：

		2010	2009	2008
现金产出单元：	报告分部：	百万英镑	百万英镑	百万英镑
印度	印度	2,300	–	–
西班牙	西班牙	–	3,400	–
土耳其	其他非洲和中欧地区	（200）	2,250	–
加纳	其他非洲和中欧地区	–	250	–
		2,100	**5,900**	

18.290　该准则允许将第 18.287 段的信息与该类资产所披露的其他信息一起披露，例如 IAS 36 所要求的不动产、厂房和设备年初及年底账面价值的调节表。[IAS 36 第 128 段]。事实上，IAS 16 和 IAS 38 都要求在调节表中披露当期所确认的减值损失金额，包括单独披露在其他综合收益中确认的损失和在损益中确认的损失。这两个准则还要求单独披露在其他综合收益和损益中确认的减值的转回。每一类资产都要作这样的披露。[IAS 16 第 16 号第 73 段，IAS 38 第 118 段]。

18.291　主体按照 IFRS 8——经营分部报告分部信息的，应该以其主要报告格式为基础，披露每个报告分部的下列事项：

■ 当期在损益中确认的以及（单独）直接在其他综合收益中确认的减值损失金额。

■ The amount of reversals of impairment losses recognised in profit or loss and (separately) in other comprehensive income for the period.

[IAS 36 para 129].

18. 292 An example of segmental disclosure of impairment losses is given in Table 18. 4.

Table 18. 4 – Segmental disclosure of impairment losses

Norsk Hydro ASA-Annual Report – 31 December 2008

Note 13 (extract)

Impairment of non-current assets (extract)

Classification by asset category:

Amounts in NOK million	2008	2007
Impairment losses		
Property, plant and equipment	1,518	150
Intangible assets	31	–
Impairment reversals		
Property, plant and equipment	(4)	(5)
Total impairment of non-current assets	1,545	145

Classification by segment:

Amounts in NOK million	2008	2007
Impairment losses		
Aluminium Metal	796	143
Aluminium Products	753	4
Corporate, other and eliminations	–	3
Impairment reversals		
Aluminium Products	(4)	(5)
Total impairment of non-current assets	1,545	145

18. 293 For impairment losses or reversals of losses that are material to an entity as a whole an entity should disclose:

■ The events and circumstances that led to the recognition or reversal of the impairment loss.

■ 当期在损益中确认的以及（单独）在其他综合收益中确认的减值损失转回金额。

[IAS 36 第 129 段]。

18.292 表 18.4 中给出了按分部披露减值损失的一个例子。

表 18.4——按分部披露减值损失

挪威海德鲁公司——年度报告——2008 年 12 月 31 日

附注 13（摘录）

非流动资产的减值（摘录）

按资产类别进行分类：

金额以百万挪威克朗表示	2008	2007
减值损失		
不动产、厂房和设备	1,518	150
无形资产	31	—
减值转回		
不动产、厂房和设备	(4)	(5)
非流动资产的减值总额	1,545	145

按分部进行分类：

金额以百万挪威克朗表示	2008	2007
减值损失		
铝金属	796	143
铝产品	753	4
总部、其他和抵销	—	3
减值转回		
铝产品	(4)	(5)
非流动资产的减值总额	1,545	145

18.293 如果减值损失或减值损失转回对一个主体整体而言是重要的，该主体应该披露：

■ 导致确认或转回减值损失的事件或环境。

- The amount of the loss or reversal.
- Where the loss or reversal is in respect of an individual asset, the nature of the asset and the reportable segment, under IFRS 8 to which the asset belongs.
- Where the loss or reversal is in respect of a CGU:
    - A description of the CGU.
    - The amount of the impairment loss or reversal analysed by class of assets and by reportable segment, under IFRS 8.
    - Details of any changes in the aggregation of assets used to identify the CGU since the last impairment review, describing both the former and current way of identifying the CGU and giving the reason for the change.
- Whether the recoverable amount of the asset or CGU is based on fair value less costs to sell or value in use.
- If recoverable amount is based on fair value less costs to sell, the basis used, that is whether it was calculated by reference to prices in an active market or in some other way.
- If recoverable amount is based on value in use, the discount rate used in the current and any previous estimate of value in use.

[IAS 36 para 130].

18.294 Many of the above disclosures are illustrated in the Tables in this section. An example that gives the nature of the assets, the impairment charge and reasons for it, line item in which charged, segments to which the assets belong, the basis of determining recoverable amount (value in use) and the discount rate used is Table 18.5. Note that the company includes two years of comparatives. It has changed the level of impairment testing retrospectively following adoption of IFRS 8, 'Operating segments', and as a consequence has recognised impairments in earlier years. Therefore, it also gives figures as at the beginning of the earliest period presented, in accordance with IAS 1, 'Presentation of financial statements'.

- 确认或转回的减值损失金额。
- 减值损失或减值损失转回针对单项资产的，该资产的性质及其按照 IFRS 8 所归属的报告分部。
- 减值损失或减值损失转回针对 CGU 的：
  - 该 CGU 的描述。
  - 按资产类别以及按 IFRS 8 该资产所归属的报告分部，分析减值损失或减值损失转回的金额。
  - 详细说明用于认定 CGU 的资产集合自上次减值复核后发生的任何变化，说明上次和本次识别 CGU 的方法以及改变的原因。
- 资产或 CGU 的可收回金额是基于公允价值减去处置费用还是使用价值。
- 如果可收回金额是基于公允价值减去处置费用的，公允价值减去处置费用的基础，即是参考活跃市场价格来计算的，还是用其他方式计算出来的。
- 如果可收回金额是基于使用价值的，披露当前和过去对使用价值进行估计中所使用的折现率。

[IAS 36 第 130 段]。

18.294　上述许多披露内容在本部分的表中予以说明。表 18.5 给出了资产性质、减值费用及原因、该费用冲减的报表项目、资产所属分部、确定可收回金额（使用价值）的基础、使用的折现率等方面的例子。注意的是，该公司列示了包含两年的比较数据，采用 IFRS 8 后，该公司改变了减值测试的层级，并进行追溯调整，从而在以前年度确认了减值。因此，根据 IAS 1，也给出了最早列报期间期初的数据。

Table 18.5 – Value in use

France Telecom S. A-Annual Report – 31 December 2009

Note 2 – Accounting Policies (extract)

2.10 Goodwill (extract)

■ **Impairment tests and Cash-Generating Units (CGUs)**

A CGU is defined as the smallest identifiable group of assets that generates cash inflows that are largely independent of the cash inflows from other assets or groups of assets.

Goodwill is not amortized but tested for impairment at least once a year or more frequently when there is an indication that it may be impaired. Therefore, the evolution of general economic and financial trends, the different levels of resilience of the telecommunication operators with respect to the decline of local economic environments, the changes in the market capitalization values of telecommunication companies, as well as actual economic performance compared to market expectations represent external indicators that are analyzed by the Group, together with internal performance indicators, in order to assess whether an impairment test should be performed more than once a year.

IAS 36 "Impairment of Assets" requires these tests to be performed at the level of each CGU or groups of CGUs likely to benefit from acquisition-related synergies, within an operating segment. This allocation is reviewed if the Group changes the level at which it monitors return on investment for goodwill testing purposes.

Impairment loss for goodwill is recorded in the income statement as a deduction from operating income and is never reversed subsequently.

■ **Recoverable amount**

To determine whether an impairment loss should be recognized, the carrying value of the assets and liabilities of the CGUs or group of CGUs is compared to their recoverable amount.

Net book values of CGUs and groups of CGUs tested include goodwill, intangible assets with indefinite useful life arising from business combinations (except for the Orange trademark which is tested separately) and assets with finite useful life (property, plant and equipment, intangible assets and net working capital). Net book values are disclosed at the level of the CGUs and groups of CGUs, i. e. including accounting items related to transactions with other CGUs and groups of CGUs.

表 18. 5——使用价值

法国电信 S. A——年度报告——2009 年 12 月 31 日

附注 2——会计政策（摘录）

2. 10 商誉（摘录）

■ **减值测试和现金产出单元（CGU）**

一个现金产出单元是指，产生现金流入的最小可识别资产组，该现金流入很大程度上独立于其他资产或资产组产生的现金流入。

商誉不摊销，但是每年至少作一次减值测试，如果有迹象表明商誉可能发生了减值的，作减值测试的次数要更多。因此，为了评估是否需要一年进行多次减值测试，除了分析内部业绩指标，本集团还要分析外部指标，包括整体经济和金融趋势的发展、电信运营商针对当地经济环境下降的不同层次的应变能力、电信公司市场资本价值的变化以及与市场预期相比的实际经济表现。

IAS 3——资产减值要求在一个经营分部之内，以可能从收购相关的协同效应获利的每一个 CGU 或 CGU 组合的层级上进行这些减值测试。为了商誉减值测试目的，如果本集团改变了监控管理投资回报的层级，应重新复核该分摊。

商誉减值损失计入利润表，作为经营利润的一个抵减项，且之后永远不能转回。

■ **可收回金额**

为确定是否应确认一项减值损失，要将 CGU 或 CGU 组合的资产和负债的账面价值与他们的可收回金额进行比较。

被测试的 CGU 和 CGU 组的账面净值包含商誉、业务合并产生的寿命不确定的无形资产（除单独进行测试的 Orange 商标外）以及有确定使用寿命的资产（不动产、厂房和设备，无形资产以及净营运资金）。以 CGU 和 CGU 组的层面披露账面净值，也即是，包含与其他 CGU 和 CGU 组交易相关的会计项目。

Con.

The recoverable amount of a CGU is the higher of its fair value less costs to sell and its value in use. Fair value less costs to sell is the best estimate of the amount obtainable from the sale of a CGU in an arm's length transaction between knowledgeable, willing parties, less the costs of disposal. This estimate is determined, on November 30, on the basis of available market information including: (i) the discounted present value of future cash flows over a five-year period, plus a terminal value, (ii) revenue and EBITDA multiples for comparable companies adjusted for a control premium, and (iii) revenue and EBITDA for comparable transactions.

Value in use is the present value of the future cash flows expected to be derived from the CGUs or groups of CGUs. Cash flow projections are based on economic and regulatory assumptions, license renewal assumptions and forecast trading conditions drawn up by the Group's management, as follows :

- cash flow projections are based on three to five year business plans;
- cash flow projections beyond that timeframe are extrapolated by applying a declining or flat growth rate over the next two years (for some CGUs), followed by a growth rate to perpetuity reflecting the expected long-term growth in the market;
- the cash flows obtained are discounted using appropriate rates for the type of business and the countries concerned.

2. 13 Impairment of non-current assets other than goodwill and trademarks

In the case of a decline in the recoverable amount of an item of property, plant and equipment or an intangible asset to below its net book value, due to events or circumstances occurring during the period (such as obsolescence, physical damage, significant changes to the manner in which the asset is used, worse than expected economic performance, a drop in revenues or other external indicators) an impairment loss is recognized.

The recoverable amount of an asset is the higher of its fair value less costs to sell and its value in use assessed by the discounted cash flows method, based on management's best estimate of the set of economic conditions.

The impairment loss recognized is equal to the difference between the net book value and the recoverable amount.

Given the nature of its assets and activities, most of the Group's individual assets, do not generate independent cash flows that are independent of those from CGUs. The recoverable amount is then determined at the level of the CGU to which the asset belongs, except where:

续表

一个 CGU 的可收回金额为其公允价值减去处置费用和使用价值两者之间的较高者。公允价值减去处置费用，是通过熟悉情况、并且自愿的当事人之间销售一个 CGU 的公平交易所能够获得的金额，减去处置费用后的最佳估计。该项估计基于 11 月 30 日可获得的市场信息来予以确定，包括：(1) 未来五年期现金流加上余值后的折现现值；(2) 收入以及经过控制溢价调整后的可比公司的 EBITDA 倍数；(3) 收入以及可比交易的 EBITDA。

使用价值是预期从 CGU 或 CGU 组产生的未来现金流的现值。现金流预测基于本集团管理层拟定的经济和监管方面的假设、许可证更新的假设和对贸易条件的预期，内容如下：

- 现金流预测以 3—5 年的经营计划为基础；
- 超过这一时限的现金流预测，按照之后两年内（对一些 CGU）下降或持平的增长率来推算，使用的增长率要能长久的反映市场预期的长期增长率；
- 针对业务类型和所在国家，采用恰当的折现率对现金流进行折现。

2. 13 除商誉和商标以外的非流动资产的减值

若由于当期发生了一些事件或者出现了一些情况（如过时、物理损坏、资产使用方式的显著变化、比预期的经济表现差、收入下降或其他外部迹象），一项不动产、厂房、设备或无形资产的可收回金额下降至低于其账面净值，则确认减值损失。

一项资产的可收回金额为其公允价值减去处置费用和使用价值两者之间的较高者，使用价值根据管理层对整体经济情况的最佳估计、采用折现现金流的方法来进行评估。

所确认的减值损失等于账面净值与可收回金额之间的差额。

考虑到资产和活动的性质，本集团大多数单个资产不产生独立于 CGU 中其他资产的独立现金流。因此在该资产所属的现金产出单元（CGU）的层级上确定可收回金额，但下列情况除外：

Con.

- the fair value less costs to sell of the individual asset is higher than its book value; or
- the value in use of the asset can be estimated as being close to its fair value less costs to sell, where fair value can be reliably determined.

NOTE 8 – IMPAIRMENT

8. 1 Definition of cash-generating units (CGUs) and level of goodwill impairment testing

During the accounting periods presented, the France Telecom Group had just under forty main CGUs, generally corresponding to a fixedline/Internet or mobile operation in a particular country. Depending on the country, convergence is gradually leading towards the merger of the cash-generating units.

Since January 1, 2009, with the application of IFRS 8 and new segment reporting (see Note 1. 2), France Telecom has carried out impairment tests on its assets, including goodwill, at the operating segment level (France, Enterprise, United Kingdom, Spain and Poland) or at the level of the countries of the segment presented under Rest of the World.

8. 2 Goodwill

The main values of goodwill and of intangible assets with an indefinite useful life appear below. The periods presented are shown in the format of the test level adopted since January 1, 2009:

(in millions of euros) At December 31, 2009	net book value	Goodwill o/w inpairment loss	Intangible asses with an indefinite useful life(1)
France	15,305	(13)	
United Kingdom	1,517	(1,786)	
Poland	1,788	(1,307)	194
Spain	4,723	(114)	
Rest of the World:			
Romania	1,806		
Belgium	1,006		
Slovakia	806		
Switzerland	673		
Ivory Coast	375	(42)	
Jordan	178	(43)	
Other	1,037	(130)	4
Enterprise	408	(639)	
International Carrier & Shared Services	68		3,133
Total	**29,690**	**(4,074)**	**3,331**
o/w continuing operations	**28,173**	**(2,288)**	**3,331**
o/w assets held for sale	**1,517**	**(1,786)**	

续表

- 单项资产的公允价值减去处置费用高于账面价值;或者
- 在资产的公允价值能够可靠确定的情况下,能够估计其使用价值与公允价值减去处置费用相近。

附注 8——减值

8.1 现金产出单元(CGU)的定义和商誉减值测试的层级

在列报的会计期间内,法国电信集团的主要 CGU 不超过 40 个,一般对应于某一个特定国家的为固话/互联网或移动运营。在不同的国家,业务趋同逐渐引起了现金产出单元的合并。

自 2009 年 1 月 1 日起,随着采用 IFRS 8 和新的分部报告(参见附注 1.2),法国电信在经营分部(法国、事业部、英国、西班牙和波兰)的层级上进行资产减值测试(含商誉),或者在列示 A 为“世界其他地区”的分部中的各个国家的层级上进行。

8.2　商誉

商誉和使用寿命不确定的无形资产的主要价值列示如下。列报期间均按照自 2009 年 1 月 1 日起采用的测试层级的格式来展示:

(单位:百万欧元) 2009 年 12 月 31 日	账面净值	其中,商誉减值损失	使用寿命不确定的无形资产[1]
法国	15,305	(13)	
英国	1,517	(1,786)	
波兰	1,788	(1,307)	194
西班牙	4,723	(114)	
世界其他国家:			
罗马尼亚	1,806		
比利时	1,006		
斯洛文尼亚	806		
瑞士	673		
科特迪瓦	375	(42)	
约旦	178	(43)	
其他	1,037	(130)	4
事业部	408	(639)	
国际运输和共享服务	68		3,133
合计	**29,690**	**(4,074)**	**3,331**
其中:持续经营业务	**28,173**	**(2,288)**	**3,331**
持有待售资产	**1,517**	**(1,786)**	

Con.

(1) Intangible assets with an indefinite useful life mainly comprise the Orange and TP brands.

(in millions of euros) At December 31, 2008 (after IAS 36 amendment)	net book value	Goodwill o/w inpairment loss	Intangible asses with an indefinite useful life[(1)]
France	15,302	(38)	
United Kingdom	1,415	(1,665)	
Poland	2,161	(893)	192
Spain	4,929	(140)	
Rest of the World:			
Romania	1,806		
Belgium	1,006		
Slovakia	806		
Switzerland	673		
Ivory Coast	375	(42)	
Jordan	183	(44)	
Other	1,176	(78)	4
Enterprise	421	(643)	
International Carrier & Shared Services	49		2,961
Total	**30,301**	**(3,543)**	**3,157**

(1) Intangible assets with an indefinite useful life mainly comprise the Orange and TP brands.

(in millions of euros) At December 31, 2007 (after IAS 36 amendment)	net book value	Goodwill o/w inpairment loss	Intangible asses with an indefinite useful life[(1)]
France	15,334	(6)	
United Kingdom	1,836	(2,161)	
Poland	2,464	(1,031)	222
Spain	5,032		
Rest of the World:			
Romania	1,806		
Belgium	934		
Slovakia	723		
Switzerland	603		
Ivory Coast	417		
Jordan	178	(42)	
Other	1,039		4
Enterprise	399	(642)	
International Carrier & Shared Services	42		3,846
Total	**30,807**	**(3,882)**	**4,072**

续表

（1）使用寿命不确定的无形资产主要由 Orange 和 TP 商标组成。

（单位：百万欧元） 2008 年 12 月 31 日 （国际会计准则第 36 号修订后）	账面净值	其中，商誉减值损失	使用寿命不确定的无形资产[1]
法国	15,302	(38)	
英国	1,415	(1,665)	
波兰	2,161	(893)	192
西班牙	4,929	(140)	
其他国家或地区：			
罗马尼亚	1,806		
比利时	1,006		
斯洛文尼亚	806		
瑞士	673		
科特迪瓦	375	(42)	
约旦	183	(44)	
其他	1,176	(78)	4
事业部	421	(643)	
国际运输和共享服务	49		2,961
合计	**30,301**	**(3,543)**	**3,157**

（1）使用寿命不确定的无形资产主要由 Orange 和 TP 产品组成。

（单位：百万欧元） 2007 年 12 月 31 日 （国际会计准则第 36 号修订后）	账面净值	其中，商誉减值损失	使用寿命不确定的无形资产[1]
法国	15,334	(6)	
英国	1,836	(2,161)	
波兰	2,464	(1,031)	222
西班牙	5,032		
其他国家或地区：			
罗马尼亚	1,806		
比利时	934		
斯洛文尼亚	723		
瑞士	603		
科特迪瓦	417		
约旦	178	(42)	
其他	1,039		4
事业部	399	(642)	
国际运输和共享服务	42		3,846
合计	**30,807**	**(3,882)**	**4,072**

Con.

(1) Intangible assets with an indefinite useful life mainly comprise the Orange and TP brands.

(in millions of euros) At January 1, 2007 (after IAS 36 amendment)	net book value	Goodwill o/w inpairment loss	Intangible asses with an indefinite useful life[(1)]
France	15,334	(6)	
United Kingdom	2,000	(2,362)	
Poland	2,274	(969)	208
Spain	5,089		
Rest of the World:			
Romania	1,806		
Belgium	934		
Slovakia	712		
Switzerland	621		
Ivory Coast	417		
Jordan	182	(47)	14
Other	1,276	(175)	
Enterprise	308	(655)	
International Carrier & Shared Services	9		4,200
Total	**30,962**	**(4,214)**	**4,422**

(1) Intangible assets with an indefinite useful life mainly comprise the Orange and TP brands.

8.3 Key assumptions used to determine recoverable amounts

The basis for calculating recoverable amounts are described in Note 2.10.

Trends in the economic and financial environment, competition and regulatory authorities decisions, or changes in competitors' behavior in response to the economic environment may affect the estimate of recoverable amounts, as will unforeseen changes in the political, economic or legal systems of some countries.

Key assumptions used to determine the value in use of assets in the telecommunications segment are similar in nature. They include:

- market level, penetration rate and market share; decisions of regulators in terms of the access and service pricing, and inter-operator tariffs; the level of commercial expenses required to renew products and keep up with existing competitors or new market entrants; the impact on costs of changes in net revenues; and
- the level of investment expenditure, which may be affected by the roll-out of necessary new technologies or by decisions of regulators in terms of licenses and spectrum allocation (and the associated fees), or network deployment obligations or obligations to open up networks to competitors.

续表

（1）寿命不确定的无形资产主要由 Orange 和 TP 商标组成。

（单位：百万欧元） 2007 年 1 月 1 日 （国际会计准则第 36 号修订后）	账面净值	其中，商誉减值损失	使用寿命不确定的无形资产(1)
法国	15,334	(6)	
英国	2,000	(2,362)	
波兰	2,274	(969)	208
西班牙	5,089		
世界其他地区：			
罗马尼亚	1,806		
比利时	934		
斯洛文尼亚	712		
瑞士	621		
科特迪瓦	417		
约旦	182	(47)	14
其他	1276	(175)	
企业分布	308	(655)	
国际运输和共享服务	9		4,200
合计	**30,962**	**(4,214)**	**4,422**

（1）寿命不确定的无形资产主要由 Orange 和 TP 商标组成。

8. 3 用于确定可收回金额的主要假设

附注 2. 10 中说明了计算可收回金额的基础。

可收回金额的估计可能受到经济和金融环境的趋势、竞争和监管机构的决定、或者竞争对手针对经济环境而改变的业务行为的影响，也会受到一些国家政治、经济或是法律体系难以预料的变化的影响。

确定电信分部的资产使用价值所使用的关键假设在性质上是相似的。他们包括：

- 市场水平、普及率、市场份额；监管机构对市场准入和服务定价以及运营商内部关税的决定；更新产品、保持与现有竞争对手或新进入市场的对手所需要的商业支出水平；收入净额的改变对成本费用的影响；以及

- 投资支出的水平，这可能受到必要的新技术的推出、或监管机构关于牌照和频谱分配（及相关费用）的决定、或网络部署的义务、或向竞争对手开放网络的义务的影响。

Con.

The value assigned to each of these parameters reflect past experience and expected changes over the timeframe of the business plan. In the economic environment induced by the financial crisis that has prevailed since 2008:

- business plans were drafted during the fourth quarter of each period in order to factor in the latest trends, particularly regarding the first year of the plans;
- the discount rate used to determine values in use may incorporate a specific risk premium to account for contingencies in the execution of certain business plans or for country risk (such as for certain African countries);
- the perpetual growth rates used were maintained, on the whole, as in the Group's assessment carried out at the end of 2009, the economic environment should not lead to any change in the long term outlook of its industry. Perpetual growth rates were revised for a limited number of Eastern European countries to factor in the effects of the financial crisis.

Other assumptions that influence the estimated recoverable amounts are set forth below:

At December 31, 2009

	France	Poland	Spain	Romania	Enterprise
Basis of recoverable	Value in use	Value in use	Value in use	Value in use	Value in use
amount Source used	Five year plans	Five year plans	Five year plans	Five year plans	Five year plans
	Discounted cash flow	Discounted cash flow	Discounted cash flow	Discounted cash flow	Discounted cash flow
Growth rate to perpetuity	0.5%	1.5%	2.0%	2.0%	0.0%
Post-tax discount rate	7.5%	10.85%	8.25%	11.25%	8.5%
Pre-tax discount rate	11.2%	12.7%	10.2%	12.95%	13.0%

In accordance with IFRS 5, the recoverable amount of assets held for sale in the United Kingdom was determined by reference to fair value less costs to sell, as measured on the basis of France Telecom's share in the enterprise value of the Orange United Kingdom and T-Mobile UK joint venture that is in the process of being created.

续表

分配给上述每个参数的价值，反映了过去的经验以及预计在业务计划的时间范围内的变化。在受到自2008年起蔓延的金融危机影响的经济环境下：

- 为反映最新的发展趋势，尤其是针对计划的第一年，商业计划于每一期的第四季度进行起草；
- 用于确定使用价值的折现率可能包含特定的风险溢价，以反映执行某些商业计划的不确定性，或者国家风险（如某些非洲国家）；
- 总体上，使用的持续增长率与本集团在2009年末进行的评估保持一致，经济环境应该不会导致这个行业的长期前景发生任何改变。几个东欧国家的持续增长率进行了修改以反映金融危机的影响。

其他影响预计可收回金额的假设列示如下：

2009年12月31日

	法国	波兰	西班牙	罗马尼亚	事业部
可收回金额的基础	使用价值	使用价值	使用价值	使用价值	使用价值
来源	五年计划折现现金流	五年计划折现现金流	五年计划折现现金流	五年计划折现现金流	五年计划折现现金流
持续增长率	0. 5%	1. 5%	2. 0%	2. 0%	0. 0%
税后折现率	7. 5%	10. 85%	8. 25%	11. 25%	8. 5%
税前折现率	11. 2%	12. 7%	10. 2%	12. 95%	13. 0%

根据国际财务报告准则第5号，位于英国的持有待售资产的可收回金额参照其公允价值减去处置费用确定，基于法国电信在英国Orange和正在设立的合营企业T－Mobile UK的企业价值份额进行计量。

Con.

At December 31, 2008

	France (fixed line and mobile)	United Kingdom (fixed line and mobile)	Poland (fixed line and mobile)	Spain (mobile)	Romania (mobile)	Enterprise
Basis of recoverable amount	Fair value (f) Value in use (m)	Value in use	Value in use	Value in use	Value in use	Value in use
Source used	Five-year plans	Five-year plans	Five-year plans	Five-year plans	Five-year plans	Five-year plans
	Discounted cash flow	Discounted cash flow	Discounted cash flow	Discounted cash flow	Discounted cash flow	Discounted cash flow
Growth rate to perpetuity	0. 0% (f) 1. 0% (m)	1. 5% 2. 0%	0. 0% (f) 3. 0% (m)	2. 0% 2. 0% (m)	0. 0% 4. 0%	0. 0%
Post-tax discount rate	7. 5% (f) 8. 25% (m)	10. 85% 8. 75%	8. 25% 11. 0%	11. 25% 8. 25%	8. 5% 11. 0%	10. 0%
Pre-tax discount rate	n/a (f) 12. 1% (m)	10. 9%	12. 1% (f) 13. 1% (m)	10. 3%	12. 5%	15. 8%

At December 31, 2007

	France (fixed line and mobile)	United Kingdom (fixed line and mobile)	Poland (fixed line and mobile)	Spain (mobile)	Enterprise
Basis of recoverable amount	Fair value (f) Value in use (m)	Value in use	Value in use	Value in use	Value in use
Source used	Five-year plans	Five-year plans	Five-year plans	Five-year plans	Five-year plans
	Discounted cash flow	Discounted cash flow	Discounted cash flow	Discounted cash flow	Discounted cash flow
Growth rate to perpetuity	0. 0% (f) 1. 0% (m)	n/a	0. 0% (f) 3. 0% (m)	2. 0%	0. 0%
Post-tax discount rate	7. 7%	n/a	11. 0%	8. 25%	8. 5%
Pre-tax discount rate	n/a	n/a	13. 1% to 13. 5 %	10. 7%	14. 0%

In accordance with IAS 36, the basis used for impairment testing (fair value or value in use) may vary from one period to another; the recoverable amount is the higher of estimated value in use and fair value.

续表

2008年12月31日

可收回金额的基础来源	法国（固话及移动电话）	英国（固话及移动电话）	波兰（固话及移动电话）	西班牙（移动电话）	罗马尼亚（移动电话）	事业部
	公允值（f） 使用价值（m） 五年计划折现现金流	使用价值 五年计划折现现金流	使用价值 五年计划折现现金流	使用价值 五年计划折现现金流	使用价值 五年计划折现现金流	使用价值 五年计划折现现金流
持续增长率	0.0%（f） 1.0%（m）	1.5% 2.0%	0.0%（f） 3.0%（m）	2.0% 2.0%（m）	0.0% 4.0%	0.0%
税后折现率	7.5%（f） 8.25%（m）	10.85% 8.75%	8.25% 11.0%	11.2% 8.25%	8.5% 11.0%	10.0%
税前折现率	n/a（f） 12.1%（m）	10.9%	12.1%（f） 13.1%（m）	10.3%	12.5%	15.8%

2007年12月31日

可收回金额的基础来源	法国（固话及移动电话）	英国（固话及移动电话）	波兰（固话及移动电话）	西班牙（移动电话）	事业部
	公允值（f） 使用价值（m） 五年计划折现现金流	使用价值 五年计划折现现金流	使用价值 五年计划折现现金流	使用价值 五年计划折现现金流	使用价值 五年计划折现现金流
持续增长率	0.0%（f） 1.0%（m）	n/a	0.0%（f） 3.0%（m）	2.0%	0.0%
税后折现率	7.7%	n/a	11.0%	8.25%	8.5%
税前折现率	n/a	n/a	13.1%至 13.5%	10.7%	14.0%

根据国际会计准则第36号，减值测试所采用的基础（公允价值或使用价值）可能在不同的报告期有所不同；可收回金额为预计使用价值和公允价值两者中的较高者。

Con.

8. 4 Sensitivity of recoverable amounts

At the end of 2009, the analysis of recoverable amounts for the main entities led to appreciate their sensitivity to the main assumptions:

- in France, Romania and Enterprise, the Group considered it improbable that there would be a change in valuation parameters that would bring the recoverable amount into line with their book value;
- in Poland, for which an impairment was booked in 2009, any decline in estimated value in use would be liable to result in an additional impairment for the France Telecom's share in TP. A change of plus or minus 0. 50% in the post-tax discount rate would increase or decrease the recoverable amount by 200 to 250 million euros for the France Telecom's share in TP. Likewise, a change of plus or minus 0. 50% in the perpetual growth rate would increase or decrease the recoverable amount by 100 to 200 million euros for the France Telecom's share in TP. Lastly, a 10% increase or decrease in cash flows after the fifth year would increase or decrease the recoverable amount by 200 to 300 million euros for the France Telecom's share in TP.
- in Spain, value in use is close to the book value and any future performance that would fall slightly short of that used to determine value in use, for example due to a persistently poor outlook for the economic environment in Spain, would be liable to result in an impairment. A change of plus or minus 0. 50% in the post-tax discount rate would increase or decrease the recoverable amount by 500 to 700 million euros. Likewise, a change of plus or minus 0. 50% in the perpetual growth rate would increase or decrease the recoverable amount by 400 to 600 million euros. Lastly, a 10% increase or decrease in cash flows after the fifth year would increase or decrease the recoverable amount by approximately 600 million euros.

8. 5 Impairment, net of reversals

	December 31, 2009			**December 31, 2008**			**December 31, 2007**		
(in millions of euros)	Goodwill	Assets with a finite useful life	Assets with an indefinite useful life	Goodwill	Assets with a finite useful life	Assets with an indefinite useful life	Goodwill	Assets with a finite useful life	Assets with an indefinite useful life
Poland	(400)	(8)	–	–	31	–	–	1	–
Spain		(2)	–	(140)	(2)	–	–	(1)	–
Ivory Coast			–	(42)	–	–			
Other	(49)	(59)	–	(88)	(38)	–	(26)	(77)	(30)
TOTAL	**(449)**	**(69)**	–	**(270)**	**(9)**	–	**(26)**	**(77)**	**(30)**

续表

8. 4 可收回金额的敏感性

2009 年年末，主要主体的可收回金额按照各主要假设的敏感性分析：

- 在法国、罗马尼亚和事业部，本集团认为不会发生估值参数变动导致可收回金额变化至等于他们的账面价值的情形；

- 在波兰，2009 年确认了一项减值，预计使用价值的任何下降将可能导致法国电信在 TP 中份额的进一步减值。税后折现率正负 0. 5% 的变动将导致法国电信在 TP 的股份的可收回金额增加或减少 200 百万至 250 百万欧元。类似的，持续增长率正负 0. 5% 的变化将导致法国电信在 TP 的股份的可收回金额增加或减少 100 百万至 200 百万欧元。最后，第五年之后的现金流量增加或减少 10% 将导致法国电信在 TP 的股份的可收回金额增加或减少 200 百万至 300 百万欧元。

- 在西班牙，使用价值与账面价值接近，未来业绩稍微低于确定使用价值时的所使用的预期，比如由于西班牙经济环境持续不佳的前景，都可能会引起减值。税后折现率正负 0. 50% 的变动将导致可收回金额增加或减少 500 百万至 700 百万欧元。类似的，持续增长率正负 0. 50% 的变化将导致可收回金额增加或减少 400 百万至 600 百万欧元。最后，第五年之后的现金流量增加或减少 10% 将导致可收回金额增加或减少约 600 百万欧元。

8.5 扣除转回金额后的减值净额

	2009 年 12 月 31 日			2008 年 12 月 31 日			2007 年 12 月 31 日		
百万欧元	商誉	使用寿命确定的资产	使用寿命不确定的资产	商誉	使用寿命确定的资产	使用寿命不确定的资产	商誉	使用寿命确定的资产	使用寿命不确定的资产
波兰	(400)	(8)	–	–	31	–	–	1	–
西班牙		(2)	–	(140)	(2)	–	–	(1)	–
科特迪瓦			–	(42)	–	–			
其他	(49)	(59)	–	(88)	(38)	–	(26)	(77)	(30)
合计	**(449)**	**(69)**	**–**	**(270)**	**(9)**	**–**	**(26)**	**(77)**	**(30)**

Con.

At December 31, 2009,
In Poland, the 400 million euros charge for France Telecom's share in TP reflects the effects of regulatory pressure and increasing competition on projected cash flows.
At December 31, 2008,
In Spain, the 140 million euro impairment charge of the fixed - line market reflects a material decline in the market valuation of revenues per broadband subscriber based on comparable transactions.

18. 295 Entities should disclose information in aggregate for each of the other impairment losses recognised and the other impairment losses reversed in the period to the extent that information is not disclosed under the requirements set out in paragraph 18. 293 above. The aggregate information should be:

- The main classes of assets affected by the losses or reversal of losses to the extent that they have not been disclosed under the disclosure requirements described in paragraph 18. 293.
- The main events and circumstances giving rise to the impairments or reversals to the extent that they have not been disclosed under the requirements described in paragraph 18. 293.

[IAS 36 para 131].

18. 296 The standard *encourages* disclosure of the key assumptions used to determine the recoverable amount of assets or CGUs during the period. [IAS 36 para 132]. Ideally such disclosures might include two that are similar to those required by IAS 36 for CGUs that contain goodwill or intangible assets with indefinite useful lives, see paragraph 18. 297. These are, for estimates of recoverable amount based on value in use:

- The period over which management has projected cash flows based on budgets and forecasts approved by management and where that period extends to more than five years, disclosure of the length of the longer period and the circumstances justifying it.
- The long-term growth rate used after the period covered by management

续表

2009 年 12 月 31 日
在波兰，法国电信在 TP 的股份发生 400 百万欧元的减值，反映了监管压力和竞争加剧对现金流预测产生的影响。
2008 年 12 月 31 日
在西班牙，固话市场发生 140 百万欧元的减值，反映了在可比交易基础上每个宽带用户收入的市场价值的大幅下降。

18.295　按照上述第 18.293 段的要求未进行披露的信息，主体应该以总计的方式披露当期确认的减值损失和转回的减值损失。总计的信息应该包括：

■ 按照上述第 18.293 段的要求未进行披露的信息，受减值损失或减值损失转回所影响的资产的主要类别。

■ 按照上述第 18.293 段的要求未进行披露的信息，导致确认这些减值损失或转回的主要事件和环境。

[IAS 36 第 131 段]。

18.296　该准则则*鼓励*披露当期在确定资产或 CGU 可收回金额时所使用的关键假设。[IAS 36 第 132 段]。理想情况下，这样的披露可能会包括类似于 IAS 36 对包含商誉或使用寿命不确定无形资产的 CGU 所要求进行披露的两项内容，参见第 18.297 段。以使用价值为基础来预计可收回金额，这两项内容为：

■ 管理层根据其已批准的预算和预测对现金流进行预期的期间，若该期间超过五年，则披露此较长期间的长度以及解释其合理性。

■ 于管理层所批准的预算和预测所包含的期间之后，所采用的长期增长率，

approved budgets and forecasts and where that rate has exceeded the long-term average growth rate for the product, industries or country or countries in which the business operates or the markets served by the business, disclosure of the growth rate assumed and the circumstances justifying it.

Such disclosures are, however, rarely given in practice. More common, particularly in the case of US registered companies is the more general type of disclosure in Table 18. 6.

Table 18. 6 – Key assumptions used to determine the recoverable amount of CGUs

Syngenta AG – Report and accounts – 31 December 2010

Application of critical accounting policies (extract)

Impairment

For the purposes of assessing impairment, assets are grouped at the lowest level at which there are independent cash inflows. This level is described as a cash generating unit (CGU). Each CGU contains tangible assets such as plant and equipment as well as intangible assets such as product and patent rights. The way in which assets are grouped to form CGU's and are related to cash flows may in certain circumstances affect whether an impairment loss is recorded. Generally, the higher the level at which independent cash flows are identified, the less likely it is that an impairment loss will be recorded, as reductions in one cash inflow are more likely to be offset by increases in other cash inflows within the same CGU. If a CGU is impaired, the impairment loss is allocated first to any goodwill in the CGU, and then to reduce the CGU's other assets pro rata.

In the Crop Protection segment, a CGU is generally defined by Syngenta at the product active ingredient level. However, where one active ingredient is sold in mixture with other active ingredients to a significant extent, the active ingredients concerned are grouped together into a single CGU because independent cash inflows only exist at this higher level. Each CGU is generally defined on a global basis reflecting the international nature of the business. Goodwill on major acquisitions, principally Zeneca agrochemicals business goodwill of US $ 549 million, is held at segment level and tested for impairment by relating it to total segment cash flows.

In the Seeds segment, a CGU is generally defined at the global crop level to reflect the fact that seed germplasm originating in one country can be used in other countries except where licence agreements are more geographically restrictive.

增长率超过该产品、行业、业务经营所在国家或业务所服务的市场的长期平均增长率的，披露所假设的增长率并解释其合理性。

然而，实务中这样的披露很少。更为常见的（尤其是美国注册的公司）的方式是表 18.6 中所作的比较笼统的披露。

表 18.6——确定 CGU 可收回金额所使用的关键假设

先正达公司——报告及报表——2010 年 12 月 31 日

关键会计政策的应用(摘录)

减值

为了进行减值评估，资产按照产生独立现金流入的最小层级分成各个组合。该层级称为一个现金产出单元（CGU）。每一个 CGU 包含有形资产，如厂房和设备，以及无形资产，如产品和专利权。在某些情况下，为确定 CGU 而对资产进行分组的方式，以及资产与产生现金流相关联的方式可能会影响到是否确认一项减值损失。一般而言，所确定的产生独立现金流的层级越高，确认减值损失的可能性就越小，因为在同一个 CGU 中，一项现金流入的减少很可能会被另一项现金流入的增加所抵销。如果一个 CGU 发生了减值，减值损失首先分摊到该 CGU 的商誉，之后再按比例冲减其他资产。

在农作物保护分部，先正达公司一般按照产品的活性成分来确定 CGU。但是，当一个活性成分在很大程度上是与其他活性成分混合在一起销售的情况下，独立现金流入只能够在这样一个较高的层级上存在，因此将所有相关的活性成分组合在一起成为一个单独的 CGU。每一个 CGU 都在全球范围的基础上来进行确定，这反映了国际业务的性质。重大收购活动所产生的商誉，主要是 Zeneca 农用化学品业务 549 百万美元的商誉，分摊到分部的层面，并基于整个分部的现金流量总额来对其进行减值测试。

在种子分部，原产于一个国家的种子胚芽能够被用于其他国家，为反映这一事实，一个 CGU 一般是基于全球的农作物层面上来确定，但是存在许可证地域性限制的国家除外。

Con.

Critical accounting estimates (extract)

Impairment review

The recoverable amount for goodwill has been determined based on value in use of the relevant CGU or group of CGU's to which the goodwill is allocated. The recoverable amounts of all material intangible assets and property, plant and equipment have also been based on their value in use.

The discount rates used to discount the estimated future cash flows included in the value in use calculations are based on Syngenta's estimated weighted average cost of capital (WACC). This is considered to include market estimates of industry sector risk premium, as Syngenta's Crop Protection and Seeds businesses both operate mainly in the agricultural sector and its non-agricultural Professional Products business is not considered a separate CGU. Because Syngenta's CGU's generally either reflect the global nature of its Crop Protection and Seeds businesses, or are located in low risk countries it is also generally not considered necessary to apply a country risk premium.

The pre-tax discount rates used were 7.0% to 8.5% except for one CGU that has been discounted at 14.8% (2009: 7.5% to 10%). The outcomes of the impairment tests were not sensitive to reasonably likely changes in the discount rate in the periods presented for any CGU or group of CGUs for which the carrying amount of goodwill was significant except as described below:

In determining value in use it is necessary to make a series of assumptions to estimate future cash flows. The main assumptions in respect of Crop Protection include future sales prices and volumes, the future development expenditure required to maintain the products' marketability and registration in the relevant jurisdictions and the products' lives. These assumptions are reviewed annually as part of management's budgeting and strategic planning cycles. The assumptions can be subject to significant adjustment from such factors as changes in crop growing patterns in major markets (for example as a result of movements in crop prices), changes in the product registration, or pressure from competitor products. The estimated cash flows are based on Syngenta management forecasts over a 5 year horizon and a terminal value which assumes a 2% long-term growth rate. Management believes, based on recent growth in agricultural markets, that there are long-term prospects for continued growth. US $703 million of goodwill is tested at the Crop Protection total segment level (2009: US $702 million). In the opinion of Syngenta, the recoverable amount is not sensitive to reasonably possible changes in any of the assumptions underlying the cash flow projections used for the impairment test.

续表

关键会计估计（摘录）

减值复核

商誉的可收回金额以其所分摊到的相关 CGU 或 CGU 组的使用价值为基础确定。所有重要的无形资产、不动产、厂房和设备的可收回金额也都是以使用价值为基础的。

在使用价值的计算中，用于对预计未来现金流进行折现的折现率以先正达公司的预计加权平均资本成本（WACC）为基础。由于先正达公司的农作物保护业务和种子业务都主要在农业领域运营，而非农业的专业产品业务根据 IAS 36 的定义不是独立的 CGU，因此该折现率被认为已经包含了市场预期的行业风险带来的风险溢价。一般而言，由于先正达公司的 CGU 或者反映了其农作物保护业务和种子业务的全球性质，或者是在低风险国家运营，所以，一般认为也没必要对其进行一项国家风险溢价。

除了一个 CGU 按照 14.8% 的折现率进行折现以外，其他 CGU 采用的税前折现率为 7.0%—8.5%（2009 年：7.5%—10%）。对于商誉的账面价值较高的 CGU 或 CGU 组，除下述情况以外，列报期间内减值测试的结果就折现率可能会发生的合理变化并不敏感：

确定使用价值时，为了估计未来现金流量，有必要作出一系列假设。农作物保护方面的主要假设包括未来的销售价格和销量，未来发展所需的开支，以保持产品的销路、在相关区域的注册以及产品的寿命。作为管理层预算和战略规划系列活动的一部分，每年对这些假设进行复核。这些假设可能会由于某些因素而产生重大的调整，例如，在主要市场中农作物生长模式的变化（例如由于农作物价格变动所导致的结果）、产品注册登记方面的变化、或来自竞争对手产品的压力。预计的现金流量基于五年期的先正达管理层预期、加上长期增长率假设为 2% 的一个终值。管理层认为，根据近期农业市场的增长情况，存在长期持续增长的前景。在农作物保护整个分部的层面进行减值测试的商誉为 703 百万美元（2009 年：702 百万美元）。先正达公司认为，可收回金额对为减值测试所使用的预测现金流量的假设可能会发生的合理变化不敏感。

Con.

A reduction in forecasted sales within management's five year forecast horizon compared to the previous year's five year forecast cycle combined with a reduction in latest forecasts of current year sales compared to the current year budget, is considered an indicator of market related impairment for CGU's to which no goodwill is allocated, resulting in the performance of detailed impairment tests. Syngenta also performs detailed impairment tests when there are asset specific indicators of impairment such as withdrawal of, or restrictions placed upon, product registrations, plans to divest products or, for property, plant and equipment, plans to restructure or close a site. Higher discount rates are used to test property, plant and equipment for impairment in the case of restructuring, because of the higher risk associated with remaining cash flows when operations are being physically relocated. The value in use calculation takes account of cash flows from the remaining period of operations and decommissioning costs. Property, plant and equipment and intangible asset impairments of US $ 15 million and US $ 17 million were recorded because of restructuring in 2010 and 2009 respectively.

In Crop Protection in 2009, one CGU which contains US $ 46 million of property, plant and equipment and US $ 36 million of intangible assets, excluding goodwill, and to which US $ 16 million of goodwill was allocated, had a recoverable amount equal to its carrying amount. In 2010, forecast future cash flows for this CGU have declined because of competitive price reductions in response to depressed market conditions, combined with increased distribution costs. This caused a US $ 4 million impairment loss to be recognized. Syngenta believes that the market sector in which this CGU operates will continue to grow faster than the Crop Protection market as a whole. The recoverable amount has been calculated assuming an 8.4% discount rate, a 5% compound annual sales growth rate (CAGR) over the five year horizon and a 3% long-term annual growth rate thereafter.

The sensitivity of the recoverable amount to these assumptions, expressed as additional impairment losses, is as follows:

1% increase in post tax discount rate	US $ 34 million
Long-term growth rate reduced to 2%	US $ 23 million
Both the above changes together	US $ 47 million

Another Crop Protection CGU, which had a carrying amount at December 31, 2010 of US $ 22 million, would have a recoverable amount equal to US $ 22 million if sales prices declined by 7% and operating expenses increased by 5% of sales compared to Syngenta's five year forecast.

续表

管理层的五年期预测中所预期的销售，比上一年的五年期预测有所降低，与此同时，近期对本年度销售的预测比本年度的预算有所降低，对于没有分摊商誉的 CGU 而言，这被认为是一项与市场相关的减值迹象，从而要进行详细的减值测试。当存在资产的具体减值迹象时，先正达公司也进行详细的减值测试，比如产品注册登记方面增加或者取消的一些限制、放弃一些产品或者不动产、厂房和设备的、重组或关闭一个运营场所的计划等。在重组的情况下，因为当运营的实物被搬迁时，剩余现金流的风险较高，所以对不动产、厂房和设备的减值测试采用较高的折现率。使用价值的计算考虑了剩余运营期内的现金流和退役成本。2010 年和 2009 年的重组，分别导致确认了不动产、厂房和设备以及无形资产的减值 15 百万美元和 17 百万美元。

2009 年，农作物保护分部的一个 CGU 的可收回金额等于其账面价值，这个 CGU 包含 46 百万美元的不动产、厂房和设备，36 百万美元的无形资产（不包括商誉），以及分摊到的 16 百万美元的商誉。在 2010 年，由于在低迷的市场条件下，出于竞争的目的进行了降价，且伴随着分销成本的增加，该 CGU 的预计未来现金流量有所下降。导致确认了 4 百万美元的减值损失。先正达公司相信，该 CGU 运营所处的市场领域的增长将仍然超过农作物分部的整体市场速度。可收回金额的计算中，假定的折现率为 8.4%，五年期内的复合年度销售增长率（CAGR）为 5%，之后的长期年度增长率为 3%。

可收回金额对这些假设的敏感性分析，体现为所增加的减值损失金额，列示如下：

税后折现率增加 1%	34 百万美元
长期增长率减少至 2%	23 百万美元
上面两项变化同时发生	47 百万美元

农作物保护分部的另一个 CGU，于 2010 年 12 月 31 日账面价值为 22 百万美元，如果销售价格下降 7% 而同时经营费用占销售收入的比重比先正达公司的五年期预测增加了 5%，则该 CGU 的可收回金额将等于 22 百万美元。

Con.

Goodwill of US $ 315 million has been allocated to the Seeds NAFTA Corn and Soybean CGU. The value in use of the CGU has been calculated based on 15 year cash flow forecasts in order to reflect the economic benefits of the full commercialization of new products. Over that period Syngenta's forecasts assume that new trait introductions by seed companies will increase total market value in both corn and soybean, and that Syngenta's traits will obtain an increased share of those markets. A 2% long-term annual growth rate has been assumed after the end of this period. At the 7.0% (2009: 8.1%) pre-tax discount rate used, value in use significantly exceeds the CGU's carrying amount. The carrying amount would be sensitive only to significant reductions in income or unidentified product related regulatory, technical or intellectual property issues which Syngenta does not consider reasonably possible at this time.

18.297 For each CGU that contains goodwill or intangible assets with indefinite useful lives and the amounts of such assets are significant in relation to the entity's total goodwill or intangible assets with indefinite lives, the standard *requires* additional disclosures. These are:

- The carrying amount of goodwill allocated to the CGU.
- The carrying amount of intangible assets with indefinite useful lives allocated to the CGU.
- The basis on which the CGU's recoverable amount has been determined, that is value in use or fair value less costs to sell.
- If based on value in use:
  - A description of each key assumption on which cash flow projections for the period covered by management budgets or forecasts are based. Key assumptions are those to which the recoverable amount of the CGU is most sensitive.
  - A description of how management has determined the values assigned to each key assumption, for example whether the values reflect past experience or, if appropriate, are consistent with external sources of information. If the values are not determined in this way details should be given of how the values differ from past experience or external sources of information.
  - The period over which management has projected cash flows using approved budgets and forecasts. When a period of more than five years has been used

续表

315 百万美元的商誉被分摊到北美自由贸易协定（NAFTA）玉米和大豆种子这个 CGU。该 CGU 的使用价值是基于 15 年的现金流量预测来计算的，以反映新产品完全商业化所带来的经济利益。在此期间，先正达公司的预测假设种子公司推出的新产品特性将增加玉米和大豆的总体市场价值，而先正达公司的新特性在这些市场的份额将实现增长。此期间结束后假设的长期年度增长率为 2%。采用 7%（2009 年：8.1%）的税前折现率，该 CGU 的使用价值大大超过其账面价值。只有当出现收入严重下降、未知的与产品相关的法规、技术或者知识产权方面的问题的情况下，CGU 的账面价值才会变得敏感，而先正达公司认为，目前来看，这些情况不具有合理的可能性。

18.297　对每个含有商誉或使用寿命不确定无形资产、且这些资产的金额与主体的商誉或使用寿命不确定的无形资产的总额相比是重大的 CGU，IAS 36 *要求*进行额外的披露，内容有：

- 分摊到 CGU 商誉的账面价值。
- 分摊到 CGU 的使用寿命不确定无形资产的账面价值。
- 确定 CGU 可收回金额的基础，即使用价值或公允价值减去处置费用。
- 如果是以使用价值为基础的：
  - 描述管理层在最近的预算或预测所涵盖的期间的现金流量预期的所有关键假设。关键假设是那些对 CGU 可收回金额最敏感的假设。
  - 描述管理层如何确定每一个关键假设的价值，例如，这些价值是否反映了过去的经验，或者，如果恰当的话，这些价值是否与外部信息来源一致。如果这些价值不是通过这种方式确定的，应该详细说明这些价值与过去的经验或外部信息来源相差多少。
  - 基于已批准的预算和预测的管理层现金流预期的期间。如果该期间超过五年，要解释为何超出五年的期间是合理的。

an explanation should be given of why the longer period is justified.

- The growth rate used to project cash flows beyond the period covered by management approved budgets and forecasts. A justification should be given for using a growth rate that exceeds the long-term average growth rate for the products, industries or country or countries in which the entity operates or for the market served by the CGU.
- The discount rate used in the cash flow projections.

- If based on fair value less costs to sell:
  - The methodology used to determine fair value less costs to sell. If the methodology is not based on an observable market price for the CGU the following information must also be disclosed:
    - A description of each key assumption used in determining fair value less costs to sell. Key assumptions are those to which the recoverable amount is most sensitive.
    - A description of how management has determined the values assigned to each key assumption for example whether the values reflect past experience or, if appropriate, are consistent with external sources of information. If the values are not determined in this way details should be given of how the values differ from past experience or external sources of information. The disclosures for fair value less costs to sell will be no less than those required for value in use if a discounted cash flow model has been used.

See paragraph 18. 297. 1 for additional disclosure requirements.

- If there is any reasonably possible change to a key assumption used in determining recoverable amount that would cause the CGU's carrying amount to exceed its recoverable amount the entity should disclose:
  - The amount by which the CGU's recoverable amount exceeds its carrying amount.
  - The value assigned to the key assumption.
  - The amount by which the value assigned to the key assumption must change, after adjusting values of other assumptions for consequential changes, in order for the CGU's recoverable amount to be equal to its carrying amount.

[IAS 36 para 134].

- 超出管理层已批准的预算和预测期间的现金流量预测中所使用的增长率。如果使用的增长率超过主体经营所处或者该 CGU 所服务的市场的产品、行业或国家的长期平均增长率的，应该解释其合理性。

- 现金流预测中所使用的折现率。

- 如果是以公允价值减去处置费用为基础的：
  - 确定公允价值减去处置费用所采用的方法。如果这个方法不是以该 CGU 可观察到的市场价格为基础的，必须也同时披露下列信息：
    - 描述在确定公允价值减去处置费用中所使用的所有关键假设。关键假设是那些对可收回金额最敏感的假设。
    - 描述管理层如何确定每一个关键假设的价值，例如，这些价值是否反映了过去的经验，或者，如果恰当的话，这些价值是否与外部信息来源一致。如果这些价值不是通过这种方式确定的，应该详细说明这些价值与过去的经验或外部信息来源相差多少。如果采用了折现现金流模式，那么对公允价值减去处置费用的披露内容不得少于对使用价值所要求披露的内容。

参见第 18. 297. 1 段的进一步披露要求。

- 如果用来确定可收回金额的关键假设的任何合理可能变动将导致 CGU 的账面价值超过其可收回金额，那么主体应该披露下列内容：

  - CGU 可收回金额超过账面价值的金额。
  - 关键假设的值。
  - 为了使 CGU 的可收回金额等于其账面价值，该关键假设值必须改变的金额，并且考虑这些变动会对其他假设造成的后续影响。

[IAS 36 第 134 段]。

18. 297. 1 Some additional disclosures are required for entities that calculate fair value less costs to sell using discounted cash flow projections:

- The period over which management has projected cash flows.
- The growth rate used to extrapolate cash flow projections.
- The discount rate(s) applied to the cash flow projections.

Example – Disclosures of growth rates and discount rates

Entity Z has 2 CGUs – wholesale and retail. After having performed the impairment test for goodwill, management is comfortable that the recoverable amount is higher than the carrying amount, that is, no impairment has to be recognised.

However, goodwill is material, so management asks what disclosure is needed.

The following is an example of good key assumptions disclosure:

Key assumptions used for value-in-use calculations:

	Wholesale				Retail			
	Euro	US	UK	Other	Euro	US	UK	Other
Gross margin	60%	59%	60%	56%	58%	56%	58%	55%
Growth rate	1. 8%	1. 8%	1. 8%	1. 9%	1. 1%	1. 3%	1. 1%	1. 4%
Discount rate	10. 5%	10%	11%	12. 8%	11. 5%	11%	11. 8%	13. 5%

These assumptions have been used for the analysis of each CGU within the business segment.

Management determined budgeted gross margin based on past performance and its expectations for the market development. The weighted average growth rates used are consistent with the forecasts included in industry reports. The discount rates used are pre-tax and reflect specific risks relating to the relevant segments. The impairment charge arose in a wholesale CGU in country B (included in 'Other countries' segment summary) following a decision to reduce the manufacturing output allocated to these operations. This was as a result of a re-definition of the group's allocation of manufacturing volumes across all CGUs in order to benefit from advantageous market conditions. Following this decision, the group re-

18.297.1 采用折现现金流预期来计算公允价值减去处置费用的主体，需要进一步披露：

- 管理层对现金流进行预期的期间。
- 推算预期现金流中使用的增长率。
- 现金流预期中使用的折现率。

示例——增长率和折现率的披露

主体 Z 有 2 个 CGU——批发和零售。对商誉进行了减值测试之后，管理层很有信心地认为，可收回金额高于账面价值，即不需要确认减值。

然而商誉的金额比较重大，因此管理层询问需要披露哪些事项。

下面是一个较好的对关键假设的披露示例：

使用价值计算中所使用的关键假设：

	批发				零售			
	欧洲	美国	英国	其他	欧洲	美国	英国	其他
毛利率	60%	59%	60%	56%	58%	56%	58%	55%
增长率	1.8%	1.8%	1.8%	1.9%	1.1%	1.3%	1.1%	1.4%
折现率	10.5%	10%	11%	12.8%	11.5%	11%	11.8%	13.5%

在对业务内的每个 CGU 进行分析时都使用这些假设。

管理层根据过去的绩效及其对市场发展的预期，确定预算毛利率。使用的加权平均增长率与行业报告中的预测一致。使用的折现率为税前折现率，反映了相关分部的特定风险。B 国（包括在“其他国家”这一汇总分部中）批发业务这一 CGU 出现了减值费用，其原因来自于一项减少这部分经营活动的制造业生产的决定。为了从有利的市场条件中受益，管理层对集团所有 CGU 制造额的分摊重新进行了定义，从而作出了此决定。作出这个决定后，集团重新评估了不动产、厂房和设备在这个国家的折旧政策，并且预计它们的使用寿命不会受到影响。除了商誉外，没有其他类的资产发生了减值。在 B 国，以前为批发 CGU 业务所使用的折

assessed the depreciation policies of its property, plant and equipment in this country and estimated that their useful lives will not be affected. No other class of asset other than goodwill was impaired. The discount rate used in the previous years for the wholesale CGU in country B was 12.0%.

18.298 The disclosures outlined in paragraph 18.297 are a formidable list of disclosures. The last of them is a type of sensitivity analysis and has precedents in the type of sensitivity analysis that companies often give when disclosing details of financial instruments, for example the effect of a one per cent increase or decrease in interest rates or foreign exchange rates. Similar variances might affect values attributed to assumptions in an impairment calculation. It also recognises that changes in one variable might affect other variables, increasing or decreasing the overall effect on the calculation.

Example – Sensitivity analysis

Management has carried out an impairment test and has discovered that the recoverable amount is higher than the carrying amount, but only by a small amount (recoverable amount is 3% higher than carrying amount). Therefore, a sensitivity analysis was done where the following parameters were changed in the calculation of the recoverable amount:

	Original assumption		Sensitivity analysis
Gross margin:	25%	- >	24%
Growth rate:	5%	- >	4%
Discount rate:	12%	- >	11%

It was determined that each of the changes would separately lead to an impairment since the recoverable amount would then be lower than the carrying amount.

What should management disclose?

If there is little headroom a sensitivity analysis has to be performed. The sensitivity analysis has to be disclosed if a reasonably possible change in any key assumption would cause an impairment to arise.

Management should disclose the amount of headroom.

现率为 12%。

18.298　第 18.297 段中列出了一个长长的披露项目清单。其最后一项属于一种敏感性分析，公司在披露金融工具的具体信息时已经经常在做这种敏感性分析了，比如，利率或汇率每上升或下降一个百分点所产生的影响。类似的变化可能会影响减值计算中所用到的一些假设的值。一个变量的变化可能影响到其他变量，从而会增加或减少对计算结果的整体影响。

示例——敏感性分析

管理层进行了减值测试，发现可收回金额高于账面价值，但是超出的金额很小（可收回金额比账面价值高 3%）。因此，管理层进行了敏感性分析，在可收回金额的计算中，下列参数发生变化：

	原始假设		敏感性分析
毛利率：	25%	->	24%
增长率：	5%	->	4%
折现率：	12%	->	11%

计算后发现，每一项变化都会使可收回金额低于账面价值，因此在每个变化单独发生的情况下，都会导致减值。

管理层应该披露哪些内容？

如果空间很小，管理层必须进行敏感性分析。如果任何关键假设可能会发生的合理变化将会导致出现减值损失，那么必须披露敏感性分析。

管理层应该披露空间的金额大小。

In addition, since the changes to the key assumptions that would lead to an impairment are minimal, they must be considered reasonably possible, so management should also disclose:

- The original assumptions and assumptions used in the sensitivity analysis.
- The amounts of changes that would result in impairment charges.

[The next paragraph is 18. 300.]

18. 300 Where goodwill or intangible assets with indefinite useful lives are allocated across multiple CGUs and the amount allocated to each CGU is not significant to the entity's total goodwill or intangibles with indefinite lives, the above disclosures are not required. However, the fact that goodwill or intangibles with indefinite lives are so allocated must be disclosed and the aggregate amounts allocated (for each of goodwill and intangibles with indefinite useful lives) must be disclosed. [IAS 36 para 135]. If the recoverable amounts of any of the CGUs are based on the same assumptions and the amount of goodwill or the amount of intangibles with indefinite lives allocated to those CGUs is significant to the corresponding totals for the entity the following disclosures should be made:

- The aggregate amount of goodwill allocated to those CGUs.
- The aggregate amount of intangibles with indefinite useful lives allocated to those CGUs.
- A description of the key assumptions.
- A description of how management has determined the values assigned to each key assumption for example whether the values reflect past experience or, if appropriate, are consistent with external sources of information. If the values are not determined in this way, details should be given of how the values differ from past experience or external sources of information.
- If there is any reasonably possible change to a key assumption used in determining recoverable amount that would cause the aggregate of the CGUs' carrying amounts to exceed their aggregate recoverable amounts, the entity should disclose:
  - The amount by which the aggregate of the CGUs' recoverable amounts exceeds the aggregate of their carrying amounts.

此外，由于很小的关键假设变化就会导致减值，这些变化必须被认为是合理可能的，所以管理层应该也披露以下信息：

- 原始的假设和管理层在敏感性分析中所使用的假设。
- 可能产生减值费用的变化金额。

［下一段是第 18. 300 段。］

18. 300　如果商誉或使用寿命不确定的无形资产被分摊到多个 CGU，且分摊到每个 CGU 的金额与主体的商誉或使用寿命不确定的无形资产的总额相比并不重大，在这种情况下，不要求进行上述披露。但是，必须披露商誉或使用寿命不确定无形资产是这样分摊的这一事实，同时必须披露所分摊的（商誉和使用寿命不确定的无形资产）金额合计。［IAS 36 第 135 段］。如果任何 CGU 的可收回金额是基于相同的假设，而且分摊到这些 CGU 的商誉或使用寿命不确定无形资产的金额与主体相应项目的总额相比是重大的，那么应该披露下列信息：

- 分摊到这些 CGU 的商誉总额。
- 分摊到这些 CGU 的使用寿命不确定无形资产的总额。
- 描述关键假设。
- 描述管理层确定每个关键假设值的方法，例如，这些价值是否反映了过去的经验，或者，如果恰当的话，这些价值是否与外部信息来源相一致。如果这些价值不是通过这种方法确定的，应该详细说明这些价值如何与过去经验或外部信息来源不一致。
- 如果在确定可收回金额时使用的一项关键假设的合理可能变动将引起 CGU 的账面价值总额超过可收回金额总额的，主体应该披露以下信息：
  - CGU 可收回金额总额超过其账面价值总额的金额。

- The value assigned to the key assumption.
- The amount by which the value assigned to the key assumption must change, after adjusting values of other assumptions for consequential changes, in order for the aggregate of the CGUs' recoverable amounts to be equal to the aggregate of their carrying amounts.

[IAS 36 para 135].

18.301 An example illustrating the disclosures set out in paragraphs 18.297 and 18.300 is given in the Illustrative examples section of IAS 36. [IAS 36 para 137, Illustrative examples, example 9]. The example is very long and detailed and indicates that the disclosures set out in those paragraphs are intended to be full and comprehensive. Boiler plate disclosure of a generalised nature will not be adequate. Table 18.7A – D are examples that give disclosure relating to goodwill allocated to business segments.

Table 18.7A – Disclosures relating to impairment reviews of goodwill allocated to CGUs

RWE AG – Annual Report – 31 December 2010

Goodwill[1]	**31 December 2010**	**31 December 2009**
€ million		
Germany	4,186	3,937
Power generation	*404*	*404*
Sales and distribution networks	*3,782*	*3,533*
Netherlands/Belgium	2,665	3,504
United Kingdom	2,968	2,877
Central and Eastern Europe	2,048	1,956
Renewables	736	441
Upstream gas and oil	25	26
Trading/gas midstream	944	434
Others		77
	13,572	**13,252**

■ 分配给关键假设的值。

■ 为了使 CGU 的可收回金额总额等于其账面价值总额，在考虑了对其他假设的后续影响后，分配给关键假设的值必须改变的金额。

［IAS 36 第 135 段］。

18.301 第 18.297 段和第 18.300 段所列出的披露内容，在 IAS 36 的说明性示例部分有一个例子。［IAS 36 第 137 段，说明性示例，示例 9］。对这个例子很长，也很详细，表明准则希望按这些段落中的规定进行全面综合的披露。模式化的一般性披露是不够的。表 18.7A－D 是关于分摊到业务分部的商誉的几个披露示例。

表 18.7A——对分摊到 CGU 的商誉减值复核的披露

RWE 公司——年度报告——2010 年 12 月 31 日

商誉[1]	**2010 年 12 月 31 日**	**2009 年 12 月 31 日**
百万欧元		
德国	4,186	3,937
发电厂	*404*	*404*
销售和分销网络	*3,782*	*3,533*
荷兰/比利时	2,665	3,504
英国	2,968	2,877
中欧和东欧	2,048	1,956
可再生能源	736	441
上游气和石油	25	26
贸易/中游气	944	434
其他		77
	13,572	**13,252**

Con.

In the reporting period, goodwill increased by €130 million. An increase in current redemption liabilities from put options resulted in an adjustment without an effect on income of € 213 million to the goodwill of the segment Sales and Distribution Networks. Declines in goodwill primarily resulted from the reporting of Thyssengas as "Assets and liabilities held for sale" (€77 million). In respect of additions to goodwill in the previous year (€3,871 million), €3,435 million resulted from the acquisition of Essent. With the assignment of Essent's trading activities and wind power generation to the segments Trading /Gas Midstream and Renewables, goodwill of € 510 million and € 285 million, respectively, was allocated to these segments. Goodwill of € 43 million was allocated to the segment Sales and Distribution Networks, based on the assignment of Essent's gas storage activities.

In the third quarter of each fiscal year, the regular impairment test is performed to determine if there is any need to write down goodwill. In order to carry out this impairment test, goodwill is allocated to the cash-generating units at the segment level. The impairment test involves determining the recoverable amount of the cash-generating units, which is defined as the higher of fair value less costs to sell or value in use. The fair value reflects the best estimate of the price that an independent third party would pay to purchase the cash-generating unit as of the balance-sheet date. Value in use is the present value of the future cash flows which are expected to be generated with a cash-generating unit.

Fair value is assessed from an external perspective and value in use from a company-internal perspective. We determine both variables using a business valuation model, taking into account planned future cash flows. These cash flows, in turn, are based on the business plan as approved by the Executive Board and valid at the time of the impairment test, and pertain to a detailed planning period of up to five years. In certain justifiable cases, a longer detailed planning period is taken as a basis, insofar as this is necessary due to economic or regulatory conditions. The cash flow plans are based on experience as well as on expected market trends in the future. If available, market transactions in the same sector or third-party valuations are taken as a basis for determining fair value.

Mid-term business plans are based on country-specific assumptions regarding the development of key economic indicators such as gross domestic product, consumer prices, interest rate levels and nominal wages. These estimates are, amongst others, derived from macro economic and financial studies.

The key planning assumptions for the business segments active in Europe's electricity and gas markets are estimates relating to the development of wholesale prices for electricity,

续表

报告期内商誉增加了130百万欧元。看跌期权导致当期回购义务负债的增加，使得销售及分销网络分部的商誉增加了213百万欧元，未影响收入。商誉的下降主要是由于将蒂森天然气列报为“持有待售的资产和负债”（77百万欧元）。上年度的商誉增加（3,871百万欧元）中，3,435百万欧元是收购艾森特产生的。随着艾森特的贸易和风力发电业务分配到贸易/中游气和可再生能源分部，商誉中的510百万欧元和285百万欧元分别分摊到这些分部。43百万欧元的商誉随着艾森特的天然气存储业务分摊到销售和分销网络分部。
每个财务年度的第三季度定期进行减值测试，以确定是否需要减低商誉的金额。为了执行减值测试，商誉被分摊到分部层级的各个现金产出单元。减值测试涉及确定现金产出单元的可收回金额，为公允价值减去处置费用或使用价值两者中的较高者。公允价值反映的是一个独立第三方在资产负债表日愿意为购买该现金产出单元支付的价格的最佳估计。使用价值是预期从现金产出单元产生未来现金流的现值。
公允价值是从外部角度进行评估，使用价值是从公司内部角度进行评估。这两项变量的确定都使用业务估值模型，考虑计划的未来现金流量。这些现金流量反过来又是基于执行理事会批准并在减值测试的时候有效的业务计划，并且具体计划的期间不超过5年。在某些可以合理解释的情况下，只要这是考虑到经济或者监管条件后认为是必要的，可以基于一个更长的具体计划期间。现金流量计划是基于经验以及对未来市场趋势的预期。公允价值的确定会基于同一领域的市场交易或第三方的评估值，如果能够取得的话。
中期业务计划以特定国家主要经济指标发展的假设为基础，比如国内生产总值、消费者价格、利率水平、名义工资。这些估计主要来自宏观经济研究、金融研究等等。
在欧洲从事电力和燃气市场方面的业务分部，其在计划中用到的主要假设是与电力、原油、天然气、煤炭的批发价格的发展情况，二氧化碳排放许可、电力和燃气零售

Con.

crude oil, natural gas, coal and CO2 emission allowances, retail prices for electricity and gas, and the development of market shares and regulatory framework conditions.

The discount rates used for business valuations are determined on the basis of market data. With regard to cash-generating units, during the period under review they ranged from 6.25% to 9.00% after tax (previous year: 6.5% to 9.0%) and from 8.0% to 16.5% before tax (previous year: 8.8% to 15.6%).

For the extrapolation of future cash flows going beyond the detailed planning horizon, we assumed constant growth rates of 0.0% to 1.0% (previous year: 0.0% to 1.0%). These figures are derived from experience and future expectations for the individual divisions and do not exceed the long-term average growth rates in the markets in which the Group companies are active. In calculating cash flow growth rates, the capital expenditures required to achieve the assumed cash flow growth are subtracted.

As of the balance-sheet date, both the fair values less costs to sell and the values in use were higher than the carrying amounts of the cash-generating units. These surpluses react very sensitively to changes in the discount rate, the growth rate and the operating result after taxes in terminal value as key measurement parameters.

Of all the segments, United Kingdom and Netherlands/Belgium exhibited the smallest surpluses of recoverable amount over carrying amount.

The goodwill allocated to the segment United Kingdom amounted to €2,968 million as of 31 December 2010. The impairment test showed a recoverable amount which exceeded the carrying amount by £1.1 billion. Valuation of the segment United Kingdom was calculated using a discount rate of 6.75% and a growth rate of 1.0%. An increase in the discount rate by more than 1.21 percentage points to above 7.96%, the assumption of a negative growth rate higher than 1.53% or a decrease of more than £85 million in the operating result after taxes in terminal value would result in the recoverable amount being lower than the carrying amount of the cash-generating unit United Kingdom.

The goodwill allocated to the segment Netherlands/Belgium amounted to €2,665 million. The recoverable amount exceeded the carrying amount by €0.9 billion. Impairment would have been necessary if the calculations had used a discount rate increased by more than 0.42 percentage points to above 6.67%, a growth rate decreased by more than 0.69 percentage points to below 0.31% or an operating result reduced by more than €61 million in terminal value.

续表

价，以及市场份额的发展和监管框架的情况。 业务估值所使用的折现率是基于市场数据来确定的。对于各个现金产出单元，在减值复核的期间内，税后折现率的范围在 6.25%—9.00% 之间（上年：6.5%—9.0%），税前折现率的范围在 8.0%—16.5%（上年：8.8%—15.6%）。 为了推断超过具体计划范围之后的未来现金流，我们假设长期增长率为 0.0% 至 1.0%（上年度：0.0% 至 1.0%）。这些数据来源于经验和对各个部门的未来的预期，且不超过本集团各公司所位于的市场的长期平均增长率。在计算现金流量的增长率时，要扣除为了达到假设的现金流增长所要求的资本性支出。 于资产负债表日，公允价值减去处置费用和使用价值均高于这些现金产出单元的账面价值。这些超出部分非常敏感，很容易受到折现率、增值率以及在终值中的税后经营业绩这几个关键的计量参数变动的影响。 在所有的分部中，英国和荷兰/比利时分部的可收回金额与账面价值相比，超出部分的金额是最小的。 于 2010 年 12 月 31 日，分摊到英国分部的商誉金额为 2,968 百万欧元。减值测试显示其可收回金额超出账面价值 11 亿英镑。英国分部的估值计算中，使用的折现率为 6.75%、增长率为 1.0%。如果折现率的增加超过 1.21 个百分点到 7.96% 以上，增长率假设为负增长且超过 1.53%，或者终值中的税后经营业绩下降超过 85 百万英镑，都会导致英国分部现金产出单元的可收回金额低于账面价值。 分摊到荷兰/比利时分部的商誉金额为 2,665 百万欧元。其可收回金额超出账面价值 9 亿欧元。如果在计算中使用的折现率增加超过 0.42 个百分点到 6.67% 以上，增长率下降超过 0.69 个百分点到 0.31% 以下，或者终值中的经营业绩下降超过 61 百万欧元，都会导致需要计提减值准备。

Table 18.7B – Disclosures relating to impairment reviews of goodwill allocated to CGUs

Thomson Reuters Corporation Annual Report – 31 December 2010

NOTE 1: SUMMARY OF BUSINESS AND SIGNIFICANT ACCOUNTING POLICIES (extract)

Intangible assets (extract)

Goodwill

Goodwill represents the excess of the cost of an acquisition over the fair value of the Company's share of the identifiable net assets of the acquired subsidiary or equity method investee at the date of acquisition. Goodwill is tested annually for impairment and carried at cost less accumulated impairment losses. Gains and losses on the disposal of an entity include the carrying amount of goodwill relating to the entity sold.

NOTE 18: GOODWILL (extract)

Impairment tests of goodwill

The Company performed its annual test for goodwill impairment in the fourth quarter of 2010 in accordance with its policy described in note 1. The estimated fair value less cost to sell of all units exceeded their carrying values. As a result, no goodwill impairment was recorded.

The Company has 12 CGUs, all of which include goodwill. The carrying value of goodwill for significant CGUs is identified separately in the table below. "All other" comprises goodwill allocated to the remaining CGU:

Carrying amount of goodwill at:

	Carrying amount of goodwill at December 31,	
Cash Generating Unit	**2010**	2009[(1)]
West	**2,894**	2,590
Markets	**13,505**	13,140
All other	**2,493**	2,400
Total goodwill	**18,892**	18,130

表 18.7B——与分摊到 CGU 的商誉减值复核相关的一些披露

汤森路透公司年度报告——2010 年 12 月 31 日

附注 1：业务概况和重要会计政策（摘录）

无形资产（摘录）

商誉

商誉，是指合并成本超出本公司享有的被购买子公司（或权益法核算的被投资方）可辨认净资产于购买日公允价值份额的差额。商誉每年进行减值测试，账面价值等于成本减去累计减值损失。处置一个主体的处置利得和损失包括与所出售的主体相关的商誉的账面价值。

附注 18：商誉（摘录）

商誉的减值测试

根据附注 1 所描述的会计政策，本公司于 2010 年第四季度进行了商誉的年度减值测试。估计的所有单元的公允价值减去处置费用均超过其账面价值，因此，未确认商誉减值。

本公司有 12 个现金产出单元，全都包含有商誉。重要 CGU 的商誉账面价值在下表中单独列示。“所有其他”包括分摊到剩余的 CGU 的商誉：

商誉的账面价值

	12 月 31 日商誉的账面价值	
现金产出单元	**2010**	2009[1]
西部	**2,894**	2,590
市场	**13,505**	13,140
所有其他	**2,493**	2,400
商誉总计	**18,892**	18,130

Con.

(1) 2009 is presented on a comparable basis to 2010, reflecting a realignment of the Company's CGUs.

The valuation techniques, significant assumptions and sensitivities applied in the goodwill impairment test are described below:

Valuation Techniques

The Company did not make any changes to the valuation methodology used to assess goodwill impairment since the last annual impairment test. The recoverable value of each CGU was based on fair value less cost to sell, using a weighted average of the following two methods to estimate fair value:

Income approach

The income approach is predicated upon the value of the future cash flows that a business will generate going forward. The discounted cash flow ("DCF") method was used which involves projecting cash flows and converting them into a present value equivalent through discounting. The discounting process uses a rate of return that is commensurate with the risk associated with the business or asset and the time value of money. This approach requires assumptions about revenue growth rates, operating margins, tax rates and discount rates.

Market approach

The market approach assumes that companies operating in the same industry will share similar characteristics and that company values will correlate to those characteristics. Therefore, a comparison of a CGU to similar companies whose financial information is publicly available may provide a reasonable basis to estimate fair value. Under the market approach, fair value is calculated based on EBITDA multiples of benchmark companies comparable to the businesses in each CGU. Data for the benchmark companies was obtained from publicly available information.

Significant Assumptions

Weighting of Valuation Techniques

The Company weighted the results of the two valuation techniques noted above, consistently applied to each CGU, as follows: 60% income approach/40% market approach. The Company believes that given volatility in capital markets, it is appropriate to apply a heavier weighting to the income approach. The selection and weighting of the fair value techniques requires judgment.

续表

(1) 2009 年是按照一个与 2010 年可比的基础进行列示的，以反映本公司 CGU 的重新组合。

商誉减值测试中运用的评估技术、重要假设以及敏感性说明如下：

评估技术

本公司用于评估商誉减值的评估方法自上一次年度减值测试后未发生任何改变。每一个 CGU 的可收回价值都是基于其公允价值减去处置费用确定的，并使用了以下两种方法的加权平均来估计公允价值：

收益法

收益法是基于一项业务在持续经营前提下产生的未来现金流量的价值所作出的预计，采用折现现金流量（“DCF”）的方法，该方法涉及对现金流量进行预计、并通过折现将他们转换为相应的现值。在折现中使用回报率，这个比率与该业务或资产相关的风险和货币的时间价值相当。这种方法要求对收入增长率、经营毛利、税率以及折现率进行假设。

市场法

市场法假设在相同行业内经营的公司拥有相似的特质，并且这些公司的价值与这些特质之间存在关联。因此，将一个 CGU 和有公开财务信息的相似公司进行比较，可以为公允价值的预计提供一个合理的基础。在市场法下，公允价值的计算是基于与每一个 CGU 的业务具有可比性的基准公司的 EBITDA 乘数。这些基准公司的数据来自于可以从公开渠道获取的信息。

重要假设

评估技术的权重

本公司对上面提到的两种评估技术的结果进行了如下加权：收益法占 60%/市场法占 40%，所有的 CGU 都运用这一相同的权重。本公司相信，鉴于资本市场波动较大，给予收益法一个比较高的权重是合适的。公允价值评估技术的选择和加权需要作出判断。

Con.

Growth

The assumptions used were based on the Company's internal budget. The Company projected revenue, operating margins and cash flows for a period of five years, and applied a perpetual long-term growth rate thereafter. In arriving at its forecasts, the Company considered past experience, economic trends such as GDP growth and inflation as well as industry and market trends. The projections also took into account the expected impact from new product initiatives, customer retention and integration programs, and the maturity of the markets in which each business operates.

Discount Rate

The Company assumed a discount rate in order to calculate the present value of its projected cash flows. The discount rate represented a weighted average cost of capital ("WACC") for comparable companies operating in similar industries as the applicable CGU, based on publicly available information. The WACC is an estimate of the overall required rate of return on an investment for both debt and equity owners and serves as the basis for developing an appropriate discount rate. Determination of the WACC requires separate analysis of the cost of equity and debt, and considers a risk premium based on an assessment of risks related to the projected cash flows of each unit.

Lower discount rates were applied to CGUs whose cash flows are expected to be less volatile due to factors such as the maturity of the market they serve and their market position. Higher discount rates were applied to CGUs whose cash flows are expected to be more volatile due to competition, or participation in less stable geographic markets.

Tax Rate

The tax rates applied to the projections reflected intercompany transfer pricing agreements currently in effect which were assumed to be transferable to another market participant. In certain circumstances, the effective tax rates, which ranged from 41% to 25%, were below the statutory tax rates. Tax assumptions are sensitive to changes in tax laws as well as assumptions about the jurisdictions in which profits are earned. It is possible that actual tax rates could differ from those assumed.

The key assumptions used in performing the impairment test, by CGU, were as follows:

	Markets	West	All other
Discount rate	9.5%	7.5%	7.6% - 11.2%
Perpetual growth rate	3.0%	2.0%	1.5% - 3.0%

续表

增长

使用的假设基于本公司的内部预算。本公司预测了五年内的收入、经营毛利和现金流，之后则采用了一个持续长期增长率。在预测过程中，本公司考虑了过去的经验、经济趋势（如 GDP 增长和通货膨胀）以及行业和市场的趋势。该预测也考虑了新产品带来的影响、客户的维系及整合项目以及每项业务所在市场的成熟状况。

折现率

为了计算所预计的现金流量的现值，本公司对折现率进行了假设。折现率体现了与相应的 CGU 处于同一行业的可比公司的加权平均资本成本（“WACC”），基于可以从公开取得的信息。WACC 是对包括债务类和权益类投资者在内的整体所要求的投资回报率的一个估计，它是形成一个适当的折现率的基础。确定 WACC 要求对权益和债务成本进行单独分析，并在对每一个单元预计现金流量相关的风险进行评估的基础上，考虑一个风险溢价。

一些 CGU，由于他们所服务的市场及其市场地位等因素使得其现金流量波动并不太大，这些 CGU 采用较低的折现率；一些 CGU，由于竞争的原因，或者处于某些不太稳定的地理区域市场中，从而预期其现金流的波动较大，这些 CGU 则采用较高的折现率。

税率

预测中适用的税率反映了当前有效的公司间内部转移定价协议，且假设这是其他的市场参与者也可以获取到的。在某些情况下，范围在 40% 至 25% 之间的实际税率低于法定税率。税法的改变、以及利润是在哪个税收管辖区赚取的假设，会对税务假设带来敏感的影响。实际税率有可能与假设不同。

按照 CGU 列示的，在进行减值测试时使用的关键假设如下：

	市场	西部	所有其他
折现率	9.5%	7.5%	7.6%—11.2%
持续增长率	3.0%	2.0%	1.5%—3.0%

Con.

The fair value for each CGU was in excess of its carrying value. The excess ranged from 17% to 898% of the carrying value of the applicable CGU. Based on sensitivity analysis, no reasonably possible change in assumptions would cause the carrying amount of any CGU to exceed its recoverable amount.

Table 18.7C – Disclosures relating to impairment reviews of goodwill allocated to CGUs

British American Tobacco p. l. c. – Annual Report – 31 December 2009

9 Intangible assets (extract)

Impairment testing for intangible assets with indefinite lives including goodwill

Goodwill of £11,331 million (2008: £11,391 million) included in intangible assets in the balance sheet is mainly the result of the following acquisitions: Rothmans Group £4,833 million (2008: £4,974 million); Imperial Tobacco £2,370 million (2008: £2,261 million); ETI (Italy) £1,463 million (2008: £1,591 million); ST (principally Scandinavia £1,103 million (2008: £1,200 million); Tekel (Turkey) £579 million (2008: £619 million) as well as £205 million relating to the Bentoel (Indonesia) acquisition in 2009. The principal allocations of goodwill in the Rothmans' acquisition are to the cash-generating units of Eastern and Western Europe, and South Africa (2008: Europe and South Africa), with the remainder mainly relating to operations in the domestic and export market in the United Kingdom and operations in Asia-Pacific.

As a consequence of the Group's new regional structure effective 1 January 2009, goodwill allocated to the Europe cash-generating unit (2008: £2,293 million) has been apportioned between the new cash-generating units of Western Europe and Eastern Europe. The goodwill on the ST transaction has been allocated between the cash-generating units of ST and Western Europe.

In 2009, goodwill has been allocated for impairment testing purposes to 16 individual cash-generating units – four in western Europe, one in Eastern Europe, two in Africa and Middle East, five in Asia-Pacific, and four in Americas. In 2008, goodwill was allocated for impairment testing purposes to 15 individual cash-generating units-five in Europe, two in Africa and Middle East, three in Asia-Pacific, three in Latin America and two in America-Pacific.

In 2009, the carrying amounts of goodwill allocated to the cash-generating units of Canada £2,370 million, Italy £1,471 million, Western Europe (includes Rothmans and other

续表

每个 CGU 的公允价值都超过其账面价值。各个 CGU 的超出部分占 CGU 的账面价值的 17% 至 898%。根据敏感性分析，这些假设的合理可能的变化不会导致任何 CGU 的账面价值超过其可收回金额。

表 18.7C——分摊到 CGU 的商誉减值复核的披露

英美烟草公司——年度报告——2009 年 12 月 31 日

9. 无形资产（摘录）

使用寿命不确定的无形资产（包括商誉）的减值测试

资产负债表无形资产中所包括的 11,331 百万英镑的商誉（2008：11,391 百万英镑）主要来自于下列收购：乐富门集团 4,833 百万英镑（2008：4,974 百万英镑）；帝国烟草公司 2,370 百万英镑（2008：2,261 百万英镑）；ETI（意大利）1,463 百万英镑（2008：1,591 百万英镑）；ST（主要是在斯堪的纳维亚）1,103 百万英镑（2008：1,200百万英镑）；Tekel（土耳其）579 百万英镑（2008：619 百万英镑）以及 2009 年收购的 Bentoel（印度尼西亚）205 百万英镑。收购乐富门时所产生的商誉主要分配给了东西欧和南非（2008：欧洲和南非）的现金产出单元，其余部分分配给了英国国内和出口市场的运营以及亚太地区的运营。

随着集团新的区域结构自 2009 年 1 月 1 日起生效，分摊到欧洲的现金产出单元的商誉（2008 年为 2,293 百万英镑）已被按比例分摊给西欧和东欧的新的现金产出单元。ST 交易产生的商誉已经分摊到 ST 和西欧的现金产出单元。

2009 年，为了进行减值测试，商誉被分摊到 16 个单独的现金产出单元——西欧 4 个、东欧 1 个、非洲和中东 2 个、亚太地区 5 个、美洲 4 个。2008 年，为了进行减值测试，商誉被分摊到 15 个单独的现金产出单元——欧洲 5 个、非洲和中东 2 个、亚太地区 3 个、拉丁美洲 3 个、美洲—太平洋地区 2 个。

2009 年，相对于商誉的账面价值总额而言，分摊到各个现金产出单元的商誉账面价值较大的为：加拿大 2,370 百万英镑、意大利 1,471 百万英镑、西欧（包括乐富门

Con.

acquisitions) £1, 208 million, Eastern Europe (includes Rothmans and other acquisitions) £1, 062 million, ST (principally Scandinavia) £991 million, South Africa £932 million, Australia (includes Rothmans and other acquisitions) £746 million, Turkey £579 million, Singapore £471 million and Malaysia £426 million are considered significant in comparison with the total carrying amount of goodwill.

In 2008, the carrying amounts of goodwill allocated to the cash-generating units of South Africa £833 million Australia (includes Rothmans and other acquisitions) £650 million , Malaysia £474 million, Singapore £516 million , Europe (includes Rothmans and other acquisitions) £2,293 million (2007: £1,697 million), Canada £2,261 million (2007: £2,046 million), Italy £1,600 million (2007: £1,218 million) and in respect of the acquisitions made during 2008, ST (principally Scandinavia) £1,200 million and Turkey £619 million are considered significant in comparison with the total carrying amount of goodwill.

The recoverable amount of all cash-generating units has been determined on a value-in-use basis. The key assumptions for the recoverable amount of all units are the long-term growth rate and the discount rate. The long-term growth rate used is purely for the impairment testing of goodwill under IAS 36 Impairment of Assets and does not reflect long-term planning assumptions used by the Group for investment proposals or for any other assessments. The discount rate is based on the Group's weighted average cost of capital, taking into account the cost of capital and borrowings, to which specific market-related premium adjustments are made. These assumptions have been applied to the individual cash flows of each unit as compiled by local management in the different markets.

The valuation uses cash flows based on detailed financial budgets prepared by management covering a one year (2008: two year) period, with growth in year 2 of 6 per cent. Cash flows for the years 3 to 10 are extrapolated from year 2 cash flows at 5 per cent per annum (2008: 3 per cent), including 2 per cent inflation, whereafter a total growth rate of 2 per cent per annum (2008: zero per cent) has been assumed.

The amendments to the approach in 2009 reflect changes in the Group's management reporting processes and greater consistency between the basis for the projected cash flows and the related discount rates.

The extrapolated growth rates are considered conservative given the Group's history of growth, its well balanced portfolio of brands and the industry in which it operates. The

续表

和其他收购）1,208 百万英镑、东欧（包括乐富门和其他收购）1,062 百万英镑、ST（主要是斯堪的纳维亚）991 百万英镑、南非 932 百万英镑、澳大利亚（包括乐富门和其他收购）746 百万英镑、土耳其 579 百万英镑、新加坡 471 百万英镑和马来西亚 426 百万英镑。 2008 年，相对于商誉的账面价值总额而言，分摊到各个现金产出单元的商誉账面价值较大的为：南非 833 百万英镑、澳大利亚（包括乐富门和其他收购）650 百万英镑、马来西亚 474 百万英镑、新加坡 516 百万英镑，欧洲（包括乐富门和其他收购）2,293 百万英镑、加拿大 2,261 百万英镑、意大利 1,600 百万英镑，及 2008 年收购的 ST（主要是斯堪的纳维亚）的 1,200 百万英镑和土耳其的 619 百万英镑。 所有现金产出单元的可收回金额都是以其使用价值为基础来确定的。所有单元可收回金额的关键假设是长期增长率和折现率。所使用的长期增长率完全是为了按照 IAS 36——资产减值对商誉进行减值测试的目的，不反映本集团在制定投资提案或进行其他评估时所使用的长期规划假设。折现率以本集团的加权平均资本成本为基础，考虑资本和借款的成本，并就特定的市场风险溢价进行调整。各个不同市场的地方管理层在编制各现金产出单元的独立现金流量时，都使用了这些假设。 评估使用的现金流量基于管理层编制的为期 1 年（2008：2 年）详细财务预算，第 2 年的增长率为 6%。第 3 年至第 10 年的现金流量在第 2 年现金流量的基础上以每年增长 5%（2008 年为 3%）来推算，其中包括 2% 的通货膨胀，第 10 年以后假设每年总体增长率为 2%（2008：0%）。 2009 年对方法的修改反映了本集团管理层报告流程的变化，以及预计现金流量的基础和相应的折现率之间更为一致。 考虑到本集团的历史增长情况、对各种品牌投资组合之间有效的平衡、及其所处的行业，用来进行推算的增长率被认为是一个保守的增长率。长期实际增长率不超过

Con.

long-term real growth does not exceed the expected long-term average growth rate for the combined markets in which the cash-generating units operate. In some instances, such as recent acquisitions or start-up ventures, the valuation is expanded to reflect the medium-term plan of management, spanning five years or beyond, with the cash flow beyond these years to year 10, extrapolated by growth of 5 per cent, as above.

Pre-tax discount rates of between 7. 9 per cent and 18. 7 per cent (2008: 7. 9 per cent to 18. 7 per cent) were used, based on the Group's weighted average cost of capital, together with any premium applicable for economical and political risks.

The pre-tax discount rates used for the cash-generating units which are significant in comparison with the total carrying amount of goodwill are 9. 7 per cent for Canada (2008: 9. 7 per cent), 11. 4 per cent for Italy (2008: 9. 8 per cent), 9. 3 per cent for Western Europe, 10. 6 per cent for Eastern Europe (2008: combined Europe 9. 3 per cent), 8. 7 per cent for ST (principally Scandinavia) (2008: 8. 7 per cent), 11. 5 per cent for South Africa (2008: 11. 5 per cent), 9. 3 per cent for Australia (2008: 9. 3 per cent), 13. 1 per cent for Turkey (2008: 13. 1 per cent), 7. 9 per cent for Singapore (2008: 7. 9 per cent) and 10. 0 per cent for Malaysia (2008: 10. 1 per cent).

No goodwill impairment charges were recognised in 2009 or 2008. If discounted cash flows per cash-generating unit should fall by 10 per cent, or the discount rate was increased at an after tax rate of 1 per cent, there would be no impairment.

Table 18. 7D – Impairment testing of goodwill and sensitivity analysis disclosures

London Stock Exchange – Annual Report – 31 December 2010

13. Intangible assets (extract)

Impairment tests for goodwill (extract)

Value in use calculations for each CGU are sensitive to changes in short and medium term revenue and cost growth assumptions, long term growth rates and pre – tax discount rates. The impact on value in use of a change in these assumptions is shown below:

续表

这些现金产出单元所处的市场组合的预期长期平均增长率。有些情况下，例如最近收购的企业或者是刚刚开办的企业，评估中将范围扩大到反映管理层超越5年或更长时间的中期计划，超出计划期之后直到第10年的现金流使用上述5%的增长率进行推算。 根据本集团的加权平均资本成本、恰当的经济和政治风险溢价，使用的税前折现率为7.9%—18.7%（2008：7.9%—18.7%）。 与商誉账面价值总额相比，商誉金额较高的现金产出单元所使用的税前折现率为：加拿大9.7%（2008：9.7%）、意大利11.4%（2008：9.8%）、西欧9.3%，东欧10.6%（2008年欧洲为9.3%）、ST（主要是斯堪的纳维亚）8.7%（2008：8.7%）、南非11.5%（2008：11.5%）、澳大利亚9.3%（2008：9.3%）、土耳其13.1%（2008：13.1%）、新加坡7.9%（2008：7.9%）、马来西亚10.0%（2008：10.1%）。 2009年和2008年都没有确认商誉减值费用。如果现金产出单元的折现现金流下降10%，或者税后折现率增加1%，不会出现减值。

表18.7D——商誉减值测试和敏感性分析的披露 **伦敦证券交易市场——年度报告——2010年12月31日** **13. 无形资产(摘录)** ***商誉减值测试(摘录)*** 每个CGU使用价值的计算中,对中短期收入、费用增长假设、长期增长率和税前折现率的变化都比较敏感。这些假设因素的变化对使用价值的影响如下:

Con.

		Impact on value in use of:			
	Excess of value in use over carrying value	5% reduction in revenues	5% increase in costs	0.5% reduction in long-term growth rate	0.5% increase in pre-tax discount rate
	£m	£m	£m	£m	£m
Borsa Italiana group:					
Issuer	0.1	(9.0)	(5.0)	(4.3)	(5.6)
Equities Trading	30.2	(20.6)	(9.5)	(11.9)	(15.4)
Derivatives Trading	21.3	(7.0)	(2.9)	(4.3)	(5.5)
Fixed Income Trading	89.2	(33.1)	(15.2)	(19.8)	(25.3)
Information & Technology Services	67.2	(26.6)	(9.9)	(16.2)	(20.8)
Post Trade Services	39.1	(66.0)	(30.1)	(37.0)	(47.4)

Management believes goodwill allocated to MillenniumIT, Turquoise and EDX CGUs is unlikely to be impaired under any reasonable changes to key assumptions. The excess of value in use over carrying value is determined by reference to the carrying value, post impairment charge, as at 31 March 2010. Revenue and cost sensitivities assume a five per cent change in revenues or costs for each of the five years in the value in use calculations.

18.302 If any of the goodwill acquired in a business combination during the period has not been allocated to a CGU by the end of that period the entity must disclose the amount of the unallocated goodwill and the reason why it remains unallocated. [IAS 36 para 133].

18.303 The standard notes that the most recent detailed calculation of recoverable amount for a CGU made in a prior period may be brought forward and used in the impairment test for that CGU in the current period – see paragraph 18.82. It states that where this is done the disclosures in paragraphs 18.297 and 18.300 relate to the brought forward calculation of recoverable amount. [IAS 36 para 136].

First-time adoption of IFRS

18.304 There are specific rules in respect of first-time adoption of IFRS, set out

续表

	使用价值超出账面价值的部分	对使用价值的影响：收入减少5%	费用增加5%	长期增长率降低0.5%	税前折现率增加0.5%
	百万英镑	百万英镑	百万英镑	百万英镑	百万英镑
意大利证券交易所集团：					
发行人	0.1	(9.0)	(5.0)	(4.3)	(5.6)
股票交易	30.2	(20.6)	(9.5)	(11.9)	(15.4)
衍生品交易	21.3	(7.0)	(2.9)	(4.3)	(5.5)
固定收入交易	89.2	(33.1)	(15.2)	(19.8)	(25.3)
信息技术服务	67.2	(26.6)	(9.9)	(16.2)	(20.8)
交易后服务	39.1	(66.0)	(30.1)	(37.0)	(47.4)

管理层认为，关键假设发生合理变化的情况下，分摊到 MillenniumIT，Turquoise 和 EDX 的 CGU 的商誉发生减值的可能性不大。使用价值超出账面价值的部分是按照 2010 年 3 月 31 日的扣除减值损失后的账面价值计算确定的。在5 年中，每一年收入或成本变动5%，会给使用价值的计算造成比较敏感的影响。

18.302 如果当期业务合并中所取得的商誉，到期末还没有分摊到某个 CGU，则主体必须披露未分摊的商誉的金额以及没有分摊的原因。[IAS 36 第 133 段]。

18.303 该准则注意到，前期进行的对 CGU 的可收回金额的最近的详细计算，可能被带到当期对该 CGU 的减值测试中使用——见第 18.82 段。该准则规定，在这种情况下，第 18.297 段和第 18.300 段所述的披露与带到当期使用的可收回金额的计算有关。[IAS 36 第 136 段]。

首次采用国际财务报告准则

18.304 在 IFRS 1 中关于首次采用国际财务报告准则作出了专门的规定。

in IFRS 1, 'First-time adoption of International Financial Reporting Standards'. IFRS 1 requires that goodwill should be reviewed for impairment at the date of transition to IFRS, regardless of whether there are indications of impairment. Any resulting impairment loss should be charged to retained earnings. [IFRS 1 App B para B2(g)]. Goodwill previously written off to reserves under previous GAAP is excluded from this requirement. IFRS 3 is quite specific and states that if an entity previously recognised goodwill as a deduction from equity, it should not recognise that goodwill in profit or loss when it disposes of all or part of the business to which that goodwill relates. Nor should it recognise the goodwill in profit or loss when a CGU to which the goodwill relates becomes impaired. [IFRS 3 para 80]. IFRS 1, 'First-time adoption of International Financial Reporting Standards', contains a similar prohibition. [IFRS 1 App B para B2(i)]. This requirement and other implications of IAS 36 for first-time adopters of IFRS are considered in detail in chapter 3.

IFRS 1 要求在过渡到 IFRS 的转换日，无论是否存在减值迹象，都需要对商誉进行减值复核。由此产生的减值损失应计入留存收益。[IFRS 1 附录 B 第 2（g）段]。此要求不包括按照原公认会计原则已经被冲销进入储备的商誉。IFRS 3 非常明确地指出过，如果一个主体以前将商誉确认为权益的抵减项，当它全部或者部分处置该商誉所对应的业务时，不得将商誉转入损益。也不得在与该商誉相关的 CGU 发生减值时将商誉转入损益。[IFRS 3 第 80 段]。IFRS 1——首次采用国际财务报告准则也有一项类似的禁止条款。[IFRS 1 附录 B 第 2（i）段]。这项要求以及 IAS 36 对国际财务报告的首次采用者的其他影响在第三章具体讨论。

PwC Assurance Service Contacts
联系普华永道审计业务部

北京 Beijing
梁伟坚 Thomas Leung
电话 Tel：+86（10）6533 2838
电子邮件 Email：thomas. w. leung@ cn. pwc. com

重庆 Chongqing
李松波 Bobby Lee
电话 Tel：+86（23）6393 7388
电子邮件 Email：bobby. lee@ cn. pwc. com

大连 Dalian
关兆文 Dorman Kwan
电话 Tel：+86（411）8379 1666
电子邮件 Email：dorman. kwan@ cn. pwc. com

广州 Guangzhou
张展豪 Albert Cheung
电话 Tel：+86（755）8261 8833
电子邮件 Email：albert. cheung@ cn. pwc. com

杭州 Hangzhou
潘振翔 Steve Pan
电话 Tel：+86（21）2323 2626
电子邮件 Email：steve. pan@ cn. pwc. com

南京 Nanjing
钱进 Jevens Qian
电话 Tel：+86（21）2323 3579
电子邮件 Email：jevens. qian@ cn. pwc. com

宁波 Ningbo
徐宏 Toby Xu
电话 Tel：+86（21）2323 3399
电子邮件 Email：toby. xu@ cn. pwc. com

青岛 Qingdao
张国俊 Kevin Zhang
电话 Tel：+86（532）8089 1818
电子邮件 Email：kevin. zhang@ cn. pwc. com

上海 Shanghai
李丹 Daniel Li
电话 Tel：+86（21）2323 3388
电子邮件 Email：daniel. li@ cn. pwc. com

深圳 Shenzhen
张展豪 Albert Cheung
电话 Tel：+86（755）8261 8833
电子邮件 Email：albert. cheung@ cn. pwc. com

苏州 Suzhou
汪超 Arthur Wang
电话 Tel：+86（512）6273 1998
电子邮件 E－mail：arthur. wang@ cn. pwc. com

天津 Tianjin
郑广安 Kwong On Cheng
电话 Tel：+86（22）2318 3003
电子邮件 Email：kwong. on. cheng@ cn. pwc. com

厦门 Xiamen
张祚诚 Douglas Chang
电话 Tel：+86（592）210 7888 * 1616
电子邮件 Email：douglas. dc. chang@ cn. pwc. com

西安 Xi'an
叶骏 Joe Ye
电话 Tel：+86（29）8720 3998
电子邮件 Email：joe. ye@ cn. pwc. com

PwC Accounting Consulting Services Contacts
联系普华永道会计咨询服务

黄家勇 Wilfred Wong
电话 Tel：+852 2289 1322
电子邮件 Email：wilfred. wong@ hk. pwc. com

金以文 Yvonne Kam
电话 Tel：+86（21）2323 3267
电子邮件 Email：yvonne. kam@ cn. pwc. com

陈保郎 Baolang Chen
电话 Tel：+86（21）2323 2555
电子邮件 Email：baolang. chen@ cn. pwc. com

陈燕华 Tracy Chen
电话 Tel：+86（21）2323 3070
电子邮件 Email：tracy. yh. chen@ cn. pwc. com

PwC China, Hong Kong, Macau , Taiwan and Singapore Office Locations and Contacts
普华永道在中国大陆、香港、澳门和台湾及新加坡的事务所

北京 Beijing
中国北京市
朝阳区东三环中路7号
北京财富中心写字楼A座26楼
邮政编码 100020
26/F Office Tower A
Beijing Fortune Plaza
7 Dongsanhuan Zhong Road
Chaoyang District
Beijing 100020, PRC
电话 Tel: +86 (10) 6533 8888
传真 Fax: +86 (10) 6533 8800

重庆 Chongqing
中国重庆市渝中区邹容路68号
大都会商厦19楼1905室
邮政编码 400010
Room 1905
19/F Metropolitan Tower
68 Zou Rong Road
Chongqing 400010, PRC
电话 Tel: +86 (23) 6393 7888
传真 Fax: +86 (23) 6393 7200

大连 Dalian
中国大连市西岗区中山路147号
森茂大厦8楼
邮政编码 116011
8/F Senmao Building
147 Zhongshan Road
Xigang District
Dalian 116011, PRC
电话 Tel: +86 (411) 8379 1888
传真 Fax: +86 (411) 8379 1800

广州 Guangzhou
中国广州市天河区珠江新城
珠江西路10号
普华永道中心18楼
邮政编码 510623
18/F PwC Center
10 Zhujiang Xi Road
Pearl River New City
Tianhe District
Guangzhou 510623, PRC
电话 Tel: +86 (20) 3819 2000
传真 Fax: +86 (20) 3819 2100

杭州 Hangzhou
中国杭州市下城区环城北路208号
坤和中心3205室
邮政编码 310006
Room 3205, Canhigh Center
208 Huancheng Road North
Xiacheng District
Hangzhou 310006, PRC
电话: +86 (571) 2807 6388
传真: +86 (571) 2807 6300

香港 Hong Kong
中国香港中环太子大厦22楼
22/F Prince's Building
Central
Hong Kong, PRC
电话 Tel: +852 2289 8888
传真 Fax: +852 2810 9888

澳门 Macau
中国澳门苏亚利斯博士大马路 323 号
中国银行大厦 29 楼
29/F Bank of China Building
323 Avenida Doutor Mario Soares
Macau, PRC
电话 Tel: +853 8799 5111
传真 Fax: +853 8799 5222

青岛 Qingdao
中国青岛市市南区延安三路 234 号
海航万邦中心 1 号楼 37 楼
邮政编码 266071
37/F Tower One, HNA IMC Center
234 Yanan Third Road, Shinan District
Qingdao 266071, PRC
电话 Tel: +86 (532) 8089 1888
传真 Fax: +86 (532) 8089 1800

南京 Nanjing
中国南京市鼓楼区中央路 201 号
南京国际广场南塔 12A 层 01 室
邮政编码 210009
Room 12A01, South Tower
Nanjing International Center
201 Zhongyang Road
Gulou District
Nanjing 210009, PRC
电话 Tel: +86 (25) 6608 6288
传真 Fax: +86 (25) 6608 6210

上海 Shanghai
中国上海市黄浦区湖滨路 202 号
企业天地 2 号楼
普华永道中心 11 楼
邮政编码 200021
11/F PwC Center
2 Corporate Avenue
202 Hu Bin Road
Huangpu District
Shanghai 200021, PRC
电话 Tel: +86 (21) 2323 8888
传真 Fax: +86 (21) 2323 8800

宁波 Ningbo
中国宁波市江东区民安东路 268 号
宁波国际金融服务中心 E 座 1203 室
邮政编码 315040
Room 1203, Tower E
Ningbo International Financial Center
268 Min An Road East
Jiangdong District
Ningbo 315040, PRC
电话 Tel: +86 (574) 8187 1788
传真 Fax: +86 (574) 8187 1700

深圳 Shenzhen
中国深圳市罗湖区深南东路 5016 号
京基 100 – A 座 34 楼
邮政编码 518001
34/F Tower A, Kingkey 100
5016 Shennan East Road
Luohu District
Shenzhen 518001, PRC
电话 Tel: +86 (755) 8261 8888
传真 Fax: +86 (755) 8261 8800

新加坡 Singapore
新加坡 048424 邮区
PWC 大厦
克罗士街 8 号 17 楼
8 Cross Street # 17 – 00
PWC Building
Singapore 048424
电话 Tel： +65 6236 3388
传真 Fax： +65 6236 3300

天津 Tianjin
中国天津市和平区
南京路 189 号
津汇广场 2 座 36 楼
邮政编码 300051
36/F The Exchange Tower Two
189 Nanjing Road
Heping District
Tianjin 300051, PRC
电话 Tel： +86 (22) 2318 3333
传真 Fax： +86 (22) 2318 3300

苏州 Suzhou
中国苏州市苏州工业园区
旺墩路 188 号建屋大厦 1501 室
邮政编码 215028
Room 1501, Genway Tower
188 Wang Dun Road
Suzhou Industrial Park
Suzhou 215028, PRC
电话 Tel： +86 (512) 6273 1888
传真 Fax： +86 (512) 6273 1800

厦门 Xiamen
中国厦门市思明区鹭江道 8 号
国际银行大厦 11 楼 B 室
邮政编码 361001
Unit B, 11/F
International Plaza
8 Lujiang Road
Siming District
Xiamen 361001, PRC
电话 Tel： +86 (592) 210 7888
传真 Fax： +86 (592) 210 8800

台湾 Taiwan
中国台北市信义区 110
基隆路一段 333 号 27 楼
International Trade Building,
27F, 333 Keelung Road, Section 1,
Taipei 110, Taiwan
电话 Tel： +886 2 27296666
传真 Fax： +886 2 27576371

西安 Xi'an
中国西安市南关正街 88 号
长安国际中心 D 座 7 楼
邮政编码 710068
7/F, D Block, Chang'an Metropolis Center
88 Nanguan Street
Xi'an 710068, PRC
电话 Tel： +86 (29) 8469 2688
传真 Fax： +86 (29) 8469 2600

如欲了解更多资讯，敬请登陆公司网站：
For more information, please visit our websites at:
pwccn. com
pwchk. com

图书在版编目（CIP）数据

国际财务报告准则实务指引. 第十八章，资产减值：汉英对照/李宜桦等编译. —北京：中国财政经济出版社，2012. 9
（普华永道国际财务报告准则实务指引系列）
ISBN 978 - 7 - 5095 - 3491 - 5

Ⅰ. ①国…　Ⅱ. ①李…　Ⅲ. ①会计准则 - 世界 - 汉、英　Ⅳ. ①F233. 1

中国版本图书馆 CIP 数据核字（2012）第 047996 号

责任编辑：蔡丽兰　　　　责任校对：王　英

中国财政经济出版社出版
URL：http：//www. cfeph. cn
E - mail：cfeph @ cfeph. cn

社址：北京市海淀区阜成路甲 28 号　邮政编码：100142
发行处电话：88190406　财经书店电话：64033436
北京财经印刷厂印刷　　各地新华书店经销
787 × 1092 毫米　16 开　23. 25 印张　390 000 字
2012 年 9 月第 1 版　2012 年 9 月北京第 1 次印刷
定价：58. 00 元
ISBN 978 - 7 - 5095 - 3491 - 5/F · 2950
（图书出现印装问题，本社负责调换）
本社质量投诉电话：010 - 88190744